Revenge

of the

Donut Boys

Revenge

of the

Donut Boys

True Stories of Lust,
Fame, Survival and
Multiple Personality

Mike Sager

Thunder's Mouth Press
New York

REVENGE OF THE DONUT BOYS:
True Stories of Lust, Fame, Survival and Multiple Personality

Thunder's Mouth Press
An imprint of Avalon Publishing Group, Inc.
245 West 17th Street, 11th Floor
New York, NY 10011

AVALON
publishing group incorporated

Library of Congress Cataloging-in-Publication Data is available.

ISBN-10: 1-56858-350-8
ISBN-13: 978-1-56858-350-1

9 8 7 6 5 4 3 2 1

Interior Design by Meryl Sussman Levavi
Printed in the United States of America
Distributed by Publishers Group West

For Miles

I have always depended on the kindness of strangers.

—Blanche Duboise, *A Streetcar Named Desire*,
by Tennessee Williams

Contents

Foreword

When Journalism Becomes Art

By Walt Harrington

> How can we know the dancer from the dance?
>
> —William Butler Yeats, "Among School Children"

I first met Mike Sager twenty-five years ago when he was a smart punk-ass kid newspaper reporter who wanted to grow up be like Tom Wolfe or Gay Talese or Hunter S. Thompson. Back then, a lot of kids wanted to be like Tom Wolfe or Gay Talese or Hunter S. Thompson someday.

Today, the smart punk-ass kids want to be Mike Sager.

Why that happened to him and not the thousands of other aspiring young literary journalists of his generation, is a lesson for those kids. Sager spent six years at the *Washington Post* learning the craft of journalism—working seven days a week whether he was paid or not, getting the facts right, never suffering from writer's block, cranking out his best on bad assignments, learning his way around police reports, financial statements, and court documents. He made himself at home in neighborhoods, bars, and towns that were like foreign countries to this suburban doctor's son. He labored to blend discordant bits of quote, fact, sight, and sound into compilations that got people to read the first sentence, then the second and the third, that grabbed people by the collars and kept them reading, made them *feel* . . . something—anger, fear, sadness, joy, whatever.

Anything to reach readers where they lived.

Anything to take readers where *other* people lived.

"Master technique," Sager once said in giving advice to young journalists, "and then listen to your heart." That, in a nutshell, is the idea at the soul of his work.

Mike Sager wasn't long for the *Washington Post*. His fascination with the contradictions of respectability, his obsession with unpleasant truths, and his stronger and stronger personal voice doomed him even at America's best newspaper. The glossy magazines, with their hip, young-adult readers, became his home. He wrote for *Washingtonian*, the now-defunct magazines *Regardie's* and *Manhattan, inc.*, then *Playboy, Rolling Stone, GQ*, and, finally, *Esquire*, where he has been a writer-at-large for years.

Revenge of the Donut Boys is a collection of Mike Sager articles exploring the confusing state of American life—its values, virtues, fantasies, and hypocrisies, circa 2000. This anthology follows an equally compelling earlier collection, *Scary Monsters and Super Freaks*. These two books, along with another planned anthology coming later, will finally make available the two-decade body of Sager's artful journalism, which is rooted in his boundless reportorial and storytelling gifts, his eye for meaningful detail, his ear for the rhymes and rhythms of unfolding life—and his unflinching belief in the beauty of humanity at its most noble and most silly, shallow and self-absorbed.

Roseanne Barr electing to reveal that she has Multiple Personality Disorder. The human's-eye view inside one of California's worst-ever wildfires. The charmed day-to-day life of a stunningly beautiful woman. A seventeen-year-old suburban boy who, for reasons unexplainable, has figured out the meaning of life. A freshly minted dot-com billionaire in the first weeks of his transformation to entrepreneurial master of the universe.

The satanic-tinged band, *Slayer*, as its evil players color-coordinate curtains and couches for their suburban condos. Struggling, neurotic actors as they suffer on the cusp of almost-fame. A wise and dignified manservant to the richest of the rich. The toughest, most decent, honorable Marine colonel in the U.S. infantry. The young and rebellious rapper Ice Cube, from the beginning, yearning to join the American parade.

A man struggling to stay confident while out of work, caring for the kids, and living off his wife. The handsome, muscled, vapid gods of the California beach volleyball circuit. Middle-class couples swinging their way to marital harmony. Football's Mike Ditka in love with his life. A ninety-two-year-old man who realizes he has been old longer than he has been anything else. And all the *other* people in America who are named Mike Sager.

A weird mix of disparate stories bound together only by Mike Sager's sensibility.

Journalism is portrayed as a craft. Learn to get the facts correct, in proper sequence, appropriately weighted and balanced for fairness and multiple perspectives, write in clear and plain language, and you don't need the unique intelligence, insight, or inquiry of a reporter/writer, because the stories will tell themselves. It is an industrial logic: Send any hundred journeymen journalists out on a given story, and they will come back with just about the same tale, because they are workers on a professional assembly line.

That has always been a silly notion. Doing anything well is mostly craft—hitting a five iron, putting a basketball through a hoop, writing a poem, building a bridge, cooking a meal. Of course, anybody can read a recipe. Yet, for reasons mystical, a few people cook a meal better and differently than most everybody else. These people are artists.

What else to call them?

They take the same raw material available to everyone and make something fresh of it: Tiger Woods curving a golf ball around a tree, Michael Jordon passing to himself in midair, the cadence of a Robert Frost poem, the majesty of the Golden Gate Bridge, the luxurious sensuality of a gourmet meal. The people who create the best in their fields know their recipes, sure, but they add to the stew their own intelligence, insight, and intuition. Ask them why they are so good at what they do, and they often cannot tell you.

They have become artists—dancer and dance, indistinguishable.

Mike Sager is an artist of journalism.

Read his story on the stunningly beautiful woman, and you are in her living room, laughing with her and her friends about penises. You can see her and smell her and taste her. Mike Sager shows you the world through her eyes, yet he never loses himself—or you—in the reverie. Always, we are reminded without words that her world is the reverse of our world. She is special because we who are not beautiful grant her special status. As we create her, we diminish ourselves. But we can't help it; beauty has power over us.

Read his story on the old man, and you will feel guilty for all you did not know about your aging mother and father. And, suddenly, you will know what is in store for you.

Read his story on the Marine colonel in the field with his soldiers and, no matter your politics on the military, you will love this man, his commitment to honor and valor and country that is absent any vainglorious pretense. And, for the moment, you will know what it is to love your country in that blind, unquestioning way.

Read Mike Sager's articles and you are taken on an ethnographic journey through the mysterious ordinary realms everywhere around you and to which you are oblivious. The stories reflect and evoke our times, yes. Yet they also reflect their author's generosity of heart and his empathy and compassion for all human beings. More than anything, these stories ask that you set aside your biases, even your deeply held beliefs, and enter the minds and worlds of others.

Although these stories are about the widest range of people, they are all really about Mike Sager, who sees in others what he yearns to see in all of us. Through his lens, we forever glimpse hope, which makes his stories not only about himself and his subjects but about all of us: Author, subjects, readers—indistinguishable, dancers and dance.

The craft of journalism raised to art.

WALT HARRINGTON is the head of journalism at the University of Illinois at Urbana-Champaign, a former staff writer for the *Washington Post Magazine*, and the author or editor of six books, including *The Beholder's Eye* and *The Everlasting Stream*.

The Multitudes of Roseanne

So there we were, all snug and cozy in the living room at Big Buck Ranch, Roseanne's mountain retreat near Lake Arrowhead, California. Night had fallen; the windows were mottled with frost, a thin blanket of early-November snow covered the grounds. Though our interview had finally commenced about six hours behind schedule, things had proceeded rather smoothly from there. Before me now lay the daunting prospect of a long, dark, treacherous drive home. I was gathered and ready to leave, but not yet able.

A fire crackled in the large stone hearth. Roseanne was shlumped in an overstuffed chair, her dainty feet clad in thick woolen socks, resting on an ottoman. I take the liberty here of using her first name only. Born a Barr; married—in chronological order—to a Pentland, an Arnold, and a Thomas; internationally famous for playing a Conner on television: Roseanne has lately found herself in a bit of a jam, name-wise, a forty-eight-year-old, Emmy-winning mother of five without a suitable appellation. As you will see, her predicament is altogether fitting. She's doing her best to sort things out.

Roseanne was dressed in faded blue jeans and a ratty, oversized sweatshirt appropriated from her current husband, Ben Thomas, her former bodyguard, a bear of a man fourteen years her junior with a trim goatee. Ben was not present at the ranch this evening, and neither was their five-year-old son, Buck, for whom the place was named. Roseanne wore no makeup, put on no airs. Her shortish brown hair was tousled. She was fat, but not too fat. Her surgically altered cheekbones looked prominent in the gauzy light, making her seem softer and more attractive than I'd expected.

Around the corner from the living room, across an expanse of faux-leopard carpeting, in the office area of the house, a man named James was searching the Internet. Tall, dark, and effusive, James is Roseanne's "publicist-slash-confidant." About an hour earlier, Roseanne had developed a craving for a particular type of pumpkin cookies popular with Mormon moms in the Salt Lake City neighborhoods of her youth. The cookies had to be soft and cakey in the middle, crunchy at the edges. Cream-cheese icing figured prominently as well. Once the recipe was secured, James and Mike, Roseanne's personal assistant, would head to the store for provisions. While they were gone, it was somehow determined, I would baby-sit Roseanne. Though no one used that word, exactly, that was my sense of things. That she couldn't or shouldn't be left alone. That my presence at the ranch had put me in the line of duty, one of the available minions.

Now Mike appeared in the living room, carrying a tray. Handsome and well-muscled, thirty-one years old, Mike was dressed in his customary uniform of flannel shirt, cargo shorts, and calf-high Caterpillar-brand construction boots. On his belt he wore two beepers and a cell phone. The tray he was carrying was a kitschy antique. On it was a kitschy antique teapot and two mugs. Every spare surface of Big Buck Ranch—a cabinesque minimanse on eight forested acres—was crammed with knick-knacks and thingamajigs, the gleanings of Roseanne's tireless and somewhat pathological *shmying*. On the front lawn sat an antique buckboard wagon. In the powder room, the mirror over the sink was framed with a leather yoke from an antique mule harness. Later in our association, I would learn of the existence of several warehouses and an airplane hangar.

Mike proffered a half dozen packets of exotically flavored coffee, fanned out in his hands like playing cards. "Which kind?" he asked.

"They're all open!" Roseanne exclaimed, annoyed.

"And . . ." Mike said elliptically.

"Who opened 'em?"

"Who do you think?"

"Did not!"

"Did too."

"Did not!"

"Okay, fine," Mike said. He let out a sigh. He's been with Roseanne and Ben for three years.

"Just gimme this one," Roseanne said, snatching the packet of Irish cream. "Do we have any chocolate?"

"I'll get some at the store."

"Well, hurry up. I'm starvin'!"

In short order, Roseanne and I were alone. She seemed happy and expansive; there was a sparkle in her smallish, dark-brown eyes. She was considerably less brassy than her well-known public persona, the loudmouthed Domestic Goddess, queen of tabloids and tattoo parlors, desecrater of our national anthem and most of our notions of good taste. Over the course of our interview, in fact, she'd been astonishingly engaging—despite her occasional tendency to call me an idiot and to point out my personal flaws—revealing herself to be intelligent and well-read if somewhat grammatically challenged, holding forth articulately on a wide range of topics, citing studies, quoting references and texts. Not to mention the sense of humor: wicked and perverse and high-end, punctuated by the occasional belch.

Though our interview was long over, Roseanne was in the mood to talk. She monologued entertainingly on a variety of deep, new-ageish subjects: her belief in the Goddess, the possibility of alien life in the galaxy, her desire to sponsor a chess tournament for Palestinian and Israeli youth. She talked and she talked and she talked. And then, suddenly, she stopped talking.

For several long minutes she stirred her coffee. Her eyes seemed to be focused on the flames dancing in the fireplace. Her spoon tinkled against the sides of the mug. At last, she turned to me. "I have MPD," she said. Her voice had the challenging tone of a bratty little kid.

"What's that?"

"MPD, stupid. Multiple-personality disorder."

"Cool," I said, vaguely encouraging.

She stared at me for several long seconds. I raised an eyebrow hopefully. A puzzled look crossed her face. "We have seven different signatures," she said.

"We?"

"We've never been comfortable saying 'I.' It's something we have to do with singletons. You know, to sound normal."

"Singletons?"

"Like you. People who don't have the gift. We consider it a gift. Those of us who—"

Just then the kitchen door swung open. James and Mike tumbled in, laden with groceries. Roseanne went silent. She darted me a nervous look, stood; moved toward the kitchen. "Did you get all the stuff? I'm starvin'!"

Linda, the cook/nanny, a smiling Filipina in a pink uniform, served coffee in china cups. It was just before noon on a sunny winter day some months later. Roseanne and I were in her office at the Big House, an architectural showcase of glass and stone with twenty-foot ceilings and waterfalls and statuary on a high ridge overlooking the Pacific.

Roseanne was sitting behind her desk in a faux-leopard-upholstered chair, enveloped in a pleasant cloud of perfume. She wore full makeup and a chic black dress; a diaphanous, bejeweled overblouse with matching head scarf; fuzzy slippers. As Linda left the room, Roseanne opened a drawer and retrieved two small paper bags. One bag contained fortune cookies dipped in dark chocolate. The other bag contained fortune cookies dipped in white chocolate. "I live on chocolate," she said conspiratorially. "It's hidden all over my house so my husband can't find it."

She took one cookie from each bag, then broke each carefully in half, shared the halves with me. She dunked her dark-chocolate piece into her coffee, took a bite, encouraged me to do the same. "Good, huh?" She took another bite, scrunched her eyes closed. She tipped back her head as if in ecstasy.

"I was thinking of changing my name to Sarah Tonin," she said next, sipping her coffee, referring to the neurotransmitter in the brain that regulates urges and moods. "My kids call me Queen Carlotta. From *Desperate Living?* John Waters? You know—they eat her in the end. When that movie came out, the part of me that was the mother was a very young part. She used to watch *Desperate Living* with the kids over and over. It's just a hideous movie. When I think now that she let those kids, when they were five years old—man! That's Buck's age now! I would never let Buck see that, though I did let him listen a little the other day to something on TV about serial killers. It was all about multiple-personality disorder, you know, and I just don't want to hide anymore. Valentine's Day is my sixth wedding anniversary, and I wanna have an anniversary/coming-out party. Because it's the same precept as coming out of the closet. You're so afraid to have anyone know who you really are, especially when you're a lot of things. I was always in conflict about conflicting parts, but I've learned how to get them to listen to each other now. I've learned how to get them to know they're on the same team, that we occupy the same body, which we never knew before."

Roseanne dunked the white-chocolate-dipped fortune cookie, popped it into her mouth. "Jews love to talk with their mouths full," she said, giggling. "There weren't many other Jews where we grew up in Salt Lake City. Our neighbor on the corner was a German. He'd come straight over from Nazi Germany after the war. He used to torture me every day. I'd come home and tell my mother, 'He's hitting me; he locked me in his garage and called me a Jew bitch and said Hitler was right!' And my mother would go, 'You're making this up!' And to show me I was wrong, she hires the guy to work at our house. That's how crazy my mother was. One time I came into the kitchen and she was lying on the floor with ketchup poured all over herself, pretending she was dead. I was real little. Can you imagine? So anyways, she hires this Nazi just to prove me wrong. That's how you get multiple-personality disorder. Or DID. That's what they call it now: dissociative-identity disorder."

She took another sip of coffee. "It comes out of being a kid, see. It's a kid's invention. There's a lot of, like, mythical heroes involved, and some people have animals, and most people have both sexes—that's a given. I know people who have dogs and stuff. It comes out of the mind, they say, between two and five years old. When you're at that emotional-development level where you really can't tell the difference between what's in your head and what's outside your head, people-wise. That's why I have trouble with assis-tants. Because I think I tell them things, but the truth is, I told it to some-body inside my head. And then I go crazy because the assistant said I didn't tell them. And I'd be: 'I did *so* tell you, you son of a bitch!'

"It's like living in a maze. It's like that old woman who keeps adding on to her house. You're continually building more and more rooms, more and more ways out. It's like putting soldiers in front of the wounded one. There's a wounded one, you know, and that one is being defended by all the parts. But the parts don't get along. And some of them have some real strange ideas about how to defend. That's why integration is such a political thing. Some people are saying you don't need to integrate, that integration is colonial bull-shit promulgated by singletons."

She leaned forward, locked my eyes. "Don't get me wrong. I'm all for integration. After ten years of hard work, I'm at the point now of having co-consciousness. I haven't had any amnesia in a while. I haven't had any blackouts for quite a while. I used to have them minute by minute. It was hard to follow through on a task. Like forgetting to call someone back for seven years. That happened! Really! This is my life, you know. I live in a different time and space than other people. I'm unstuck in time. That's why I have that great big calendar up there." She pointed to the wall behind me, to one of those large whiteboard planning calendars. "See where it says 'Christmas'?"

I let the question hang a moment. "I think it's already January."

Roseanne cut her eyes toward the calendar, furrowed her brow. "It *is* January, isn't it?" she said, somewhat abashed. Then she shrugged her shoulders. "I'm hungry. Are you hungry? Where do you feel like eating?"

A few weeks later, toward the end of January, Mike was leading the way through a back-alley entrance into Roseanne's new studio space, a storefront on the main drag of El Segundo, a quaint little throwback of a beach town tucked into the rolling landscape just south of the Los Angeles airport. We filed through a hallway, past a pair of Hispanic maids mopping the floor, into a large main room.

"Look at all this!" Roseanne trilled. There must have been a hundred linear feet of industrial garment racks crammed to capacity with women's clothes. She threw out her hands gleefully, twirled around like Mary Tyler Moore. "Oh, my God! I forgot about all this shit! Where's my furs?"

"Here's some of 'em right now," Mike said wearily, indicating about eight linear feet of fur coats.

"Where's my other minks?"

"Still in storage, I guess."

"You guess?"

"Like I said, you have at least two times this much still to come."

Roseanne dropped her pink plastic Hello Kitty knapsack—a match to the floor mats and steering-wheel cover of her Lexus—and approached one of the shiny chrome racks. "Wow. Here's my rubber minidress! Oh, good Lord—these are my favorite pants!" She moved through the merchandise like a politician through a crowd, touching and feeling and reveling. So many long-forgotten pieces of her wardrobe, each with a story to tell: her Christian Lacroix gold leather jacket, her purple Chanel suit, her Swiss milkmaid's lace apron. Knit sweaters, distressed jeans, designer frocks. A very naughty nightie. "Oh, look at this thing!" She laughed uproariously, rearing back her head. "My idiot ex-husband wanted me to wear this in *Vanity Fair!*"

Just then, Mike interrupted: "Hey, R., I gotta get going."

Roseanne's face fell. "But . . . I'm . . . *hungry,*" she said, haltingly, beseechingly. She seemed to have forgotten all about the garment she was holding up beneath her chin on a hanger, a black lace corset with nippleless cups.

"Go next door and get something if you want," encouraged Mike.

"Um, well, okay," Roseanne said, pulling herself together, noticing now the garment beneath her chin, as if seeing it for the first time. She shrugged her shoulders and arced the hanger back onto the rack, a practiced parabola, a ringing metal clank. "Everybody out!" she commanded.

Roseanne and I successfully navigated the trip next door, returning with large greasy orders of French fries and onion rings sprinkled with copious amounts of salt. We settled into a black leather sofa in a little waiting room at the studio, a historic place where Buster Keaton once made movies.

"Okay!" Roseanne said. "We're gonna get something done here. I have total control of my mind today. For the next twenty minutes, probably. I hope, anyway."

"Should we try to meet the alters?" I asked.

"God," she said. She ripped open a paper bindle of salt with her teeth. "That's heavy shit."

"I'll go easy. You tell me how."

"Tell me what you want and I'll go there."

"It would be logical to make a sort of roster and meet all the characters, I think."

"*Nnnnn,*" she said, a wholly negative sound hummed through her nose. She made a face as if she were tasting lemons. "That's a real freak show. A real *uncomfortable* freak show."

Roseanne munched a fry, long and crispy and bow-shaped, starting at the tip, taking small chipmunk bites with her front teeth until it was gone. "Everybody thinks I'm Roseanne Conner," she said thoughtfully. "Right now I have no name. I need a last name. When you're like me, you have a lot of names. I have a lot of biblical names. A lot of Jewish names. And a lot of aliases. And I don't know how many signatures."

"You said seven, right?"

Her eyes blazed. "Shut up," she sneered, a little scary. "You've gotta be the one who knows something, don't you?"

"Pardon?"

"Every time I'm in the mood to talk, people interrupt me."

"Sorry."

"There's this book, *A Confederacy of Dunces?* My favorite quote is where he goes: 'He wiped a tear as he contemplated his Godlike mind.' I love that quote. I love that his mother sold the book after he committed suicide. I knew I was fascinating at a really young age. I have the ability to transcend time and space. And become peers with people they claim are dead."

"Cool," I said.

"I love being in this house," said Roseanne, speaking over her shoulder in a husky whisper, stepping gingerly around a coiled garden hose. "We bake cookies here, we barbecue with the neighbors. It makes me feel normal."

Ten blocks from the studio is Ben's Doghouse, a rich guy's sentimental take on a typical, upper-middle-class dwelling, with the requisite gym and vaulted ceiling, a guesthouse for the nanny. Ben stays in the Doghouse when Roseanne kicks him out of the Big House—like that time last New Year's, when he drank too much and started doing front flips off the furniture. Or when he just needs a break from the whirlwind of their life together. Roseanne married Ben because he loved and protected her, and he still does, fiercely, playing the stern father to her troubled teen, supervising her movements and affairs, calling her on her cell phone every hour.

With the Big House roof undergoing repair, the family was staying at Ben's Doghouse. It was late February. The anniversary/coming-out party had not come off. Roseanne had been avoiding me for weeks, busy with myriad projects: her movie (a film version of *Rubyfruit Jungle* by Rita Mae Brown), her three screenplays, her Web site (RoseanneWorld.com), her painting, her cabala studies, her book on DID with her shrink, a renowned M.D. who had a hand in writing the American Psychiatric Association's official clinical definition of DID, said to be suffered by 1 percent of the U.S. population.

Although Ben had suggested we use the guesthouse for our interview, Roseanne was restless there. At length she decided we should walk along the shore instead. It was further decided that the way to get to the shore was not through the house, as you would normally surmise, but through the property's service entrance, on the west side of the double-deep lot, cluttered with tools, muddy from recent rains.

Maneuvering around a wheelbarrow, Roseanne made her way along the side of the house. Inside, in the dining room, the two Hispanic maids were busily cleaning. They averted their eyes as their missus tiptoed past the large windows, dressed in camouflage pants and an olive-drab shirt. Roseanne kept her eyes averted, too, as if not looking was nine-tenths of not being seen. On her face was a giddy, exhilarated grin—that teenage girl, sneaking out her window on a school night.

Two houses down, the street dead-ended. We climbed a little hill to a concrete bicycle path, beheld below us the sweeping view of the cobalt Pacific. In the foreground was a picture of the Golden State seldom featured in movies: huge metal holding tanks and pipeworks and Erector Set cranes, tall concrete stacks belching white smoke, high-voltage transformer towers—an oil refinery, a power plant, a water-treatment plant.

Roseanne picked up a three-foot stick from beside the path and tapped it idly along the ground as we walked. A guy rode past on an expensive racing bike, headed in the opposite direction. Roseanne's head swiveled, then she turned and walked backward, watching him recede, pretending to use her stick as a spyglass. "Do you wanna hear the story of how my parents had to go to therapy to get me a bike when I was twelve?"

"I'm on the clock," I said.

"My father always said that we couldn't have a bike because his best friend had been killed riding a bike. My father has seen so many horrible things in his life. He saw his baby sister burned to death. They were playing with matches and she caught on fire. He had a hard life, my father. He was terrified of bikes. He'd go, 'Don't you understand? My friend was eating peanuts, and when the car hit him, I ran over and there were peanuts coming out of his eyes.' Finally my parents went to this headshrinker, and the guy put a spell or something on my dad, and one day my dad came home with a bike. I was so happy. That was my freedom. The minute I got that bike I was gone. I have the strongest leg muscles to this day. Look," she said, proffering her leg. "Feel."

It was a big, strong muscle and I told her so, and she seemed satisfied. She resumed walking, banging the stick on the ground now, shortening it splinter by splinter. After a time, she stopped and turned toward me. "Disneyland," she said, as if reciting the title of a poem at a slam.

"Okay," I said.

"There are so many of these; this is one of the nicer ones." Her eyes were fixed on the horizon. "See, my dad got a hair up his ass and had two hundred bucks or something and his fuckin' broken-down car, and it was me and my sister and my brother was a baby, and my other sister wasn't born yet. We all drove from Salt Lake out to California, to Disneyland.

"We're driving over Donner Pass and it's snowing. Did I mention it was winter? That's my parents. Disneyland in winter. They had to booby-trap everything. Anyway, we got there. My sister is seven, I'm eight. My brother is probably thirteen months old. He's in his little snowsuit; he has to be carried. My dad decides he wants to go on the gondola. So me and my mom go in the first gondola. My dad and my little sister and the baby go in the one behind us. We start out, and then we hear my father shouting. He's like, 'Helen! Helen! Look!'

"My mom turns around. And then she turns right back, and she just goes totally stiff. She hisses to me, 'Don't turn around! Whatever you do, don't look at him!' Because to him everything was funny, you know? You didn't want to encourage him because whenever he was fucking doing something like that, something would always go horribly wrong at the end because he's such an idiot.

"So of course I turn around. My father is holding the baby out the window of the gondola. He's holding him under his little arms, you know, dangling him there in his yellow snowsuit.

"My mother is digging her fingers into my leg. And my sister is screaming and the baby is screaming and my mother is screaming, and my father is laughing this maniacal laugh, and I just kind of snapped. I was eight years old. I let my father have it. I fuckin' barraged him with the kind of language—I mean, the words that came out of my mouth, I didn't even know I knew them! I just kept yelling and yelling, and it lasted forever, but finally my father sort of snapped to. He looked at me funny, and then he looked at the baby. And then he just pulled my brother back inside and it was over.

"And then we get off the gondola, and my father's like, 'Line up! We're taking a family picture!' And I'm shaking. I think I had gone to the bathroom in my pants. I'm just standing there. I'm totally spaced out. I'm totally dissociated out. And he comes over, like he always did, and he cracks me in the back of my head with the palm of his hand and then pushes me over there to take the picture. And then he goes, 'Okay, everybody, let's have a great big smile!'"

We walked together in silence for a while. Roseanne raised her stick into the air like a twirler's baton, worked it through her fingers with surprising verve. "That day I had a big split," she said. "I had two parts that came out. One was a real tough part that would protect the softer parts, a fighter part that would always go up against my father."

"Who was the other one?"

"All my parts came out in twos. There were always mirror images of mirror images, because it all started in my gramma's bathroom. I was so little I'd climb up and stand in the sink, and I'd look in the mirror, and there was a mirror behind my head. And I'd pull the mirror back and I'd count how many me's there were. And it just went on and on and on. So for every part, there is a mirror image. One equals two, you see? And then there's a whole freaking numerical system that I made up when I was just a kid, all based on fours—it was like a code. And when it came time to become integrated, I had to crack the code and then find the box where all the stuff was locked away. And in the box was ONE. ONE was in the box. That was the part of me that I had always been protecting."

"ONE—is that the original self?"

"No," she sneered. "That's horseshit!"

"Then what?"

"It was a scared part of me that everybody else protected."

"Do the parts come out and stay out? How long do they stay?"

"You never know. Sometimes a while. Sometimes a second. When there's a certain kind of perceived danger, different ones come out. I had a lot of protectors. A lot of fighters. And I couldn't control when they came out. If something would feel threatening or whatever, they'd just come out."

"Like having an arsenal of weapons?"

"No, more like having a system. And the system is intelligent. It sends out the right face at the right time."

"When an alter comes out, does it stay for a long time?"

"That's TV crap. Anything can happen, really. It's called rapid cycling."

"Can you get them to come out whenever you want?"

"I can now, pretty much. That's integration. It's also why I'm working on so many things at once. They all want a chance. Like when I look back, I can see which part did what. I'd have one part writing comedy and one part writing poetry. There were performers, businesspeople, mothers, protectors, children—lots of children. And they all worked independently, so basically they would all sabotage each other all the time. Like, I'd have a business meeting with someone, and then another part would call them back and just fuck everything up. The parts were very fluid. It took a great amount of energy each day just to hide the disorder from other people. Because you don't want people to find out that you're crazy."

"That must have been really tough," I said.

She cut her eyes at me. "Funny," she sneered.

The next morning, Roseanne and I sat together on the black leather sofa in the media room of Ben's Doghouse. The maids were busily cleaning the kitchen. Ben was out front, hooking a trailer to his truck. I pulled a beat-up hardback from my bag.

"What's that?" Roseanne asked.

"Your second book, *My Lives.*"

"It's falling apart."

"Published 1994. Used to be a library book."

"Scary, huh?"

I turned to the last chapter, to the very last page. There, a seeming afterthought to the text, was a list of names, "the people who share my body": 2, Baby, Cindy, Susan, Nobody, Somebody, Joey, Heather, Roger, Kevin, Evangelina, Vangie, Martha, Mother, Piggy, Fucker, Bambi, Rosey, Roseanne, ONE.

I pointed to the list. "Can we talk about these people?"

She made her lemon face. "They're not there anymore."

"Can we talk about who is?"

"It's dull to talk about that."

"But you've been so elliptical. You allude to everything."

"I like alluding. I'm a mystic."

"But you have to give people a little help."

Roseanne sighed. She looked out the big picture window into the lush green garden, where a small, brown-skinned man was weeding the flower beds. She was quiet for several long minutes. I busied myself hooking my lavalier microphone to her collar. The wire was about two feet long. At the center was a little switch box that turned the power on and off. She took up the cord of the mike and began fiddling with it, wrapping it absently around her fingers. A range of emotions crossed her face.

"Okay," she said at last. The tone of her voice was quiet and conversational, a bit forceful, slightly chiding. "You want MPD? I'm showing you MPD. So you better . . . fucking . . . check it out, 'cause I ain't gonna do it again. And the other ones that you want to talk to"—and here her voice changed, becoming formal and ladylike, schoolmarmish, and she sat forward primly on the edge of the sofa, her legs pinned at the knees, crossed at the ankles—"I'm afraid, dear, that you can only get them by phone. That one can't be in a room with men and talk that way. Nothing to do with you, it's just that part of me is terrified of males, that part of me"—and here her voice changed again, became that of an innocent little girl, and she flopped back into the sofa and pulled her legs up beneath her, until she was sitting Indian style, all squirmy, bouncing a bit in place—"I'm scared of males, 'cause they done the weirdest things, and you never know. The things they do are so weird, okay, like when they spit"—and here her voice changed again, becoming loud and brassy, the Roseanne we know from TV—"Why do they need to spit like that? *Haaaaaaa-tooooooey!* They must think you need to do that to clear your sinuses. Or maybe they just don't want to swallow the stuff when it runs a little bit down their throats. I myself have always swallowed. And that's why I'm in the position I'm in today. Because I needed the fifty bucks! That was—" and here, I would later learn, is where one of the parts turned off my microphone.

For the next seventy-some minutes, Roseanne presented a range of different characters. She talked passionately, seriously, hilariously, tearfully. She talked about being hospitalized, about "waking up" in the middle of sex with strange, dirty men she'd picked up at gas stations, about gouging holes in her thighs with her fingernails, about the male alter who was crushed when the shrink challenged him to wisen up and look at himself naked in the mirror. There was a cast of different players I couldn't definitively chart, distinct yet indistinct, slightly butch or fem, old or young, preachy and know-it-all, vulnerable and scared, all of them unidimensional, fragments of personalities, really, each with its own agenda. There seemed to be a funny one, an innocent one, a prophetic one. There was one who was holier-than-thou, one with a trash mouth, one who wished to save the earth, one determined to bring females to their rightful place in the world family. As she shifted between the different parts, her voice would change subtly, her mien would change subtly—her body language, her gestures, her hairstyle, all of it would change ever so subtly—or sometimes the change would be jarringly abrupt, from a whisper to a yell, from self-conscious to grandiose, from hushed revelation to claws-bared attack. Most remarkable was the constant fiddling with her eyeglasses, a pair of antique cat's-eye frames, taking them on and off, on and off. Later, speaking with two of her children (who believe each of them has a different alter for a mother, the reason they rarely get together with her all at once), I learned that some of the alters need glasses and some do not.

And then Roseanne, or one of her alters, wanted to read something to me, so I unhooked her from the mike and we went upstairs to her office. She found the notebook, then stood before me, assuming a sober, theatrical voice, a bit overly portentous, like a serious young writer at a reading. She went on for a few minutes. Then she came to this:

"So this is my life, my true E! Hollywood story. It's the story of a multiple, multifaceted girl woman boy poet dancer comedian singer freedom-fighter warrior message-bearer performer mother sex-partner wife actor producer director pioneer autistic-child survivor-of-post-traumatic-stress borderline bipolar overweight Tourette's-sufferer multiple-personality-disorder obsessive-compulsive victim-of-psychiatric-planting-of-false-memories heretic witch crone—take your pick, there's about three hundred diagnoses, which proves: Shrinks have been my only friends."

Jessica and Jennifer are two of Roseanne's daughters, thirteen months apart. The older one, Jessica, is dark and artsy. At twenty-five, she looks like a young, thinner Roseanne—Roseanne before her surgeries, they like to joke. Jennifer is brown-haired and green-eyed. She is married and has a seven-month-old son, Roseanne's first grandchild. We were in her apartment, a small architectural gem in the Fairfax district of Los Angeles. Morning light streamed through the windows. We drank coffee at the dining-room table.

"I remember when Mom told me she had MPD," Jess was saying. She has an art-deco bracelet tattooed onto her wrist. "I was on a home visit from boarding school. She took me into her bedroom and said, 'I have something to tell you.' She brought out one of her alters, Cindy, the little girl. And Cindy's like, in a real baby voice: 'The lady's sad 'cause you're leaving.' And I was like, *what?*"

"I don't remember when she told me," Jenny said. "I remember being in the hospital. Before the boarding school, we got locked up, like, a lot."

"It was trendy in the eighties."

"Mom and Tom had good insurance."

"It was tough growing up," Jess said. "She had three of us in diapers at the same time."

"Sometimes, you'd wake up, and Mom wouldn't make us go to school," Jenny said. "We'd stay home and play all day. She'd take us to Denny's and let us have coffee."

"And then you'd wake up the next morning, and all hell would break loose. It was like, 'Okay, do your chores! We're on a merit system!'"

"I used to just think she was moody."

"She's 100 percent better than she used to be," said Jess.

"What can you say about something so complicated?" said Jenny.

A week after my last visit with Roseanne, in early March, I got a message to call.

"Hi," I said. "You wanted me to talk to one of the parts."

"I don't give a shit," Roseanne said.

"Is this she?"

"No. Everybody's always here. What do you want?"

"You said to call."

"I thought you wanted to ask me specific things."

"Ah, no," I said, a bit confused.

"Ummm," she hummed, and then she went silent. Thirty full seconds passed. I waited her out.

Finally, she spoke: "This is, ah . . . I'm, ah, the person that you want to talk to. Just don't be all fuckin' geeky about it and shit."

It was a shy, quiet, halting voice that seemed to be struggling to find words. "I'm kind of like, um, the whadayacallit—the switchboard-operator type. I'm the one who knows what goes on and all that shit."

"You have something you wanted to say?"

"Yes. Um. Ah . . . see, here's my little speech: I was not aware for a long time that I caused harm to other people. And the fact that you're not aware of it is so horrifying. There's not a lot of people in this world who get a chance to become conscious. There's not a lot of people who get the chance to actually take stock of what's happened and make an effort to heal. Every war and every conflict that exists in the world is just a physical manifestation of the war inside each and every one of us. We are all so divided. We need to be integrated—as males and females, as nations, as religions. For some reason, I was chosen to act out my shit on a huge fucking platform. Most people just act out on their own family, but I had to do it big."

"You did it big, all right."

"I know. And now I look back and say, Boy, was I fuckin' crazy or what?"

Esquire, August 2001

Is Something Burning?

Bob Younger whispered into his wife's ear. There was alarm in his voice. "Honey, wake up."

Sandra Younger blinked awake. She found herself on the sofa, still wearing her Hawaiian shirt and kukui-nut lei.

It was early Sunday morning, October 26, 2003. They'd just returned from a Halloween party hosted by their Newfoundland-dog club. Their two black Newfs—large and slobbery and affectionate—had worn leis, too. "I must have dozed off," Sandra said. She sat up, gathering her wits. "What time is it?"

Bob looked at his watch, then thought about it a moment. Tonight was the time change: fall backward. Had he changed his watch?

"1:05," he said definitively.

Sandra sniffed the air. Her brow wrinkled. "Is something burning?"

"There's a glow on the horizon. Over the hills, to the northeast."

They'd just spent $10,000 clearing brush. "Did you call the fire department?" she asked.

"Lakeside had a recording: 'Please call back during business hours.' I finally got a human at Barona. He said there's a fire up near San Diego Country Estates."

Sandra frowned. After nineteen mind-numbing years in the suburbs, they'd only recently moved to Wildcat Canyon. She counted her blessings every day: coyotes and deer, hawks and hummingbirds and rattlesnakes. Fragrant sage, thorny cactus, stately oaks. Huge granite boulders, rounded over the eons by wildfire and erosion, peeking out like dinosaur eggs from thick nests of impassable brush. To the east was El Capitan mountain; to the west, the San Vicente Reservoir, a breathtaking basin of deep-blue water surrounded by undulating foothills that stretched off in all directions, a no-name range. The sunsets were mesmerizing; you could see the Pacific twenty miles away. At night, a million stars—you could see the lights of Tijuana. The sunrise bathed the sky in extraordinary light, a lovely pastel shade of peach. The previous owner had gone so far as to custom blend the stucco to match.

"How far away is that?" she asked.

"About fifteen miles as the crow flies. Some hunter got lost in the Cleveland National Forest. He lit a signal fire."

She rolled her eyes. "So what do we do now?"

Bob stroked his beard. "The Barona guy said not to worry. He said we should go back to bed."

Irene Hurst woke herself coughing at 3:00 A.M. The air was gritty and hot. She felt as if she'd just inhaled a lungful of ashtray. She shook her husband's shoulder. "Jimmy?"

He had spotted her the first day of junior high. It took him a whole semester to approach. Times were different then. People said it would never work, this big Okie boy and his pretty little Mexicana. A lot they knew. In April, they'd celebrated their fortieth anniversary.

Jimmy got out of bed, padded naked to the back door. Sixty years old, with a barrel chest and thick white hair, he still worked full-time as a longshoreman. Irene also worked full-time, in accounting at a marine-construction company. They had eight payments left on their mortgage. After that, they were free and clear. Maybe they'd do a little traveling.

The house itself was nothing special—a small wooden rectangle on a slab foundation, built many years ago as a hunting lodge, part of the M&M Ranch. Over the past six months, Jimmy had been renovating the bathroom. He'd put in brand-new copper pipes, rewired the whole thing himself. The tub had just been re-enameled. It was outside, leaning against the house, wrapped in plastic. The floor was next. He was hand-cutting the marble tiles. He promised to be done by Christmas.

The rest of the place was Irene's domain, chockablock with her collections: Blue Willow dishes; cobalt-blue glass; antique tins; china pieces Jimmy had brought back from overseas when he was in the Marine Corps; a picture of her great-grandmother from the days when she carried a gun and rode with Pancho Villa; and all of her music—CDs, tapes, and vinyl 78s, 45s, LPs, from Sinatra to Queen, every recording she'd ever owned. You name it, Irene collected it. Every report card. Every essay and painting by the kids. Every Christmas card. Trunks of the stuff. "Every used snot rag," Jimmy liked to joke. Everything was there in that house.

Across a little courtyard was a rustic barbecue, around which there'd been many gatherings over the years, and beyond that was a little guesthouse; their two sons had shared it growing up. Surrounding the little compound was a tall, lush grove of old shade trees. Nearby were the remains of a stagecoach mail route that once linked San Francisco to St. Louis. When he first bought the place in 1979—ten acres for $122,000—Jimmy had to evict the last stragglers from a hippie commune that had taken up residence. They lived in shacks and in old vehicles scattered around the property. In a draw nearby, facing the reservoir, they grew high-quality marijuana. The field had since been reclaimed by nature—a tangle of fire-adapted plants that covered the chaparral like fur—part of the nine-acre plot Jimmy had sold off years ago to pay some bills.

Now he returned to the bedroom, got back between the sheets. "Couldn't really see nothing through them trees," he reported.

They lay there a few minutes in the dark. The smoke was thick. They'd lived in Wildcat Canyon for twenty-four years. Many times they'd sat on lawn chairs and watched fires burn on a distant ridge—whole hillsides engulfed, planes dumping red fire retardant, and them sitting there drinking beers. Never once had they evacuated.

A few more minutes passed. They tried to go back to sleep.

"Damn," said Jimmy, coughing.

"I know," said Irene.

"How 'bout a little quickie?" Jimmy suggested.

Afterward, it was even smokier. Jimmy put on his sweatpants and his Ugg boots. This time, he ventured outside the perimeter of their cosseted little grove.

His mouth went instantly dry, as though someone had stuffed it full of cotton. *Holy shit!*

A half mile away, the northeast wall of the canyon was fully engulfed.

Even from this distance, he could see that the flames were towering. He could feel the heat. He could hear it moving toward him, like a jumbo jet approaching the runway, still a ways off, coming fast. The wind was blowing hot and strong from the east, a Santa Ana.

This is a monster! he thought, scanning the ridgeline.

And then he thought: *We're gonna lose our fuckin' house.* There was no insurance.

Before he could think of anything else, he noticed something. Though the houses in Wildcat Canyon were few and far between, there was a semblance of a neighborhood down by Jimmy's place, several houses that shared the same private road. All of them were newer and more grand than his, made of stucco with vaulted ceilings and large, dramatic windows. They occupied high spots here and there, the better to command the stunning views. There were the Fritzes (a horse corral, a 360 degree sunset), the Irwins (husband and wife USPS mail carriers), the Piorkowskis (he was a bond trader who rose early with the Eastern markets), the Mumfords (he'd made a good living leasing office plants to downtown businesses; her family owned five hundred acres of Wildcat Canyon). Everyone kind of kept to themselves, but everyone was kind of friendly, too. There was the occasional pick-up basketball game at Professor Hanson's. A beer and a smoke beneath Ghost Rock. Halvsies on a piece of heavy machinery to clear some brush or move some boulders. It was the way of the backcountry; no one lived here by accident.

Now, however, with the fire advancing, Jimmy noticed that all of his neighbors' houses were dark. It had been hot lately. All of them had air conditioning. Was it possible they hadn't smelled anything? Could they still be asleep?

He ran back into the house, grabbed the keys to his truck. He told Irene to pack a few things and get out. "Don't wait for me!" he said, turning to leave. "I have to go warn the others!"

Bob Younger opened his eyes. It was 3:05 A.M. The room was aglow, bright as day, an odd but beautiful shade of orange. He went to the window.

"Whoa!"

Sandra sat bolt upright. The fire was two hundred yards away. She threw on some clothes. She couldn't find any shoes to wear. She was looking for sneakers; all she could see were dress shoes. She grabbed a laundry basket, began filling it with family photos. "Get your negatives!" she reminded Bob, an avid photographer.

"I can't find my glasses or my keys!" he called.

"We'll take the Acura!" she called. His glasses were on her head.

"You get the dogs!" he called. His keys were in his pocket.

Then all the lights went out.

She reached the garage, herding the dogs in front of her. Bob was right on her heels, which were still unshod. She dropped the laundry basket; he tossed a load of negatives toward it. A bunch missed and fell to the floor. He bent down to gather them, using one hand. In the other hand he held a heavy, three-million-candlepower flashlight. There was no need to turn it on.

Sandra opened the driver's-side door of the Acura. The smaller of the two dogs, Terra, jumped right in. Charter was not so sure. He was a silly-goosey puppy who didn't always mind. Seventeen months old, he stood twenty-eight inches at the shoulder, weighed 140 pounds. Sandra swept him up and shoved him into the car, slammed the door. Then she went around and opened the trunk, stashed the laundry basket. She found a pair of tennis shoes and put them on, took a seat behind the wheel. Normally, when she and Bob went places, he drove. He *always* had to drive. But now here they were in an emergency and *she* was driving. In the middle of everything, she reflected upon this little irony. She started the engine.

Bob popped the safety latch and heaved open the heavy garage door, careful to lift with his knees. As the door slid up and over, taking its familiar path, making its familiar sound, the railroad-like click clack of rollers plying a track, he had the sensation of opening an oven door—the way the heat hits your face when you go to check the turkey. He estimated the temperature to be about 600 degrees. (In truth, the fire would reach upwards of 1600 degrees, fanned by the winds, feasting on the abundant brush. At that temperature, automobile engines melt into puddles; granite rocks crack and flake, a process called spalling, the reason for the dinosaur-egg shape of the boulders, testament to the countless similar fires that had ravaged Wildcat Canyon over the ages.)

He jumped into the car, slammed the door shut. His knees hit the dashboard; the seat was too far forward. Sandra eased it into gear—*Lord Jesus, don't let me stall.*

Riding the clutch, she goosed the gas pedal nimbly with her toe, just like her father had taught her when she was fifteen. Slowly, she backed out of the garage.

By now the fire was in the yard. It was on the front porch. It draped itself upon the familiar landscape of the Youngers' life, possessing the trees, the shrubs, the lawn chairs, devouring all.

Then she slammed on the brakes.

"Chelsea!" she exclaimed. Her eyes were wide with alarm.

Bob ran back inside.

Laureen Redden was everywhere at once. Throwing on clothes and grabbing the fireproof file box containing their important papers. Running up and down the steep steps to the garage, getting the five cats and the two dogs into the car, rousing her mom and stepdad, Judy and Gordon, who lived with them now in the new addition.

Hurrying about her business, focused and distracted at once, trying to remain calm, Laureen came to a sudden halt outside the master bedroom. *What on earth?*

Her husband was standing like a statue in the dark. His feet were set at shoulder width. His muscular arms were interlocked heroically across his chest. He was looking out the window, watching the fire approach.

"Larry?" She was twenty years his junior. They'd met in a country-western dance class—the last time either of them had danced. "Are you coming?"

"No," he said.

"No?" Her tone was incredulous.

"We're better off here," he said matter-of-factly.

A former lifeguard and a mountain endurance runner, Larry Redden had only recently retired, after thirty-five years of service as a captain in the San Diego Fire-Rescue Department. Had it not been for a slight misstep in a smoky stairwell with a three-hundred-pound man across his shoulders, he might still have been on active duty. As it was, three surgeries later, he was back to exercising every day. He was taking a woodworking class, planning a waterfall behind the house. He'd just bought a new band saw.

Laureen gave him a look. "We're *going*," she said. It sounded like an order. There was no sense arguing. Like the T-shirt says: SHE WHO MUST BE OBEYED. Larry shrugged. "All right then, let's go."

They got into their cars: Gordon and Judy in their matching cabernet-colored Jaguars, Laureen in her fingernail-polish-red '93 T-bird, Larry leading the way in his burgundy Buick Regal, a beefed-up fire chief's special.

The night was dark. The smoke was thick. Visibility was next to nil. The heat sucked the moisture from their bodies; their lips felt instantly cracked and dry. Burning debris flew through the air, sticks and leaves and branches, pelting the cars like flaming chunks of sideways hail. *It's like the tornado in* The Wizard of Oz, *only everything's on fire,* Laureen thought.

Turning out of the driveway, they climbed along the narrow strip of private blacktop that was the only way in or out of Lake View Hills Estates—ten solitary homesteads set lovingly, spectacularly, into the steep and rugged terrain overlooking the San Vicente Reservoir less than a mile southwest from Irene and Jimmy Hurst's little neighborhood. Laureen followed Judy's taillights. Judy followed Larry's. Gordon brought up the rear.

At the top of the hill, at the wrought-iron gate that marked the entrance to the community, the Redden caravan encountered several of their neighbors stopped haphazardly on and off the road.

The Hamiltons were in two cars: Steve had Alexander, the toddler; Jodi, who was pregnant, had Libby, the boxer. Cheryl Jennie was in her blue Acura. Trembling in her lap was her Lhasa apso, Muffie. Cheryl was waiting for her partner of twenty-three years, Steve Shacklett—for some reason, they'd never gotten around to marriage. He had a broken leg, was wearing a thigh-high cast. A bear of a man with an easy smile and a bushy goatee, he was headed this way in his thirty-foot motor home with his two Irish wolfhounds. Behind Cheryl were the Shoharas—James, Solange, and their thirty-two-year-old son, Randy, a handsome, biracial dude with an asymmetrical haircut who spent a lot of time skateboarding, body surfing, and riding dirt bikes. The Shoharas were the newest to the area. Both worked as correctional officers. Their sprawling stucco house was designed to incorporate the principles of feng shui. It also boasted a gazebo, a koi pond, and a custom-built library for their cherished collection of books. Lifelong suburbanites, they had never before experienced a firestorm, much less one of this magnitude. Behind them were the Dalys, a retired couple, unwilling or unable to attempt a maneuver around the pack.

Larry Redden slowed briefly and squinted through the windshield, through the smoke, trying to assess the situation, which was obviously time-critical. *Nobody's doing anything!* he thought. *Everybody's just sitting here like a bunch of chickens—buck-gawk!* He honked his horn several times. *Let's go, let's go, let's go!*

Taking the initiative, Larry drove off the asphalt and around the confused knot of his neighbors, his Buick's heavy-duty suspension serving him well. His family followed: Judy, Laureen, Gordon.

Recognizing the retired fireman as he went past, Cheryl fell into line behind Gordon. The Shoharas did the same, followed by the Dalys, and at last, here came Steve Shacklett, rumbling up the road in the motor home. They drove slowly down a little hill, then up a little rise. The smoke was thick; debris pelted the cars. Everything was glowing an eerie orange. It brought to mind a science-fiction movie, something postnuclear, cataclysmic.

Then, around a curve, they met the fire.

The flames were more than three stories tall. The thick brush and man-zanita and oak that normally overhung this section of Muth Valley Road like a canopy—shading it in summer so effectively, so romantically from the sun—were fully engulfed.

Even through the windshield, Larry Redden could feel the heat like sun on sunburn, burning his knuckles and forearms.

No way, he thought.

He pulled a U-turn.

"Go back home!" he hollered at the others, his head out the window of his Buick, burning embers stinging the back of his neck. "We can't make it out this way! Go back! It's our only chance!"

One after the other down the line, like the tuba section of a marching band pulling a featured movement, each vehicle followed Larry's example and made a tight U-turn. Everyone except Steve Shacklett.

A U-turn in the camper was out of the question. He decided to push on.

Bob Younger ran from his burning house toting a little cage. Inside was Chelsea, their cockatiel.

"Pop the trunk," he yelled.

With Chelsea secured, Sandra backed the white Acura out of the driveway, seventy-five feet uphill to the road. The fire raged all around them.

It was four-tenths of a mile from their house to Wildcat Canyon Road, the main artery through the canyon. Popular with triathletes and competitive cyclists, it ran in a northeasterly direction, from the Lakeside Rodeo Arena to the Barona Indian hotel, casino, and drag strip, and then up to the Cleveland National Forest, where the fire had started.

Ten and a half hours earlier, at about 5:50 P.M., a San Diego County Sheriff's search-and-rescue helicopter had spotted the lost hunter who'd set the blaze. Sergio Martinez, thirty-three and heavyset, had been lost for seven hours. He was dehydrated and delirious. According to newspaper reports, when asked if he'd set the fire, he said no. Then after a moment, he said, "I'm sorry about that. I thought I was going to die out there."

At the time of the rescue, the pilot recalled, the fire covered about fifty square yards, or one and a half basketball courts. Driven by seventy-mile-an-hour winds, supercharged by the physics of the canyon's contours, the fire would consume up to 12,000 acres an hour—195,000 acres over the next thirty-one hours.

Within minutes of the rescue, another sheriff's-department helicopter was speeding toward the fire with something called a Bambi Bucket, an accessory that can hold hundreds of gallons of water. However, due to regulations that prohibit flying within thirty minutes of sunset—6:06 on that day—the U.S. Forest Service denied the pilot permission to dump water on the fire.

By 7:00 P.M., about three hundred firefighters had responded to the blaze. Because of the rough terrain, they were unable to bring their equipment any closer than half a mile. Owing to the point of origin of the fire—a dry creek bed below drought-stricken Cedar Creek Falls—the blaze would be dubbed the Cedar Fire. It was one of several wildfires that erupted within hours of one another that hot, dry, windy day across southern California. In all, the Cedar Fire would claim fourteen lives and more than twenty-two hundred houses. Over eleven days, it would burn an area covering 280,000 acres—the largest single wildfire in California history. More than a month later, in late December, amid the political fallout and finger-pointing, San Diego firefighters would still be extinguishing the last embers of the blaze. Martinez, the hunter, was issued a misdemeanor citation for setting an unauthorized fire. He faces a fine.

The road between the Youngers' driveway and Wildcat Canyon Road had no name. It was wide enough for only one car. Part of it was paved, part of it dirt and gravel. There was a steep falloff on one side, a drainage ditch on the other. From the Youngers' driveway, the no-name road led back past their house, up a hill, around a giant boulder, then down the other side of the hill, where the road became extremely steep and narrow. At the bottom of the hill, the pavement ended. From there it was a straight shot to the main road.

Now, reaching the end of their driveway, Sandra swung the Acura's nose around, faced it east. The smoke was thick. "I can't see a thing!" she said.

"Whatever you do, don't stop!" Bob said. The fire was all around them. He was sweating profusely. He reached over and set the air conditioner to recirculate.

They proceeded along at five miles an hour, maybe less; it seemed like great speed. Both of them hunched forward to see; the visibility was no more than ten feet. Up the hill, around the giant boulder. They had lived here seven months. Sandra willed herself to visualize the route.

"Where are we?"

"Don't wreck the car!"

"What if the gas tank heats up?"

"I'm more worried about the tires melting!"

Somehow, slowly, they made progress, Bob calling out directions, Sandra gripping the wheel, riding the clutch, her right foot poised to slam on the brake pedal the moment they encountered the stalled car or downed tree trunk or live power line she was sure was lying in wait for them just beyond the shadows.

Toward the bottom of the hill, in the hollow where the pavement ended, the smoke was at its worst. She slowed the car to a stop.

"What do I do?" asked Sandra.

"I think we go left."

"Are you sure? I think—"

Just then, something bolted in front of them.

It jumped out from the cover of darkness, a flash of silver fur, fast and graceful, like footage from a *National Geographic* special. . . .

And then it was gone, dissolved like a ghost into the curtain of thick smoke.

"Did you see that?" asked Bob.

Sandra said nothing. She'd seen that bobcat before. It was morning, she remembered, somewhere right around here. She was headed to work. Suddenly, a bobcat had bolted in front of her car. She could still see it in her mind's eye, a flash of fur, a silver-and-black streak. He'd run down the very center of the gravel road. The very center. *How bold!* she'd thought to herself at the time, amazed at the glory of God's creation, this exquisite creature. *He's running right down the middle of the road, just like he owns it.*

Now she decided to follow.

Aman Vogel woke to an eerie glow. The smoke was thick. His clock said 4:30 A.M. Fifty-eight years old, Aman (pronounced *Ah*-mon) had lived an eventful life by anyone's yardstick: He'd hit a grand slam to lead his team to the finals in the 1957 Little League World Series in Williamsport, Pennsylvania; he'd shared an apartment with the Pointer Sisters in San Francisco; he'd lived off the grid as an IRS fugitive and subsistence farmer with a woman he'd taken up with after accidentally shooting her in the leg with a .357 Magnum. (She eventually left him, the only woman who'd ever broken his heart.) Of late, he was earning his living as a contract dentist: great money, no overhead, no responsibility. And a never-ending supply of fresh females, as he liked to say with a wink.

Aman was many things, but one thing he was not was the kind of guy who goes around changing clocks the night before daylight saving time ended. In truth, no two of his clocks were ever the same. He lived in the caretaker's house of an old estate called High Meadow Ranch. The main house had long ago burned to the ground; the vast acreage had once been slated to become an exclusive private golfing community. His ramshackle little house was set in a meadow beside a grove of towering oaks. It was thought by all who visited to be a tiny slice of heaven.

Sharing his bed with him that night were his cat and two of his dogs. Two more of his dogs were curled up on the floor. Calahan, the cat, had been with him for more than eighteen years. The dogs were all orphans, abandoned in the canyon by families who didn't want them anymore.

Now he sat up, swung his feet over the side of the bed. He walked five steps to the door that led outside. He turned the handle . . .

The door imploded.

Aman flew through the air, slammed against the opposite wall, ten feet distant. He slid down to the floor. He felt a stabbing pain in his side—a cracked rib.

He lay there a moment, dazed, thinking that he needed to get up and close the door, when all of a sudden, all the windows in the house exploded inward. The sound was deafening. Tiny shards of glass flew everywhere. The curtains billowed inward, fully in flames. He looked up. The roof was gone.

Out the door he could see a huge funnel of fire headed toward the house, toward him. It looked like something alive, like a monster from a comic book. The meadow behind the house, the grove of ancient oaks, all of them more than a hundred feet tall—everything was on fire. Every single leaf was burning. Every single blade of grass. Every shrub, every flower—everything. It reminded him of one of those nuclear explosions you see on television, when the bomb goes off and all the trees bend way over and then flip back up as if blown by gale-force winds, only it was fire instead of wind.

With some effort, he rose and walked back into the bedroom. His knees felt funny. He was bleeding from a dozen tiny cuts made by the glass. His rib hurt; it was doubly hard to breathe the smoky air. His arms felt singed and tender. On the bed stand was a fireproof safe he'd bought recently at Sears, guaranteed to 1000 degrees. Inside was $35,000 he'd won at the Indian casino up the road. Next to the safe was his Glock 9mm pistol. As he passed the bed stand, he thought to himself, *I should get the money. I should get the Glock.* For some reason, he didn't. He just kept going.

Out of the bedroom, through the living room. Two steps up into the kitchen.

With some of his winnings from the casino, he had recently purchased a 1990 Toyota pickup. It was beige, with four-wheel drive, a real cherry. Now he looked up. The two front tires and the engine compartment of his new truck were sticking down through what remained of the roof and the kitchen ceiling.

He wheeled around. Everywhere across the living room there were little fires, hundreds of them, lighting every nook and cranny. It was a beautiful sight, really. For a second, he thought about this chick he once knew. She loved candles. She liked him to dribble hot wax on her skin.

It was getting hotter and hotter in the house. He estimated it to be about 500 or 600 degrees. He stood there, paralyzed. The smoke was thick. There was fire all around him, blocking every exit. There was nowhere for him to go. *I'm gonna burn to death,* he thought. *This is how it's gonna be. I'm gonna die burning.*

An odd feeling of calm came over him. *Well, shit. I don't have a wife. I got no kids. I've had a good life. I've done a lot of things. I'll be okay. I hope it doesn't hurt too bad.*

And then he thought about some of the stuff he'd learned in premed. In his mind, he saw a picture of a hospital burn ward. And then he thought about the Glock. It was loaded. One in the chamber, like always. It was on the bedside table, next to the money.

Larry Redden led the caravan back down the steep hill. He turned into his driveway, followed closely by his mother-in-law, his wife, his stepfather-in-law, and Cheryl Jennie. The other families—the Shoharas, the Dalys, and the Hamiltons in their two vehicles—continued on down the hill, toward their houses, toward the reservoir.

After directing his group to stay put in the living room, Larry went up to the attic, broke out his Nomex fire suit. Returning downstairs, he found Laureen outside in a short-sleeved shirt attempting to beat out a small fire with a throw pillow. He ushered her back inside.

He knew there was no point in turning on the hose; he had two five-thousand-gallon cisterns, but the electricity was off. No pump, no pressure. He settled for a pair of two-gallon buckets.

He drew water from the swimming pool, carried it back up the hill to the deck, dumped it on the fire, did it again—a one-man bucket brigade. In short order, he was joined by Laureen. She was worried about her husband, about his surgically repaired rotator cuff, about his seemingly extra-large heart. Laureen had a Web business selling vintage clothing. She'd changed into a long-sleeved denim shirt. It looked cute with her black leather Enzo Angiolini loafers.

Side by side, the Reddens fought the fire. The house itself—stucco with a tile roof and safety windows—was basically fireproof. But the decks were wood, as were the ten cords of fireplace fuel—laid in for the upcoming cold season—that was stacked nearby. They threw buckets of water on the bougainvillea and the acacia, buckets of water on the she-oaks in the grove, buckets of water on the outdoor cathouse, on the lawn furniture, on the ice plant all around their property, which they'd planted because it was supposed to be fire retardant. They'd douse one little fire here, only to notice another little fire starting up there. Bucket after bucket. Haul and tote and throw. Back and forth. They worked as though they were possessed. . . .

Farther down the hill, the fire was getting closer to the Hamiltons' large Spanish house. According to a story in the *Los Angeles Times*, Jodi was on the phone with her mother in Connecticut, complaining bitterly that Steve, a construction-company executive, was wasting precious time moving work vehicles and heavy machinery out of the garage. She wanted to flee. Her mother told her to drive to the reservoir. Leave Steve behind if you have to, she said. Jodi hung up. She went ahead and loaded Alex and the dog into Steve's vehicle. Steve pleaded with her to stay, as the professional firefighter had advised.

They argued, precious seconds ticking away. At last, they reached a compromise. He wet the vehicle down with water and they drove out into a nearby open flat, a place in the road with a turnaround, sparsely landscaped. For the next hour or so, as the *Times* further reported, he raced the vehicle back and forth, dodging the flames, hoping like hell that the gas tank wouldn't blow. "Hot! Hot!" shrieked little Alex in the safety seat.

Jodi was petrified. She was angry at her husband. She still thought they should go to the reservoir. *This must be what hell is like*, she told herself. . . .

The Dalys, Barb and Bob, returned to find their house fully in flames. Bob was a retired electrical engineer, an inveterate tinkerer. Barb still played tennis regularly. Last year, despite the SARS epidemic, they'd insisted on keeping their travel plans to China.

Faced with their present situation, Bob took out his wallet, placed it carefully on the patio table. Then he and Barb jumped fully clothed into the pool.

They floated there, between the shallow and the deep, where they could still touch the bottom with their toes. They could hear propane tanks exploding all across the canyon, windows imploding; the apocalyptic roar of the fire cannot be overstated. Burning debris—the substance of their lives together—flew through the air, which was scorching hot. Each breath was an effort, like breathing in an overheated steam bath, only instead of steam, this was acrid smoke that made you cough and sneeze.

They took turns dunking their heads beneath the chlorinated water.

Down below, everything was cool and quiet and calm.

Aman walked back into the burning bedroom in search of the Glock, a man on a mission. Reaching toward the bedside table, he felt something furry against his leg. It was Calahan, his cat. In the eighteen years Aman had owned him, Calahan had never once nuzzled his leg. He was never a cuddler, never a lap sitter. There was never even any petting and purring. Like Aman, Calahan always just did his own thing. He was a very independent cat.

Aman bent down. Calahan jumped into his arms. He was trembling. Aman held him as tight as he could, the cat's head wedged forcibly into the soft hollow beneath the man's chin. Aman whispered into his ear: "Don't worry, pal. I'm gonna get you out of here."

As dawn broke, the fire burned its way out of Wildcat Canyon, heading in a southwesterly direction for Eucalyptus Hills, an oldish, densely populated suburb named for the highly flammable Australian shade trees planted thickly throughout.

The smoke began to clear, pushed off by the same Santa Ana wind. From their vantage point high above the reservoir, Laureen and Larry Redden—he in his Nomex fire suit, she in her denim work shirt and muddy Italian loafers—looked out on the remains of their beloved canyon.

All that was left of the thick brush were brittle charcoal skeletons. The huge granite dinosaur eggs were naked now against the brown earth, dusted with ash and charcoal. At the feet of the larger boulders could be seen piles of spalled rock—large flat shingles that resembled giant fish scales. The Dalys' house was gone, as was the Shoharas'. The Reddens' was fine, as was the Hamiltons'; they had been able to ride out the firestorm in their vehicle.

Now Larry walked down the road, carrying two buckets of pool water, intent on checking on the Dalys. He found them by their toolshed. There was a fire in the roof. Larry gave Bob a hand trying to knock it down; the fire turned out to be in the wall. When they were done, Bob went up to the pool to retrieve his wallet. There was no sign of it. Neither was there any sign of the patio table on which he'd left it.

Looking down toward the reservoir, Bob spotted the remains of the Shoharas' car. He and Larry walked down.

In all the neighborhood meetings, Larry had always told people that in the event of a fire, they should *never* drive toward the reservoir. There was something called a chimney effect. You never want to head downhill into a fire.

The Shoharas, of course, were new to the neighborhood. They'd never attended any of those meetings. Before getting into his pool, Bob Daly had tried to warn them. They chose to go anyway.

Bob and Larry found Solange and Randy Shohara still sitting in their seats, two charred skeletons frozen in repose. All the flesh was gone.

They found James a hundred feet up the road.

Two weeks later, Sandra and Bob Younger sat on a donated sofa in the living room of a rental house. Along with the Hursts, the Mumfords, the Hansons, and Aman Vogel—among many others in Wildcat Canyon—their house was burned to the ground, all their worldly possessions gone. They were thankful they escaped with their lives.

Such was not the fortune of Steve Shacklett, the man in the motor home with his two Irish wolfhounds. After finding the Shoharas, Larry Redden had driven out in search of Shacklett, whose common-law wife had weathered the storm in his living room. He found Steve's remains in a ditch beneath the back end of the vehicle, where he had attempted to take cover, moving with some difficulty, a cast on his leg.

"You keep thinking, What if?" Sandra Younger said. "What if Bob hadn't woken up? What if we'd kept sleeping? What if our brush contractor hadn't decided as an afterthought to clear ten to fifteen more feet of brush on the side of the house where the fire came through? That may have been the few extra minutes Bob needed to get out of there when he went back for the bird.

"And what if he hadn't come out? I wouldn't have left without him. There was this couple, twenty-eight years old, who lived near us. They found her in the car; he was coming out of the house with the dog in his arms. Essentially, that was us. Bob coming out with the bird. They both died on the spot.

"And what if I hadn't had LASIK surgery in March? I wore glasses for fifty years. I grabbed the wrong glasses. And I ended up driving. What if I hadn't just recently had the tires on my car replaced? Before that, they were worn to the tread. What if the fire had made them blow out? What if Bob had found his car keys and we tried to go out in two cars? Some people didn't make it out because they got separated in the smoke. One car ran into the ditch, the other one tried to stop and help. There are so many little variables. If you ran the numbers on all those permutations and combinations, it would be—it's just miraculous that we got out. All of the people who died were so near us geographically. They were all doing the same things in the same time frame that we were trying to do. There are all of these little things that could have gone the other way.

"You know, I told my dad about the bobcat. And then the next time I talked to him, he said, 'Honey, I've been thinking about your bobcat.' And I said, 'Yeah, me, too, Daddy.' And he said, 'The Lord sent one of his wildest creatures to lead you out of the fire.' And you know what? I think he's right.

"Things like this happen. There's just really nothing we can do," she said, shaking her head in sadness, in resignation, in wonderment.

Esquire, March 2004

The Secret Life of a Beautiful Woman

She loves big silver cowboy buckles and chewy red Swedish fish, three-inch Gucci stiletto heels and Lamborghini trucks. She hates being alone. She doesn't kiss on the first date. She feels high highs and low lows, often in rapid succession. Sometimes she'll push you away because she wants you to try again. She's been offered $30,000 for one night.

Her toes are long, like fingers. One of them sports a silver ring. She has a tiny tattoo of a cottontail bunny on the nape of her neck, a souvenir of a drunken night on the town with her two best friends, former *Playboy* centerfolds. She loves backgammon, bowling, dive bars, sunbathing in the nude, gambling in Las Vegas: blackjack, baccarat, *pai gow.* She loves French lingerie, always in matching sets, and scented candles, oodles of them, all over the room. She loves the word *love*—and the words *romance, ambience, intimacy,* and *hot.* She's been kidnapped by a bodybuilder, stalked by a Persian nightclub owner, electronically surveilled by an Israeli mobster, relieved of her worldly possessions by a family of wealthy Egyptians, sued by a downstairs neighbor who claimed that her vocal lovemaking destabilized his energy.

She has dark eyes and dimples, bright teeth and full lips, a beauty mark on her right cheek, the beginnings of fine lines in the various localities across her heart-shaped face that register emotion. She is the girl next door grown up, feet planted firmly on the summit of her prime, looking expectantly, tentatively, hopefully toward the future. Her speech is punctuated with musical exclamations—*Oh my God! Holy shit! Rad! That's the bomb!*—and though she hardly moves her lips when she talks (she can, in fact, carry on a conversation while a makeup artist applies lipstick with a brush), her tonal range is preternatural, from alto to coloratura, church mouse to screaming meemy. She invents adjectives: *froggy, foofy, fugly*. Her take on language is like her take on life: She makes it fun, she makes it fit her needs. She doesn't always care if others understand.

Her primary goals in life are marriage and motherhood. She's been engaged four times. She thinks it's probably better to marry someone who loves you more than you love him. No man she's ever been with has truly known how much she cared. She is ardent and enthusiastic, nurturing and sincere, spontaneous and insatiable. When she was young—a coltish, buck-toothed tomboy who gave up cheerleading to play football—she collected Matchbox cars, which she still keeps in their original carrying case, stashed inside a large antique hope chest, along with her old photo albums. Her first car was a cream-colored Porsche convertible. Her first night in Los Angeles was spent locked in a laundry room in a house in the Hollywood Hills, seeking refuge from an erstwhile acting teacher. She listens to Kool & the Gang, Mariah Carey, Kenny G, Shania Twain, Isaac Hayes. She likes tank tops and shorty shirts, cashmere and soft leather, baby-doll nightgowns and black garters, handbags by Chanel. She believes that men and women can be friends. Friends have given her clothes, diamonds, plane tickets, a Jaguar and a Jeep, three months in her own suite at the Ritz-Carlton. She's still friends with the Israeli mobster. He took his ring back with a shotgun. He is currently in prison. They correspond.

She owns her own condo in Santa Monica. She can watch the sun set over the Pacific Ocean from a hammock on her private rooftop deck, which doubles as a doggy latrine and could use a good cleanup. She can maneuver her black Lexus SUV through freeway traffic, talk on her cell phone, look up numbers on her palm computer using her fingernail as a stylus, and still manage to flip off an errant driver. She's never tried to flirt her way out of a speeding ticket. She's never found the guts to say, "No, honey, please don't go. Let's work this out." She thinks it would be nice, for once, to figure herself out, to understand herself better, to be more sure, to integrate more fully the things she knows with the things she feels.

She is a Virgo. She was born in 1972. She was born in 1971. She was born in 1970. Her grandfather was a Portuguese sailor. Her father split when she was two. Her mom worked three jobs. Her stepdad parked his car in front of the side door so she couldn't sneak out of the house at night. She used the window. She was an ugly baby, eggplant-colored and hairy, sick all the time. She still coughs like a croupy infant, with a hack like a hound from hell, though somehow it works for her, as does the dog-bite scar on her cheek— a cocker spaniel named Lucky—endearing little flaws that take her down a few pegs from perfect, make her seem more real. She giggles freely, laughs conspiratorially, grazes your arm lightly with her fingernails, leans her forehead into the space near yours. She rarely cries. Her most arresting feature is her eyes: deep, glittering orbs in almond-shaped settings. She says thank you to every compliment, no matter how small, no matter how tangential. She pays scant attention to things that don't involve her. She doesn't watch the news or read the paper; she doesn't remember names. When she's eating and wants to say something, which is often, she holds her left hand delicately in front of her mouth while she speaks. She hates her name: Brooke Burke. The way it looks: the busty double B's, the cutesy double e's. The way it sounds—like chicken talk: *Buk Buk.*

Brooke won her first beauty pageant at fourteen. She had her first boob job at nineteen. At twenty-two, she had a pocket of fat removed from just below the cheekbone on either side of her face. Once, in a mall in Tucson, where she grew up, a guy was so busy staring at her that he walked into a pole and knocked himself out. Once, crossing a street in Beverly Hills, she caused a four-car accident. Her likeness has smiled down upon Sunset Boulevard from a billboard. She's appeared on *Star Search* and *Jenny Jones,* in *Sport* magazine's swimsuit issue. She does a lot of catalogs for swimwear and lingerie and a television commercial now and then, most notably the stylish spots for Bally Total Fitness. An inventory of her catalog shots can be found on two unofficial Web sites posted by fans. She makes a minimum of $1,500 a day for print work. She will not bare her nipples or her kitty for any price; she is not that kind of girl. She has no interest in becoming an actress; she is not that kind of girl, either.

She is cute as a button, pretty as a picture, eminently fuckable, totally unavailable. Barring one regrettable incident, she is a confirmed serial monogamist, a one-man woman. Since the eighth grade, when the first love of her life deliberately flunked in order to stay behind in the same school with her, she has never gone more than a month without a boyfriend. Her current boyfriend drives a Mercedes V-12 convertible, a $120,000 car. She recently misplaced it in a shopping-mall parking lot. His name, Garth, is tattooed on her instep. He's forty, a plastic surgeon, one of the best in Beverly Hills, a blue-eyed graduate of Ole Miss known for his sweetness and good looks, for his pioneering techniques in scalp flaps and breast augmentations. On their fifth date, they went to Hawaii. They've been together every night since—nine months so far. The tattoo, in blue cursive letters, was a birthday gift. She knows it was risky, but it felt like the right thing to do. She calls it her public confession. Garth was flattered and pleased. One thing he loves about Brooke is her capacity for giving. The other day, for no particular reason, she bought him an alligator watchband from Cartier. His last girlfriend required a monthly stipend. Her price for cohabitation was a diamond ring. She never gave him anything but a hard time.

Brooke and Garth have talked about taking the next step—or at least about taking the step after the next step, because the next step will be moving into the house he is building, a $2.5 million, seventy-five-hundred-square-foot "estate home" with a three-story atrium entryway and a fireplace in the master bath. Just yesterday, in fact, four days before Christmas, while she was visiting his office, stopping by for a few moments to drop off a picture of herself in a red satin Santa suit, a little holiday surprise for his desk, Garth's great good friend and business manager came right up and gave her a big hug. It was no ordinary hug, this one. It was a huge, strong, lingering hug—you might even say a pregnant hug—followed by a chaste little kiss on the cheek, followed by an arm's-length biceps squeeze and a knowing look. *That* had never happened before. Never, ever. Never! *Holy shit!* Come to think of it, everyone in the office was acting weird. The receptionist, the nurses, even the techs. Looking at her funny. Smiling oddly. Strange. Really strange. And then the business manager just walked right up and wrapped her in this bear hug and then kissed her and wished her well and then looked at her like, like—

Oh my God!

Oh my GOD!

Oh. My. God.

Something's up, she is sure.

Brooke strolls with her pit bull down the sunny side of the street, a trendy little avenue of boutiques and palm trees just east of the beach, wearing large Donna Karan sunglasses and a vintage leather jacket, unzipped to reveal the low-cut neckline of her tan knit shirt, the hemispheric swell of her breasts. Her long brown hair luffs behind her in the gentle salt breeze, trailing the aroma of Coco Chanel.

"Excuse me. Excuse me? *Hellooooo.*"

He is tall, mid-twenties, handsome like a college quarterback. He carries a gym bag and a cell phone, wears a baseball cap and a crooked grin. He passed her one block back and his eyes bugged. He stopped, turned, watched her for a few moments, transfixed, the muscles of her taut thighs and high ass undulating subtly beneath her faded Levi's, and then he took off after her in a leisurely pursuit. Now he's three yards back and holding steady, matching her step for step. "Hey!" he calls, a tad beseeching. "Just a minute."

She accelerates, lengthening her stride imperceptibly, pretending not to hear. It is three days before Christmas and she has presents to buy, much on her mind. There are curtains and colors and fireplace fittings to be chosen for the new house; she needs to find someone to sublet her condo. She has a go-see at two, her test shots for her new comp card are ready for pickup at the photographer's studio, her reservations for New Year's Eve at the doggy hotel have yet to be confirmed. She's still undecided about her outfit for Garth's office party tomorrow night—will the backless be too much? Maybe the black lace would be better. Or the leather pants. Something's up; she wants to look smashing. To top it off, her best friend, Neriah, one of the tattooed triumvirate, is due home this afternoon from Las Vegas. She's been gone for a while visiting her man. She called this morning, said she was flying in, said she had big news. Last time, the big news was a brand-new Mercedes convertible. *Oh my God!* What could it be?

"Excuse me," calls the quarterback, throttling up a notch, hailing her like a coast-guard vessel on the high seas, trying to come alongside and cast a line. "Pardon me! Please?"

She adjusts the strap of her handbag over her shoulder, loops a stray hair behind her ear with a manicured nail, stays a brisk but nonchalant course down the sidewalk. In a town teeming with beautiful women, Brooke is still a magnet, a prime example of what she likes to call the BBD—the Bigger Better Deal, the kind of woman who makes men restless and noncommittal in their relationships, the kind of dream date they like to think is waiting just around the corner, anxious to enter their lives. Once or twice a day, someone stops dead in his tracks and stares at her, or someone says something, tries to meet her, to get her number. They call to her from car windows across two lanes of traffic, make small talk about ibuprofen at the drugstore cash register. Maybe because Brooke is not particularly tall. Maybe because she's not particularly famous, or because she's brunette instead of bombshell blond, and men tend to want to date blonds but marry brunettes. Maybe because when she smiles, she lights up a rather large area around her. Whatever the reason, there is something about Brooke that seems approachable, that draws people in. Men see her and think for just a moment that it might be possible to have a pinup girl of their very own, the perfect woman with whom to share all their toys.

When she first came to Los Angeles from Arizona, if someone looked her way, she'd gaze into his eyes and smile her best smile, not to invite conversation or approach, just to be friendly, to be the best person she could be. She rarely does that anymore. There have been too many invitations to parties that turned out to be intimate dinners, too many business meetings with Joe Blow and his cousin Sam the writer, too many psychos and too many restraining orders, too many long nights of giggling at stupid jokes, acting as if she wanted to be somewhere she didn't want to be, acting as if this sweaty dodo with his smelly cigar might really have a chance with her when the night was through. Over the years, she's become more discreet, more careful, not nearly so nice. It pains her to say this—being the kind of person she's always been, a woman who finds her deepest solace in the company of a man, a man's woman—but a girl like Brooke needs to protect herself. A girl like Brooke needs a house alarm, a dog, a gun, and caller-ID blocking.

The quarterback closes the gap, reaches out and taps Brooke on the shoulder. "Excuse me," he says again. She wheels around. They almost collide.

"Can I help you?" Her tone is businesslike, cool but not cold, short but not indignant, a little wary.

"Um, uh—hi!" he stammers.

The pit bull growls. "Sit, girl," she tells the dog, a thick-bodied, brown-black bitch on medication for a thyroid problem.

"So," he says, searching for an opener. "What do you do?"

"That's kind of personal, isn't it?"

"I guess," he says. He shuffles his feet. He beams. It is clear that his looks are his usual route in, but the door isn't opening. He's at a loss.

"So what do you want?" she asks.

"I, uh—well, uh—"

"Yes?"

"Do you think it would be possible for us to dine together?"

"Dine together," she deadpans. She smiles a fake smile, a kind of grimace. She shakes her head. "I don't think so. I'm engaged."

"Engaged?" he asks. "Really." He lifts a skeptical eyebrow, points with his cell phone at her left hand. A chunky gold bracelet slides down his wrist. "Where's your ring?"

"My ring?"

"Yeah. Your engagement ring."

"Who says you need a ring to be engaged?"

"Most people, I guess."

"Well, I'm not most people."

"So what do you think?"

"About what?"

"About dinner."

She sighs again. "Listen, I'll tell you what. See that coffee shop over there?"

Shielding his eyes with the cell phone, he squints across the street. "You mean that one?"

"I'll meet you there in an hour, okay?"

"Great! Excellent! Okay!" His face breaks into a big smile. He shifts his weight from foot to foot. "One hour from right now." He taps his watch. "Say, one-twenty?"

"Perfect. One-twenty will be perfect."

"Okay!"

"Okay."

"Okay! Well! I guess I'll see you then!" He waves goodbye, begins backing away.

"Let's go, Cali," she says to the dog.

"Wait a minute. What's your name?"

She calls over her shoulder, headed south: "I'll tell you when I see you."

"I'll be waiting," he croons.

Late afternoon in Brooke's condo, a dramatic one-bedroom with a vaulted ceiling and two-story windows. The sun has set, the Cabernet is poured, the scented candles are lit, oodles of them, all over the room.

Brooke and Neriah sit facing each other on either end of an overstuffed sofa, legs crossed Indian-style, each of them nuzzling a cat. A little more than a year ago, between men, feeling sad and mighty froggy, they roomed together here for a while. Brooke had just broken off her engagement with a German model named Stefan, a strapping piece of manhood with shoulder-length hair and deep brown eyes—*Oh my God!* Their relationship was pure adrenaline: extremely volatile, very chemical, very unhealthy. The thought of him still makes her roll her eyes and pretend to swoon. Neriah had just fled a long relationship with a youth pastor from her tiny hometown in northern California. One night he just went off, calling her the devil, trashing their log cabin, vowing they'd never marry, because she'd appeared naked in three million magazines. It was a dark time for both women, and every evening, schedules permitting, they'd rendezvous at sunset, break out the wine and one of Brooke's ornate weed pipes, and take their respective seats on the deep, velvety sofa. They called it the Therapy Couch.

Neriah has just returned from Las Vegas with a five-carat diamond ring on her finger. When the initial wave of shrieks and hugs and *Oh my Gods* subsided, they immediately called Nikki, the third of their triumvirate. Now Nikki is here with them in voice and spirit, via speakerphone. She recently married Ian Ziering, an actor on *Beverly Hills, 90210.* The rule among these women is that your man comes first; it's been quite a while since they've all been together in the same room. The decibel level is deafening.

"Neriah! You're getting married! Oh my God!" shrieks Nikki.

"Isn't this the best!" squeals Brooke.

"I know. I know. I *know!*" cheers Neriah, throwing a fist in the air.

"So what are you gonna do, man, live in Vegas?" asks Nikki. A former dental hygienist from Orange County, Nikki was Miss September 1997, pictured in her centerfold in front of a fun-house mirror. She is a blond of the bombshell variety, known in her circle of friends for her devilish laugh, her quick tongue, her ability to recite the fifty states in alphabetical order in less than a minute.

"I'll probably keep my place here," says Neriah, another beautiful blond, buxom yet athletic, another petite girl made larger than life through surgery. In her *Playboy* layout (March 1994), she was pictured as a hippie chick, outdoors in the desert. She is famous among the kind of men who read *Playboy* as the Playmate Who Split the Scene. Shortly after her pictorial ran, she found God (and the youth pastor) and refused to participate in any promotions. Her disappearing act served unwittingly to create a cult following. Recently, the license plate from the scooter pictured in her centerfold sold for more than a thousand dollars to an anonymous collector. You can find her on her own Web site, in catalogs, in guest spots on TV.

"You could always stay with us when you work," offers Brooke. "You know you'll always have a room wherever I live, bunny."

"Ahhhh!" groans Neriah, anguished. "I don't know. I don't *know!* Bunnies! I'm starting to get sad now, guys. I am not moving away!"

"Don't get sad," soothes Brooke. "You're *not* moving away."

"You're not moving away, but you *are* getting married," advises Nikki, somewhat stern, the voice of experience. When Nikki came home at 4:00 A.M. after that fateful night out with the girls, tattooed and wasted, her husband was none too pleased. They'd been married barely a month. She'd converted to Judaism for him, and Jews, he informed her as the sun began to rise, don't believe in tattoos. Two days later, she had a laser treatment; she was scheduled for three more but didn't keep the appointments. Her cottontail bunny still shows, albeit faintly.

"You mean I don't get to keep my own apartment?" asks Neriah, playfully baffled, putting on a breathy Marilyn Monroe voice.

"You mean she has to actually *live* with him?" asks Brooke, playfully incredulous, putting on a cute-little-girl voice.

"Yes, bunny!" says Nikki in her Betty Boop voice.

They met several years ago at a Frederick's of Hollywood catalog shoot. There was Brooke and Neriah and Nikki, a few others, including the Tenison twins, Rosie and Reneé, the latter well-known as the 1990 Playmate of the Year, the first black woman ever selected. The chemistry worked so perfectly that the Frederick's people signed them all for a lengthy campaign, and with the regular gigs came familiarity and then friendships quite rare in their business—phone calls and lunches, solidarity and hand holding, uproarious nights of dancing, karaoke, bowling, expeditions to Playboy Mansion West. Brooke stands out from the rest in the Frederick's catalog by virtue of the fact that she doesn't stand out quite so much, a sort of princess among sex kittens, a beauty among the bombshells—smaller, subtler in proportion, tending to beam into the camera rather than smolder, tending to shy away from the more outrageous and revealing outfits.

While their exact ages remain a bit murky, it is clear that Brooke functions as a kind of den mother or elder sister to the group, a counselor and adviser, a trail master who gathers the wagons for a night out, an authority on diamond grades and auto leases, dinner parties and foreign cuisines, hairdressers and clothing stores, style and business and relationship tactics. She believes that shoes make the woman, that nails should never be fake, that candles and good smells make a home intimate and inviting. She preaches that sweetness is the utmost virtue, that the way you carry yourself dictates the way you're treated, that you shouldn't accept as a gift something you couldn't afford to buy yourself, unless you're sure there are no strings attached, or at least no strings you can't handle.

It was Brooke who first came up with the whole bunny thing. Whenever one of the girls was sad, Brooke would look at her and say, "Don't be a sad bunny," and then she'd place her hands at the top of her head like ears and let them droop. Over time, the bunny thing has taken on a life of its own. If someone is curious, one bunny ear goes up. If someone is blown away, both bunny ears go back. Sometimes the ears become horns.

Now, sitting in her spot on the Therapy Couch, celebrating Neriah's good news, eyeballing that diamond ring, that rock, that huge symbol of lifelong care and commitment glinting there on the third finger of her left hand, Brooke is beginning to feel a little like the odd bunny out. Nikki is happily married. Neriah is next. Something is up with Garth, she is sure. She is excited—*Oh my God!*—is she ever. She is ready and willing. She can hardly stand it. But she has also been around way too long to count her chickens. She's been proposed to nine times. She ducked out of one wedding less than a month before the date. *Que será, será,* as her mother used to say. Brooke loves her career, takes it very seriously. But she will tell you in a minute that modeling to her is just a nice way to make a living, a fun game of dress-up, a glamorous means of killing time. She knows you can't model forever. A few more years and she'll be through with this phase of her life, and that will be perfectly fine. She has never regarded herself as the prettiest girl in the room. Look at her friends—*Holy shit!*—they're all tens. She got into modeling to see how far she could go. She's gone pretty far. Now she's just about ready for something new. When she gets out of modeling, she wants it to be a happy time. She wants it to seem as if she's making a positive change, growing into another life, moving up to another level. Her dreams and values and ambitions have always been focused upon being a wife and a mother. She was born to these tasks, she believes, was put on the earth for these things. Looking at her, you can hardly disagree. She raises her glass, takes a deep draft of wine. "When are you gonna have a baby, Nikki?" she asks, her voice winsome and far away.

"You guys, I've been craving one myself," croons Neriah.

"Guys! Listen to this!" says Nikki. "I had this dream last night. I was watching someone's baby. It was a little girl. And she looked up at me in my dream and—I know this sounds, like, really corny, but it broke my heart. She says to me, in this tiny, baby voice: 'I'm a really good girl.' "

"Ohhhhh!" swoons Neriah.

"Ohhhhh!" coos Brooke.

"And I was like: I love you!" squeals Nikki. "But then the parents came and took her away. I felt soooooo empty. Bunnies: I want a baby soooo baaaaaaad!"

"Just hold off for a little while," says Neriah. "I think we should all be pregnant together."

"Definitely!" pronounces Brooke, her blues receding at the very thought of it. "Oh my God!"

"Think about it," says Nikki. "Do any of us want to be fat alone?"

"No way!" says Brooke.

"Swollen ankles!" says Nikki.

"Fat thighs!" shrieks Neriah.

"We could get a three-for-one group liposuction discount with Garth!" says Nikki.

"We all know which bunny is going to be next!" sings Neriah, sly and teasing. She reaches over, gives Brooke a playful shove.

"You think it's gonna be Wendy?" asks Brooke, laughing, deflecting, bringing up the name of one of their friends. "Is she still with that producer guy?"

"I was just talking to her," says Nikki. "She says he's really boring."

"Then why is she dating him?" asks Brooke.

"Is he rich?" asks Neriah.

"He's got a really big dick!" squeals Nikki.

"Nooooo!" shrieks Neriah.

"And the biggest balls she's ever seen!"

Bunny's feeling froggy. It is Christmas Eve, and the sky is a glorious canvas of pink and orange and magenta. A cold front has descended over the beach, and there is an almost wintry chill in the air, a strong smell of woodsmoke and pine needles and potpourri. Brooke has just returned to her condo, laden with gifts for Garth. There is a pair of royal-blue silk pajamas, special-ordered from Barneys in New York. A Hugo Boss lambskin coat, a Ralph Lauren alligator business-card holder, a book of poetry called *The Language of Love*, a Felix the Cat refrigerator magnet, a traveling coffee mug from Starbucks. And there is the Big Present: a huge, soft, fluffy, luxurious sheepskin rug. She has plans for that rug. Candles and wine and nakedness are involved. She declines to elaborate further. She sits now at her dining-room table, awash in wrapping paper and bows and ribbons and lace of every color and variety, her head resting in her hands.

Though shopping usually makes her happy, though Christmas usually makes her very happy, though she's going home to visit her family tomorrow and that usually makes her extremely happy, she's a little down at the moment, has been so for the last two days. Shortly after she and Neriah had gotten off the phone with Nikki, Garth came home and went straight to the bedroom, didn't even say hello. When Brooke told him about Neriah's engagement, he barely reacted. When she tried to show him her new photos, he smiled wanly and told her he was tired, would look later. The photos were the culmination of more than a month of frustrating effort. She'd changed agencies a while back, and they thought she should update her comp card, the six-by-eight-inch photomontage that is shown to potential clients. She'd done test shoots with three different photographers at her own expense. The results looked great on the contact sheets. Blown up, however, they were disappointing, to say the least. You could see the beginnings of tiny character lines near her dimples, near her nose, beside her mouth, a bit of puffiness under her eyes, and traces of crow's-feet. For the first time in her career, she resorted to airbrushing. Those pictures were important to her in a lot of ways; Garth didn't get it. He didn't seem to care one iota. She has a thing about men not taking her seriously. She may not have finished college, but she's done pretty well for herself, making the most of her God-given talents. She's been to Taiwan and South Africa, Ibiza and Tahiti. For much of her work, she acts as her own agent, is known among clients for being professional and easy to work with, for driving a rather hard bargain. She's not just another pretty face. Her man, of all people, should know that. He made her feel really bad.

But being the kind of woman that she is—a nurturer, a caretaker, a giver, an optimist of the highest sort—she decided to give him a break, to let it pass. A man can have a hard day at the office, she knows very well. He's under pressures she can't even imagine. She swallowed her dismay, set about trying to cheer him up while Neriah waited in the living room. After a little hand holding and TLC, Garth agreed to come out of the bedroom and go to dinner with Neriah to celebrate her good fortune. He spent much of the evening, before the food came, with the collar of his sweatshirt pulled up over his nose. It reminded Brooke of that idiot guy in the bubble-gum comics. She went to bed angry, something she rarely does.

The next night was the big office party: lobster and filet mignon and dancing in a special room at Trader Vic's. She wore a clingy black tube dress with a slit up the side. She was clearly the most beautiful woman in a room of beautiful women. They ate and they drank and they were merry. Drank quite a bit, in fact—she fell asleep on the living-room floor afterward. But nothing special occurred. Nothing out of the ordinary. If something was up, it didn't happen. She must have been imagining things. She must have read things all wrong—the reactions the other day in the office. Now she's questioning her instincts. She doesn't know what's going on, if anything is going on at all. The truth is, the timing for a proposal is all wrong. A house and a diamond and a wedding all at once? It seems pretty exorbitant. Way too much to expect. Or even to want. It's almost disgusting if you think about it. *Holy shit!* What is going on?

Adding to her distress this afternoon, as if she needed something else, is the presence of something new in her life, a big honker of a pimple that has taken up residence between her eyebrows, a virtual third eye. It reared its ugly head before the party. She used some special stuff to kill it, but it burned her skin. Now it looks all brown and crinkly—a giant mess, totally fugly. When it rains, it fuckin' pours.

Life's little dramas. Every day can't be a holiday—even if this really is a holiday—even for Brooke, who tries her darndest to keep to the sunny side of the street. She raises her head from her hands, regards the array of holiday paraphernalia before her, lets go a large, cleansing, sibilant sigh. She chooses a roll of wrapping paper, lays the book of poems on top, cuts the paper to size, sets about folding and taping and tying an elaborate bow.

Things will get better. They always have. They always do. Hell, things aren't so bad, anyway. Not if she really thinks about it. "I know what it looks like," she says. "I'm a model. My man is a Beverly Hills plastic surgeon. We drive nice cars. We're moving to a big house in Bel Air Crest. It's kind of sick, but you just have to put it in perspective. I never asked for all of this. It all came naturally, and I'm thankful. I'm a happy person. I'm a grounded person. I'm an honest person. I'm living the best life that I could ever be living. And if some of that is because I'm beautiful, I mean, *holy shit!* I am what I am, you know?"

She finishes wrapping the book and the magnet and the pajamas and then gets up from the table, carries the packages across the room, past the Therapy Couch, toward the six-foot potted palm in the corner, near the windows. It is strung with tiny white lights, hung with ornaments: their California Christmas tree. Underneath are a bunch of presents. This morning they weren't there.

"Holy shit!" exclaims Brooke, happiness dawning over her face like the sun on a brand-new day. "When did *these* get here? And look at the tags! They're all for me! Oh my God! I can't believe him. What a sneak! What a sweetheart!"

She drops the presents she's just wrapped carelessly at her feet, bends over to the sprawling pile of cheerful packages surrounding the tree. At the very top is a small box—a cube, two by two by two.

"Oh my God! Holy shit! Holy Moly!" she squeals, retrieving the box. "I wonder what *this* is?" She holds it suspended in the air before her eyes, turns it this way and that, brings it up to her ear, shakes it. "Diamond earrings, I bet you!" she declares, the decibels rising. "It's gotta be diamond earrings. It's not a ring box. I don't *think* it's a ring box. If it was a ring box, it would have the round velvet hump on the top. Unless! Oh my God! Unless the ring box is *inside* of a bigger square box! Holy shit! That way, the top would cover the hump! It can't be a ring box. Could it be a ring box? Should I open it? The tape is a little loose right here. I could probably unwrap it and—"

Oh my God!
Oh my GOD!
Oh. My. God.
Should she open it? What could it be?

Esquire, April 1999

The Man of Tomorrow Goes to the Prom

Sweaty and dejected, as smelly as a man, Jesse is slumped in his regular chair at the kitchen table. It is late afternoon in the suburbs. The dishwasher churns, *SportsCenter* plays on the wide-screen TV in the seating area adjacent. His elbows are propped upon the wooden table, his cheeks rest heavily in his palms. His lower lip protrudes a bit, fleshy and pink, a teenage version of a pout.

"Oh my God!" he exclaims, pure anguish in his voice, a reedy tone, a clarinet. He is wearing an Old Navy T-shirt with a blue jalopy on the chest, Gap cargo shorts (the waistband riding low on his slender hips, exposing green plaid boxers), and Reebok DMX basketball shoes, well-worn, perhaps in need of replacement, a souvenir of his days as the starting point guard on the sophomore team. His eyes—large and arresting, described by his older brother as "babe magnets: supercool neon green and turquoise with flecks of brown"—are bugged out of his long, thin face, an expression known well to his family and friends, reminiscent of the thousand-yard stare associated with veterans of combat, emblematic at the moment of Jesse's supreme frustration, his total disbelief, the kind of primal, elemental, unmitigated outrage that only a seventeen-year-old can feel.

He buries his face in his hands. His fingers are tapered and rangy, neither those of a boy nor those of a man, callused but unwrinkled, devoid of any hair, skilled with balls and clubs and bats, with the sterling-silver Cross pen-and-pencil set he keeps in his Jansport backpack, with keyboards and joysticks and remote controls, with other stuff left unsaid. His skin is the blue-white of alabaster. His veins show. He burns easily in the sun, unfortunate when you live only twenty minutes from the beach. He's always slathering himself with SPF 50, always leaving bits and dollops on the corners of his prominent nose or in his biggish ears. His girlfriend—half Japanese, one year older, soon to graduate and leave for college—likes to strum the veins on the inside of his forearm like guitar strings.

"*Ahhhhhhhhhh!*" he moans, a pitiful sound. It resonates within the chamber of his hands, leaks out into the room, which is painted a warm shade called Smoky Taupe. A ceiling fan turns slowly overhead.

Jesse's mother looks up from the dishes in the sink. A small woman with auburn highlights in her hair, Meryl Epstein, fifty-two, is dressed in her exercise clothes: black leggings and a simple white tee. Out the window, the sun is bright, the sky is storybook blue. A lawn mower drones in the middle distance. In the shade of a palm tree, a trio of indigenous rabbits nibbles at the foliage bordering the lawn, leaving behind turds the size of Milk Duds. To her left, beneath the natural-wood cupboards, is an ugly gouge in the dry wall where a contractor made a new problem while trying to fix an existing one. He has promised to return. She'll believe it when he shows.

Jesse is her second son, six years and two miscarriages after the first. Adam is twenty-three, a graduate of UCLA. He has a job editing movie trailers. Jesse's was a difficult birth—twenty-four hours of labor followed by a C-section. Meryl always loved the name Jesse because of Jesse Colin Young. She saw him recently in concert. She can still remember buying her first Young-bloods album in 1969. *C'mon people now / Smile on your brother.* She was in college at the time, in Amherst, Massachusetts, a fine-arts major, a huge mistake. "The teachers all had their heads up their asses," she will say, in the "potty language" she likes to employ out of earshot of kids and fellow members of the PTA executive board. After she graduated, she never painted again. An old canvas hangs over the mantel. It mocks her every day. One more year and Jesse will be off to college himself. Her forehead wrinkles, moderate alarm. "What's wrong?"

Jesse raises his face from his hands. "We had this three-on-three basketball tournament at school."

"And you lost?"

"We were *ahead!*" The volume rising again. "We were *waaaaaaay* underdogs! They were *seniors!*"

She throws an admonishing look. "I didn't know you were playing in a tournament."

"I forgot to tell you," he deadpans. He reaches up and smooths one of his eyebrows with his fingertips. Among the things about which Jesse is self-conscious—the possibility of food residue in his teeth or on his face, which compels him to use at least three napkins during the course of a meal; or an eruption of pimples, for which he uses two different prescription acne creams; or bad breath, the reason he is always chewing gum, specifically Wintergreen Ice Breakers gum, not the blue kind, death to the blue kind, though all they have in stock right now in the Epstein pantry is the blue kind, because that was the kind on sale and his mom, a devoted clipper of coupons, can't resist a sale—the thing about which he is most self-conscious are his eyebrows, which bring to his mind images of caterpillars or Groucho Marx. He's always combing them back, going like this with his fingertips, trying to get them, like, pushed into place, a reflexive action, seemingly involuntary, performed absently during those times in which he is not absently cracking the joints of his fingers and his toes, or absently drumming on the table, or absently jazz-snapping his fingers, or, rather, absently *attempting* to jazz-snap his fingers, as he has, inexplicably, only recently learned how to jazz-snap and he's still not that great at it, so he practices all the time, as is his nature, all the time, no matter where he is: looking into the colorful flat screen of his computer, checking his fantasy-league baseball scores; lying on the tan leather sofa watching *PTI* on ESPN, his favorite show besides *The Simpsons, Gilmore Girls,* and *Six Feet Under;* sitting in one of his four Advanced Placement classes at Capistrano Valley High School, in Mission Viejo, in Orange County, California, where he is a second-semester junior, number ten in a class of 531, and where his rainbow assortment of classmates—all of them identically clothed in a sort of SoCal-surfer-hip-hop-retro-Britney chic that transcends body type and racial origin—are in constant and continuous motion themselves, a kinetic collection of raw promise and raging hormones, of tapping feet and pistoning knees, all of them fidgeting and adjusting and grooming and whispering and playing with their hair. Jesse's own thick black hair is cropped short and needs no care whatsoever. At the crown of his head, arranged in a circular pattern, is a curious sprinkling of white hairs, perhaps a hundred in all. Through the years, teachers have always told his parents that Jesse is a bright kid, a nice kid, an exceptionally mature kid. Somehow his skullcap of prematurely gray hairs seems apt, an odd genetic misfire marking his particular gift—a head for reason and logic and unswerving good sense, which is, in his own estimation, sometimes his best asset and sometimes his worst.

"So tell me," Mom probes. "What was this tournament?"

"A sophomore fundraiser."

"Who was on your team?"

"Me and David and Ajay. We drew a hard first-round game and we lost."

"I'm sorry," she coos.

"We were up ten to nine, game to eleven. And then I missed, like, *two shots!*" He stares into his traitorous hands. *"Ahhhhhhhhhh!"*

"You dog!" Steve Epstein, fifty-eight, pads into the kitchen in his stocking feet, bringing with him his usual energy and good humor, some of it learned, no doubt, during the course of his first career, as a teacher of emotionally disturbed kids. The son of a Depression-era traveling salesman, Steve now works as a regional sales director for a pharmaceutical company. He spends two days a week on the road, the rest of the time in his home office; he pulls down a little over six figures a year, plus bonuses. He is wearing Gap cargo shorts like his son's; Meryl does all the shopping. A green T-shirt brings out the green in his eyes, which everyone in the family agrees, with a wink, are not nearly as cool as Jesse's. The family also likes to lampoon Steve's thick Boston accent, the way he gets food on his face and talks with his mouth full, the way his spare tire seems to be growing lately, the way he never knows where anything is kept. Every family has its Homer; Adam and Jesse call him Homer to his face. Steve doesn't mind. Not even when he tells a joke and his wife and sons exchange mournful looks among themselves, then burst out laughing at how bad the joke was. Being a good dad means being taken a little bit for granted. The bottom of the totem pole is the base.

"You *never* miss the last shot," Dad says.

"It was *this* close!"

"You *dawwwwwwg!*" says Dad, changing up on the pronunciation this time, being that he is the fun type of parent—as opposed to Mom, the worrywart disciplinarian—the kind of dad who peppers his speech with an awkwardly deployed range of somewhat outdated vernacular like *Tight!* and *Bad!* and *Cool!*; the kind of dad who has just realized that his earlier exclamation, *"You dog!"* really sounded, on second thought, like something that could be construed by his son as a negative value judgment on his ability to put the rock in the hole. The last thing he wants is the kid on a couch in ten years blaming the old man for his woes. He lays his hands on Jesse's shoulders. He still wakes him gently for school each morning at 6:45 with a kiss. "Was it a good fundraiser at least?"

"They probably made a lot of money!" Mom adds brightly, shutting off the water at the sink, taking up station behind the granite-topped island in the center of the room.

"I just keep replaying that shot! Over and over in my head!"

"What about the shots you made?" Mom asks.

"I should have taken him off the dribble!"

"*What if* doesn't count," Mom says.

Jesse's eyes bug. Really wide this time.

"Don't worry about it," Dad chuckles, trying to lighten the mood. "We'll still feed you."

"Really?" The word shoots out of his tight lips like a dart from a blowgun.

Dad issues his own look. "Why don't you go take a shower?"

"Would you like me to make you a sandwich?" asks Mom.

"*Ahhhhhhh!*" He buries his face in his hands.

If Jesse Epstein were writing a speech for a school election—something he's done twice recently—he might be inclined to point out that the junior year of high school is a crossroads in a boy's life. It wasn't very long ago that he was down on the carpet with sticky hands, playing with his favorite Hot Wheels, making car noises with his lips. Now he's sharing those lips with his girlfriend, Kina, driving her around in his silver Mercury Cougar, formerly his dad's company car, free to roam at will the twenty square miles and three highway exits—home, the mall, school—that make up his world.

Over the past six weeks or so, the future has begun to show itself to Jesse. In rapid succession, he has taken the SATs and the ACTs. He has taken four Advanced Placement exams, high scores on which can be redeemed for college credits. And this weekend he'll be taking the SAT II's—three individual tests: English, math, and Spanish. Not to mention last week's state-mandated STAR exams in every subject. And his regular homework—he has a ton. The semester is almost over. Finals are next week; grades are on the line—the grades that will go out to colleges. In AP English he's reading both *Macbeth* and Jim Carroll's *Basketball Diaries*. A mock college essay is due tomorrow morning at 7:45. In AP Spanish IV he's reading *Don Quixote*. There's a ton of busy work assigned; some of it involves scissors and paste. In AP Environmental Science, there's a research project: habitat loss and urbanization. (Watch those footnotes: Mr. Redding runs entire sentences through Google.) And in AP Calculus, as usual, there is a test looming: integrals and anti-derivatives. He gets it. He guesses he gets it. He doesn't exactly get why. He sincerely hopes someday to have the opportunity to travel to the Land of Calculus so he can put some of this crap to use.

If you ask him directly, Jesse will tell you that the future is no big deal, that he doesn't feel any pressure, no way. His general attitude, he says, "is to try and do my best. Whatever happens, happens. I'm not one of those stress cases because, frankly, it takes all the fun out of everything, and having fun is my number-one objective in life—right now at least." Jesse says he doesn't mind school, doesn't mind taking standardized tests—although he hates the sweaty, shaky feeling he gets when he doesn't know the answer to a question. He also says he doesn't mind homework—although that's not entirely true. One day recently, he and his friend Jon spent upwards of two hours musing about how great it would be to wake up one morning and find themselves metamorphosed into . . . Jon's golden retriever, Elvis. What a life! Take a nap, play some fetch. Pee anywhere. And never do any homework again. Ever.

Of course, they were just joking around. That's pretty much what you do when you're seventeen. You hang around and you joke around. You hang around in your room by yourself or in the rec room with your parents, or in somebody else's bedroom or rec room or driveway, or in the grass by the courts or the diamond, by your locker, in the food court at the mall—which, to Jesse's total derision, is called the Dining Veranda at the Shops. You joke around about the way Jesse asked his English teacher, Jewel Kamita, to be the alternate player on his three-on-three hoops team, how he did it with a totally straight face and she believed him for a minute. How Natalie is totally hot; too bad she's Mormon. How Mrs. Smith, the principal, is totally hot; *those legs!* How Seña Martín (Seña is her own made-up title—sort of like *Ms.* in *Español*) tried to give Jesse a cookie after they had an argument over extra *creditos.* How Jesse refused both the cookie *and* the extra *creditos.* And what's with those braces? She looks like an eighth grader. How Dan's girlfriend, the Oh My God Girl, wrote him a mushy note decorated with all these stickers. How time passes so slowly in calculus: You look at the clock and it's 10:15, and then you look again ten minutes later and it's 10:14. How this friend of theirs hid in the closet while this couple was, like, hooking up: *Silver Dollar Nipples!* How this girl they know is sort of hot but has a tragic case of FUPA: Fat Upper Pussy Area. How this other couple did it for the first time on prom night. After the deed, the girl was put in charge of getting rid of the empty condom box. At four in the morning, she sat on the toilet seat in her bathroom and tore the cardboard into a zillion tiny pieces. Then she put the pieces in a glass of water and let them soak until all the color dissolved. As the sun rose, she went outside and threw the mushy mess over the fence into her neighbor's yard.

But even as Jesse tries to do his work and keep his cool, even as he tries to hold on to his comfortable role as a kid—which he has only recently become old enough to really appreciate, now that it's almost over—everyone around him is beginning to freak out. The teachers, the parents, even some of the other kids: Everyone is acting like everything, suddenly, is *So Fucking Serious.* Everything! *Everything! Ahhhhhhhhh!* Grades, scores, activities. Essays and recommendations. Quotas and affirmative action. Loans and scholarships. A hook. You gotta have a hook. The college you choose, the major you choose, the city you choose—blah blah blah: monumental decisions that will affect the outcome of his entire life. For years he's been hearing people talk about the senior year of high school. Senior Year This and Senior Year That. The Best Year of Your Life. For years he's been watching it happen, watching the older kids go through it, one class after the next, those kids who once seemed so big and so old, so grown up, with their mustaches and beards, the girls with their huge—oh my God! The first day at Capo? Ninth grade? He felt lilliputian. Like a little insignificant ant that someone was gonna step on. Lower than an ant. Like someone was gonna pick him up at any moment and shove him headfirst into a trash can. And now it's almost here. He's almost a senior. It's his turn . . . almost. The grown-ups are always saying how time flies. How was he supposed to know it was true?

Later now, Jesse is upstairs in his room, shlumped over his desk, as his mom says. His fingers spider across his computer keyboard, a modified sort of touch-typing he taught himself. Open in his lap is his copy of *Don Quixote*; the teacher calls it *DQ* to make it sound more hip.

Like the rest of the house—a buff-colored Mediterranean contemporary with a ceramic-tile roof—Jesse's room is neat and sparsely furnished, painted Smoky Taupe, with an accent wall in Victoria Falls. The ceiling is vaulted, a way of making a small space seem larger. A fan circulates slowly overhead. It is controlled by a remote on Jesse's night table. On high it blows wind like an airplane propeller.

Two framed Ansel Adams landscapes hang over the touchingly small single bed. A framed poster of the Boston skyline hangs above the wood-and-metal desk, a hand-me-down from Dad, fully depreciated as home-office furniture some time ago. Several prom pictures are taped around the light switch. Kina was late from work that afternoon and didn't have much time to get dressed. She felt stupid for being late; she felt retarded having her picture taken in a public park with a group of other prom kids. The strain shows in their faces. In the end, things turned out pretty well. They had the sort of night you see in movies.

As Jesse types on his iMac, the desktop screen automatically switches scenery—Pacific island . . . snowy mountain . . . sunbaked desert. Now and then an Instant Message pops up, announced by a signature clarion. No one e-mails anymore—just IMs and text messages. The antenna on Jesse's cell is gone. He uses both thumbs simultaneously to work the keypad. He has customized the screen to read "Kobetime." The cell phone is on the desk, next to the household extension. Both ring intermittently. At the foot of the bed are an old nineteen-inch Sharp color TV (tuned to a baseball game on ESPN; one of his fantasy-league pitchers is on the mound) and two outdated game consoles (Nintendo 64 and Super Nintendo). A metallic-blue electric guitar, a recent acquisition, stands in the corner; Kina is teaching him to play. There are precious few things that thrill his parents more than the sound of Jesse singing in the shower. One can only imagine their faces last weekend, when Kina's parents came over for dinner and the lovebirds sang a duet. Jesse sings all the time, everywhere, songs by the Red Hot Chili Peppers or the White Stripes or the Beatles. His mom says that back in the old days, you were either Beatles or you were Rolling Stones. Jesse doesn't get it. He likes them both. They are part of a musical continuum that has no past and no future, all of it available to download. Kina herself is an accomplished songwriter. She's thinking about majoring in music next year at USC. This guy she met wants to help her make a CD.

Whenever Mom comes into Jesse's room to check her e-mail, she straightens the inside of his drawers. Jesse doesn't mind. He has nothing to hide. Nothing that can fit in a drawer, anyway. Cigarette smoking is his number-one pet peeve. He has tried beer but has never been drunk; Kina is so antialcohol that she doesn't even like *seeing* other people drink. It's gotten to the point where Jesse won't go to a party if he suspects his friends might be drinking; it feels like he's cheating on Kina. (If you want to cheat on someone, you should just break up. It means you don't like her anyway.) He's never tried marijuana or any other drugs: waste of time. He's known four kids who committed suicide, three in the last two years. One was his locker partner in middle school. He was a twin. He went into the garage one day and shot himself with his dad's shotgun. Every year, the mom of another suicide kid talks at an assembly. Every year she cries. Jesse can't see taking his own life, but he does understand the pressures that could cause it. He thinks that a lot of the problems kids have can be traced back to their parents. He knows he's lucky to be from a family like his. He gets the concept: He could have been born in Calcutta.

Jesse is five feet nine and three-quarter inches tall; he weighs 138 pounds. His height was the main reason he quit basketball. His brother, Adam, played varsity—sat varsity. Jesse didn't want to be second string. Some people work better from a position of strength; Jesse is one of them. Instead he joined the JV golf team—free golf daily at some of Orange County's finer courses. He became more active in school activities, won the two elections. Next year he'll be president of the National Honor Society (succeeding Kina) and also vice-president of the student government. (He sang his speech to the tune of the Chilis' "Californication.") He's also thinking about playing tennis next year, joining David and Ajay on varsity.

Jesse's only household chore is making his bed. When he needs money, he asks for it; he has no part-time job. Steve says Jesse's job is going to school. A child doesn't ask to be born, he believes. He shouldn't have to pay his own way. At the present moment, Jesse has thirty-seven cents in his pocket and seventeen dollars in his wallet, along with a Triple-A card. Recently, at about four o'clock on a Saturday morning—he was volunteering for this program where you drive drunk kids home from parties—he discovered that a Triple-A card covers a particular driver rather than a particular car. The woman on the phone was such a bitch. Couldn't she just have *pretended* he was Steven Epstein?

Like his dad, who is three inches shorter, Jesse throws with his left hand, writes with his right. When his mom speaks, he admits, he sometimes lets it go in one ear and out the other. In a Mexican restaurant, he asks his mom what he should order because he can't remember what he likes. He has no idea what size shirt he wears. He is Jewish. He believes in God because he's been brought up to believe in God. He doesn't really have a picture of Him in mind. As for organized religion, that's simple: He wishes it was nonexistent, or that everyone was just the same religion. Because religion leads to so many pointless deaths, so much hate. The way religion is the basis for all your beliefs—it doesn't, like, make any sense. What happens when one religion doesn't agree with the other? How can one be right and one be wrong? The answers are unknowable anyway, right?

For school, Jesse wears size 11 Airwalk Andy Macs, skateboarding shoes, though he hasn't actually skated since middle school. He's not really a daring kind of person. He doesn't like doing crazy stuff—taking big risks, putting himself in a position where he could get injured. The worst he's ever been hurt was when he fell off his bike. He was eight. He went over the handlebars and hit his face on a rock. It was the coldest feeling. It hurt so bad. He screwed up his chin and chipped a tooth. That whole *Jackass* thing? Doesn't get it. Why would you want to hurt yourself *deliberately?*

Sometimes he hates kids. "I'm a self-hating kid," he says. The way they leave their lunch trash all over the floor at school. The way they come unprepared to class. The worst feeling ever is being unprepared, not having your homework done, not understanding what's going on. When that happens to Jesse, he gets this feeling like he's a failure. Like he's not accomplishing things. Sometimes kids can be so dumb and mean and stupid. Like those eighth graders when he was in seventh. They called you a *sevi.* They would make you move from your lunch table. They would treat you like dirt just because they could. As a policy, Jesse believes in treating people well. "Making people happy is more fun than having yourself made happy," he says. He likes to hang out with "smart, nice kids." All of his best friends have two parents living at home.

Jesse hates people who chew with their mouth open. He hates that they've stopped selling sodas in the machines at school. He hates it when he wakes up tired. He hates it when his mom bugs him about making his bed, especially when it's morning before school and he's doing some last-minute studying for a test. He hates it when friends spread rumors and don't keep secrets. And he really hates it when Kina makes him pull teeth to find out what she's thinking.

The thing Jesse probably hates the most—aside from the way Seña Martín gives you extra *creditos* but doesn't let you *use* them to bring your grade up to an A—is affirmative action. Now, he knows how this sounds. But the whole thing is just not fair. It's just, like, why can't everyone be evaluated on their actual achievements? What you've done, he thinks, shows who you are. He works really hard. He does what he's supposed to do. Why shouldn't everyone else have to also? Shouldn't *that* be the measuring stick? Race is insignificant. He doesn't even look at race. His girlfriend is Asian. Ajay's parents are from New Delhi. Omeed is Persian. Check out his English class: Every single race you can think of is there, sitting side by side in those hard, uncomfortable desk/chair thingies. Close your eyes. They all have the same SoCal accent. And every one of them, like, says *like* too much.

Jesse loves to argue. He gets it from his mom. It's something they do together, like a sport. Jesse is known among his peers for his logic, his reason, his arguing. His friend Scott, with a hint of awe, says that "even when he's wrong and I'm right, he finds a way to make it sound like *he's* right. It's wild. I usually just go ahead and agree with him." Jesse will argue about anything. About a point in Mario Tennis. About the score in a game of Tip It. About the kind of chicken pasta he and David ordered last time at the Cheesecake Factory. His eyes bug out. His alabaster skin flushes pink. His reedy voice hits its upper register. Not that he's an asshole. He's a really nice guy. He just wants you to understand his point of view. And he'll make you understand it, goddammit! The best argument he ever had was with his friend Cameron. Even the parents became involved. It lasted for months, each side periodically producing new evidence: Cucumbers—fruit or vegetable?

Jesse hasn't seen Cameron much since he started dating Jesse's old girlfriend Samantha. Once, out of the blue, Cam called seeking Jesse's advice on girlfriend stuff, as do a lot of guys. Before Kina, before Sam, Jesse went out with Allie for two years, from the summer of eighth until the summer of tenth. While there was much speculation at the time, Jesse would only say that "gentlemen don't tell." Cam wanted to know what to do when, "like, at first she's the coolest thing in the entire world, and then the next week, you're kinda so-so." Jesse talked to him about infatuation and how a real relationship took things to the next level. "Your girlfriend needs to be, like, your other best friend," he told Cam.

If Jesse could go out with any woman on earth, he'd choose Cameron Diaz. Or more specifically, her character from *There's Something About Mary*. "She goes to the driving range and she says, 'I just want a guy who likes going to baseball games and can handle a few hot dogs'—that's my ideal woman," says Jesse. He also likes Amanda Peet. But in general, he doesn't like to focus on celebrities because there's no chance of him ever getting one; he's just more of a realistic person than an idealistic one. And besides, it's a moot point, because he's in love with Kina, who is deathly afraid of every kind of ball. She does, however, run the mile in 5:41; last year she was on the track team.

Though he claims to have a horrible memory, Jesse can remember things as far back as his infancy in the Boston suburbs—the color of the family house, the cold taste of snowflakes on his tongue. He remembers sitting on the front stoop, his dad tying his baseball cleats extra tight. His dad moaning beneath the palm tree, the ladder on the ground, his arm bent the wrong way. The catch at first base, Tournament of Champions, 1998. Last inning, two outs, guy on third, hard grounder to short. The throw was high. Jesse had to extend his arm as far as he could, keeping his foot on the bag. Somehow he snagged it. The whole team mobbed him. Winning the MVP of All Stars. He drained shot after shot; he was unstoppable. When he got home, his brother, who'd never given him a compliment in his life, told him, "Good job, dude." Mom catching Jon and him watching *Real Sex* on HBO. He was thirteen and had just gotten the TV for his room. Jon was sleeping over. It was late. They were flipping channels and came to this show; this guy was going down on this girl. They were amazed. They knew about blow jobs, but they had no idea the guy could do it, too. And then Jesse's mom came in! The eagle at Tijeras Creek, on hole number two. A 9-iron from 140 yards. It bounced once and rolled in. Coming back to class with toilet paper stuck in the waistband of his jeans. Kissing Kina for the first time. They were sitting on his narrow bed in his room. Their faces were really close. He was trying to listen to what she was saying, but at the same time he was thinking, *I have to kiss her now!* What's weird was that they were talking about whether or not they should kiss for the first time. She was saying stuff like "What if you don't like how I kiss?" and "What if I'm a bad kisser?" and he was trying to assure her it would be fine. On and on it went. On and on. Finally, he just told her to shut up. "Shut up," he said, just like that. And then he kissed her. And it was great. Really great. Probably the happiest moment of his life—that and getting his SAT scores: 1440!

Now, in his room, Jesse is shlumped over his desk, not a memorable night perhaps, but a night like many others. His fingers spider across the keyboard, doing the sentence-completion exercises for *DQ*.

A signature clarion sounds. An IM pops up. He reads it and responds. *Clicka click clack.* Then he picks up the phone.

"Hey," he says to Kina. Officially, the two have been dating since October 22, 2002, though their attraction was kindled the previous Valentine's Day, when Jesse went to her house for an NHS project.

What Kina loves about Jesse is his intelligence. He is so real and down-to-earth and laid-back and *really* smart. The kind of guy who's friends with everyone, despite what group they're in. She loves his dry humor, the way he jokes around and yet is dead serious at the same time. And even though he's a year younger, he has this certain way of looking at things that has really benefited her. She tends to stress out a lot and become overly concerned with people and issues and random stuff; he's always there to help her rationalize things. He's also helped her let loose a little more, just have more fun in her life. Together they've opened some doors, built a relationship, a secret life conducted out of range of their families, a sort of marriage with training wheels under two separate roofs.

"I just can't believe we lost the game!" Jesse agonizes. "I'm sooooo crushed!" His eyes bug. "I had the last two shots! It just keeps playing over and over in my head. What if I'd done this? What if I'd done that? I'm plagued with it. It's, like—"

He falls silent, listening for a moment. Then his furry eyebrows rise. "You're like that, too?"

Jesse pads into the kitchen in his stocking feet, absently jazz-snapping his fingers. It is nearing dinnertime. The wide-screen TV is tuned to Fox News; the scent of salmon wafts in from the gas grill in the backyard. Mom is at the granite island, preparing to make her famous chocolate-peanut-butter balls.

Jesse takes his usual seat. He rustles through the assortment of newspapers, magazines, and coupon inserts scattered over the kitchen table, settles on the sports page. While he is aware of current events, kind of absorbs it subliminally from all the media that surrounds him, he doesn't really know all the details and stuff, doesn't really care to know. It's just, like, all that stuff out there—AIDS, earthquakes, terrorism, SARS, the ozone layer—it doesn't bother him. It's out there and he knows it. He's not trying to bury his head. It's just, well . . . if it happens to find him, then, fuck, you know? He's out of luck. What can he do about it? You can use a condom to prevent AIDS. All the rest of it is out of your hands. He's got enough on his plate as it is. Why worry about things you can't control?

Now Steve pads into the room, the commute downstairs from his office having proved uneventful. Two blocks away, just outside their tidy subdivision, Oso Parkway is stop-and-go. "You gonna watch the Ducks game tonight?"

Jesse brightens. The Anaheim Ducks are in the Stanley Cup finals. "I'm *sooo* there!"

"Oh, wait," says Mom, opening a Tupperware of sugar. "We're supposed to go to Debbie's."

Dad hits his forehead with the palm of his hand. *D'oh!*

"I hope you can come," she says to Jesse, laying on a little guilt. "It would be really nice. Her father died, you know."

"What time is *that?*"

"Seven-thirty."

"But the Ducks!" he pleads. "I have to write my college essay!"

Jesse's favorite sweatshirt is a blue hoodie from UCLA, where Adam went to college, where he'd like to go, too. With his grades and activities, he could probably get into a good school back east, maybe an Ivy League. But UCLA is a good school. It's close, convenient, and relatively cheap. A whole world away but only an hour away. (And across town from Kina at USC.) It's so cold back east, you know? He thinks he'd like to study law or communications. His dream job: sports agent like Arliss or Jerry Maguire.

Beyond that, Jesse's dreams are modest: a nice wife—perhaps Kina, perhaps not; it's a longtime off. A house somewhere in southern California, a cool kid or two, hopefully a boy who likes sports. And enough money that he doesn't have to think about money: low six figures, he estimates. He doesn't care about being rich, about amassing a lot of things. When you ask him what makes him jealous, he doesn't mention clothes or cars, looks or girlfriends. Unexpectedly, he says he's jealous of kids who seem sure of themselves—kids who are willing to take risks. "I like to play it safe," he explains. "I like to be sure of things. I'm always underestimating myself. I always think that I'm not going to do that well, even though I usually do." As he gets older, he reckons, he'll probably have to take more risks. You can't get far in life without taking chances. If you don't, you're never going to experience all you can. Like David and Dan and them. They used to go at night to this place with a giant swimming pool. They'd break in, jump off the high dive. Jesse would never go. In a way, he wonders what it was like—to climb the fence, to jump. In a way, he thinks it would be cool to forget about being so logical sometimes, to forget about the rules, to have more guts to try stuff. Perhaps he will someday.

But right now, at six o'clock on a Wednesday, a school night near the end of his junior year, all of that crap doesn't matter. Being a kid means living in the moment, having fun in the here and now. He is old enough to realize that this childhood thing has been a really good deal. He knows that soon all the serious stuff will begin: college applications, big decisions, graduation, blah blah blah. But not quite yet. Not just yet. *Not yet!* For the moment, he will savor his waning childhood the way he savors a Milky Way, making a game of making it last, trying his hardest to keep the future at bay. For the moment, he's finished the Spanish, he's reviewed the calc. All he really has to do right now is one lousy two-hundred-word college essay. A mock college essay—he'll rip off something after dinner. This summer he'll get to the real thing in earnest.

"What do you think I should write about?" Jesse asks his mom.

She concentrates, scooping the sugar into a mixing bowl.

"It's due tomorrow." The volume rising. "I still have no idea what I'm going to write!"

No response.

"Mom?"

"Wait a minute!" she snaps.

"What!" snaps Jesse, indignant.

"I'm counting!"

"How was I supposed to know!"

"Oh my God!" she exclaims. "I think I lost count!"

"You wonder why I get mad when I lose in basketball. Listen to her!" He mimics Mom: "Oh my God! I lost count of the flour."

"Sugar," she says.

"What?"

"It's sugar." She puts down the scoop. "You do that all the time, by the way." She mimics him: "Oh my God! Oh my God!"

"No shit!" says Jesse, pushing a bit, getting into the game. The only person who loves to argue as much as Jesse is his mom. "Who do you think I get it from?" he challenges.

She ignores the profanity; he is, after all, seventeen. Already he is gone much of the time, unleashed on the world, plying his own judgment. A year from now, he'll be getting ready to leave home. But not quite yet. Not just yet. *Not yet.* "You don't get it unless you want to pick it up," she ripostes.

Jesse's eyes bug. His fleshy pink lips curl into a smile, a teenage version of absolute relish. He knows he's got her now.

"That's a lie," he proclaims. "That's a pure false statement and you know it!"

Esquire, October 2003

Yeaahhh Baaaaby!

Forty stories over Dallas, a gleaming atrium, the sky lobby at the Petroleum Club. A bumptious guy in Bally loafers holds court before a rapt semicircle of Harvard Business School alumni. Bankers and lawyers, cattlemen and oil execs, they've cleared their calendars and paid twenty dollars each to hear him speak. They crowd around him like schoolboys around a pro quarterback, hands reaching, faces aglow, like pilgrims around a prophet, a messenger from the promised land of three-comma personal worth.

"How you doing there, Mark?" drawls a sixtyish man in a gray suit, casing his way to the front.

"Just tryin' to keep out of trouble," says Mark Cuban, shrugging his shoulders. Six feet two and 205 pounds, with a heavy brow and a crooked grin, a silk-knit pullover clinging nicely to the health-club topography of his shoulders, he does look a bit like a quarterback, the kind who's just found out he's going to Disney World. His friends call him Cubes. "Your buddy in the *Wall Street Journal* tells a great story about you ordering a Gulfstream," says the man in gray, referring to a piece in this morning's paper.

"You got to have the plane," says a man in pinstripes.

"Absolutely!" affirms another man.

"Did you consider one of those share planes?" inquires another.

"I did," says Cuban. "But then I thought: What's the reason to buy it? And the answer was: Because I can."

Forty-one years old, a few degrees south of handsome, Mark Cuban is a recent addition to the *Forbes* 400 list of the nation's wealthiest, ranked 199, higher than Ed Bass and Barry Diller, just below Donald Trump and Charles

Wang. His personal worth today totals about $2.5 billion. Two thousand, five hundred million dollars—enough to spend a million a day, every day, for almost seven years. Not bad for a guy who started his career in business selling garbage bags door-to-door. His nickname back then was Pudgy. His date to the senior prom was a cold call.

On this blustery afternoon in early winter, with the market surfing another tsunami, Cubes has about him the air of a man complete, or nearly so, a man who is feeling pretty darn good about himself just now, as if he knew all along his life would someday come to this: his thumb hooked casually over his alligator belt, his ultralight Sony VAIO notebook computer cradled under his arm, a bevy of fawning Ivy League admirers surrounding him, basking in the hot light of the fabulous possibility he embodies. If he could do it, they are figuring, they can, too. They lean forward almost imperceptibly, hanging on his every word, straining for some pearl, some crust, some clue.

"So you really ordered a GV by e-mail?" asks the man in the gray suit.

"Sure," says Cubes. "I sent them an e-mail and told them I wanted to test-ride it and check it out first, and if I liked it I would buy it. And they were like, 'Excuse me, who are you again?'"

"So what did you say?"

"I said: 'I'm a guy who's gonna write you a check for $40 million, that's who I am.'"

The chorus erupts with delight, nodding approval all around. "If you're gonna buy yourself anything for Christmas, that's the thing," says the man in pinstripes.

"I have my little list of toys," says Cubes, smirking like a rowdy frat boy on spring break, a role he played frequently during his college days, a role he hasn't quite outgrown. "It was one of the three things I wanted. The first was the house. The second was the plane."

"What's the third?"

"Ah, ah, ah!" says Cubes, his voice rising, childlike, playing at mystery. "I'm keeping that private just now."

Eleven in the morning, sunny and cool. Birds sing in the bare trees of Preston Hollow, a storied North Dallas neighborhood also known as the Golden Corridor. Deep lots, Corinthian columns, high walls and stone chimneys, old money and new, the pickup trucks and step vans of maintenance workers parked everywhere, tender craft servicing a landlocked fleet. Outside an imposing iron gate, you push a button on a call box. You wait.

Leaves skitter across the quiet streets. Traffic drones in the distance, an undertrack of white noise, a faint smell of exhaust. A long black limo rolls past. A Humvee. A pair of red Porsches. Dot-com Dallas: a city with many past lives—cattle, oil, real estate, software—a city yet again reborn. Through the ornate scrollwork of the gate, you can see down the cobbled drive, past the carriage house and guard station to the brand-new French Renaissance–style house, cast stone with a slate roof—a baronial twenty-four-thousand-square-foot mansion hunkered down upon seven lush acres of wooded grounds, complete with a guesthouse, a wine cellar, an eight-car garage, and, by the pool, a three-story party pavilion crowned with a stately Jeffersonian rotunda. Gas lamps flicker outside the front portico. The waters of a fountain dance serenely in the center of the circular driveway, where sits Cubes's black '96 Lexus SUV, along with a golf cart and several cars. Gardeners are fanned out across the property, planting ground cover, finishing the job the previous owner left undone, after two years and $20 million. Once a national leader in home-mortgage refinancing, he's facing bankruptcy now—another time, another IPO, another bubble. Cubes paid $15 million for the place. The moment he took possession, he made $5 million. You push the button on the call box once again.

At last the gates swing slowly inward. You drive in, park, climb several steps past a pair of stone urns. The double front doors are massive, carved mahogany, twelve feet tall, reminiscent of a castle. One door is cracked open a few inches. As you step in, pushing with some effort, you are greeted by the unmistakable sonic assault of the custom-built, club-quality sound system that Cube has just installed throughout the house, on the basketball court, by the pool—the heart-thumping, earsplitting decibel rave of vintage funk bouncing off the white hand-cut-marble floors, swirling around the apex of the dramatic three-story entryway, vibrating the crystal teardrops of an immense chandelier that overhangs the only piece of furniture in evidence, a large rectangular dining table with room for at least twenty: George Clinton's *Hey Man . . . Smell My Finger.*

Cubes boogies over in jeans and stocking feet. "What did I tell you?" he shouts, a guy in a nightclub trying to be heard. "Is this the fuckin' greatest?" He does a little dance, eyes shut, head bopping. "Were you out there long?"

He pops a spin, a neat 540, then skates across the slick floor toward a doorway, hand aloft, finger waggling, the boogie-woogie billionaire. Back in college, before he bought the bar, before the bar was closed down by authorities for staging wet-T-shirt contests—or rather, for awarding first prize one night to a sixteen-year-old who was on probation for prostitution—Cubes hired himself out as a dance instructor, teaching the bump and the hustle. As a youth, despite his husky size, Cubes studied ballroom dancing, Russian dance, and ballet. He took piano lessons, played football and basketball, engaged in marathon wrestling matches with his younger brothers, meanwhile maintaining a thriving business in door-to-door sales—fire extinguishers, magazine subscriptions, Junior Achievement serving trays. An avid stamp and coin collector, he put himself through his first two years of college with the proceeds of his hobbies.

From an early age, Cubes was a super salesman, with the gift of gab and a winning way, a nose for a hidden vein, a firm conviction that it was nearly impossible to turn down a kid who knocked on your door with a useful product. As he always told his middle brother: "You don't need the showroom to sell the Cadillac." A fierce competitor, a rabid sports fan— the kind of guy who likes to sit courtside and yell at the refs and the players, who takes particular glee when one of them turns and glares— Cubes has never seen money as the ultimate end. It's great, sure, and he's been doing an excellent job lately of spending it, having written checks for more than $60 million over the last two months for various toys. But like Gordon Gekko in *Wall Street*, one of his favorite movies, Cubes sees business as something far more epic than the story of the bottom line. Business, like life, is strictly a matter of winners and losers, he believes. Somebody wins and somebody loses and everything else flows from that. Part Andrew Carnegie, part Peter Pan, Cubes is a man who marches to his own perverse little tune. He takes great pride in doing things, as he says, *backasshalfwards*—things like moving into a college fraternity house during his senior year of high school, or ordering a $40 million Gulfstream V jet by e-mail, or buying a twenty-four-thousand-square-foot mansion and leaving it nearly empty of furniture. His motto, his philosophy, his raison d'être, can be summed up in three little words: Because I can. As they said in the movie *Risky Business*, another of his all-time favorites, "Sometimes you gotta say, 'What the fuck.'"

Cubes skates on across the floor, through a doorway, eventually reaching the restaurant-sized kitchen. It is an awesome room, with every available amenity and gadget and fixture. The house can be accessed by computer from anywhere in the world. Cubes can even call up the security cams. He hasn't lived here long, but the possibilities for that little wrinkle seem endless, he says with a wink. Living in such grand circumstances hasn't really changed his life much, he says, pointing to his propensity for playing Wiffle ball with his buddies in the formal living room. He does admit that he's had to alter his habits somewhat. For instance, he's begun taking a bottle of water to bed with him. It's just too far to hike in the middle of the night. Ditto eating in bed, heretofore his custom. By the time he makes himself a plate in the kitchen and carries it back to the master suite, the food is gone and he has to reverse his steps and return the plate. And while he has always preferred to rise in the morning, make himself a bowl of high-fiber cereal, and sit naked in front of his computer, answering his e-mail, he has found the house to be a bit drafty.

Had Cubes moved into this house ten years ago, things might have been very different. They'd have had to close down all the strip joints in Dallas, he muses, because all the girls in town would have been working for him right here. As it is, he's had great fun initiating each and every room of the place. In deference to his pretty blond girlfriend—a twenty-seven-year-old Dallas-born advertising exec named Tiffany Stewart—he declines to give the specifics of that fun-filled weekend, except to mumble something about little blue pills. Cubes is devoted to Tiff. Sometimes he thinks he ought to get married, ought to have kids. It's not like the old days, when every night was a party. But, hell. As a friend of his put it recently, Cubes has in his possession that ultimate cologne, eau de wallet. There are a lot of ways to define "conquest." Settle down? Have fun? Who knows? It's an interesting time in his life, to say the least.

Now, in the kitchen, Cubes grabs an elaborate remote, tones down the sound, turns to the business at hand, a conference with his assistant, Stacy, and a guy named Bob, a wardrobe consultant from Lombardo Custom Apparel.

Cubes walked into the store a while back on a lark, thinking he'd buy some custom threads. Looking around, he realized he didn't know what he liked. "Just give me one of everything," he told them. By the time he left the store, he'd placed an order for $80,000. He'd always wanted a closet like Richard Gere's in *American Gigolo*. Now he has one—row upon row of shirts and pants, sport coats and suits, all of it hanging neatly, arranged by hue. Some of the stuff will eventually be shipped to his two other residences, a house in Manhattan Beach, California, and a studio apartment on Central Park West. You know you've really made it when you can travel without luggage.

"So where were we?" asks Cubes.

"Shoes," says Bob. His mission, he says, is to make Cubes more "wardrobe mature." Cubes has responded nicely. This morning he placed an order for thirty-seven pairs of shoes, in various styles, for $12,000.

"I wear 11 ½."

"Right. 11 ½ D."

"And the clothes—just keep on bringing the shit like you do and I'll just—"

"Just weed 'em out and tell me what you don't want," says Bob, interrupting. "And I made up some shirts for you—on me. I think you'll really like them."

"Did you see that picture of me in the paper on Sunday? I was wearing all your stuff."

"I appreciate that," says Bob. "So you're in good shape with belts?"

"Yeah, belts are cool."

"But you need knits."

"Yeah, the knits, and also something fun. I need some fun clothes and more solids. I like solids. And something bizarre, you know, something *superfunky*."

"I'll see what I can do," says Bob, looking puzzled.

"What about socks?" asks Stacy, in the mother-hen tone of the highly effective personal assistant. "He's always out of socks, and then he's bugging me."

For the longest time, Cubes didn't wear socks, one of his many superstitions. When he was jetting around the country pushing the IPO, he had lucky pants, a lucky shirt, lucky shoes. Cubes is a great believer in the "butterfly effect—the notion that one little action can change the karma." He's a big tipper ($150 on a $250 check), a patron of charities (particulars off the record). He still has the same cheap desk and credenza he bought when he started his first business. He still owns the first house he ever bought, and the first warehouse, on the outside wall of which is painted a mural depicting the high points of his life—Cubes lofting a big trophy after a college rugby tournament; Cubes in Red Square, when he was teaching business to the budding new capitalists; Cubes at dinner with his parents and his two younger brothers; Cubes wearing a T-shirt, upon which his girlfriend had scrawled, "I want you to pin my legs back like a Safeway chicken"; Cubes and his friends partying in Vegas, in Acapulco, in Puerto Vallarta, at the Final Four in New Orleans, at the Dream Team finals in Barcelona.

At his parents' house in Pittsburgh, Cubes keeps a pair of size 38 jeans from ninth grade, when he was five feet eight and 210 pounds and had silver caps on his bottom teeth. On a numbered Web site, he keeps hundreds of snapshots, with file names like "drunk and happy on 40th birthday" and "foxxxy lady." On a shelf in the closet of his home office, he keeps the tortoiseshell Coke-bottle glasses he used to wear before he got contacts. Last year, he finally had corrective laser surgery. When the doctor finished and Cubes looked across the room for the first time and could see clearly the outline of the light switch on the wall, well . . . it was amazing, incredible, *unfuckingbelievable.* It was one of those moments, a defining moment, something he will never forget. Like the moment he turned the key in the front door and walked into his bar for the first time, a twenty-one-year-old college senior in possession of a state-issued liquor license. Or the moment he became a billionaire—1:16 P.M. EST, January 8, 1999. Or the moment, sitting at a bar in the airport, having a celebratory beer after the sale to Yahoo was announced, that his image appeared on the TV news and everyone in the bar noticed. Or the moment he climbed aboard his Gulfstream for his inaugural flight. Or the moment yesterday afternoon when he cranked up his new sound system for the first time and felt the house fairly lift off the ground, fairly hover, a booming chorus of "Atomic Dog" that made him want to dance, to shout, to throw a fist in the air and scream, *Yeahhhhhhhhhhhhhhh baaaaaaa-byyyyyyy!* Tears of joy welled in his eyes; he actually cried—a deep, wrenching, singular sob.

Cubes knows full well that he's a lucky motherfucker. He's forty-one years old. He's a bachelor. He's on the *Forbes* list, for chrissakes! He's doing what he likes, how he likes, when he likes, all because he can. Sometimes you gotta say, *What the fuck.* He'd have to be pretty stupid to lose $2.5 billion. He could lose a billion and still be golden. Hell, he could lose two billion. Nevertheless,

Cubes is no fool. Most of his wealth is on paper. You never know what life holds, and he is acutely aware of that mystical fact, and he takes care not to anger the gods. In his wallet he keeps a lucky penny. He picked it up off the street in New York on the day in 1998 that his company, Broadcast.com, went public. Since then, he has never picked up another. He wants someone else to be able to find a lucky penny, too.

"He has plenty of socks," says Bob.

"I'm trusting you on this," says Stacy, shaking a finger in his direction. A frenetic, dark-haired young woman with a sweet Beaumont drawl, Stacy's been working for Cubes for three years, his loyal gal Friday. She keeps his schedule, makes his bed, runs the house, pays his bills, stocks the refrigerator with his preferred staples—precooked chicken breasts, yogurt, diet Snapple, Lite Ice beer, Ragú Light, sport-top bottles of spring water. Though Stacy prefers going to the store herself, Cubes has lately got her ordering household supplies off the Web. He wants her to do the same with groceries, but she has resisted. It's triple value on coupons on Wednesdays, she keeps reminding him. Waste not, want not, you know?

Despite her tendency toward frugality, Stacy made a killing when Broadcast.com went public, as did many of Cubes's other employees. She doesn't really have to work. But she loves the job, the excitement, all of it. Never a dull moment at Cuban Crest, as she likes to call the house.

"The socks are great," says Cubes, assuring Stacy. "They match the pants! They're awesome!"

"Can I bring you more dress shirts, that kind of stuff?" asks Bob.

"Not really. Just more casual stuff, and stuff I don't have to worry about trying to match. And I need more—"

The phone rings and Cubes stops midsentence. He moves for it, then hesitates, then looks at Stacy. She picks it up on the third ring.

"It's the guy," she says cryptically, cupping her hand over the receiver. "About the thing."

"I'll take it in the office," says Cubes, skating out of the room in stocking feet.

If you are looking for a clue, you could say it all began with a pair of basketball shoes. You remember the kind: suede Pumas—the lust object of preteen jocks in the early seventies, the Rosebud of our tale. Norton Cuban was an auto upholsterer, the son of a Russian-Jewish immigrant named Chobanisky, a proud man of modest means who was not about to spend twenty-five dollars on a pair of sneakers. "When you make your own money, you can do whatever you want," the father told the twelve-year-old.

Cubes stood there a moment, wheels turning. "Whatever I want?" he asked.

And so began the garbage-bag route, which began the notion: Because I can. By his junior year of high school in Pittsburgh, he was taking a psychology class at the University of Pittsburgh. By his senior year, he was a full-time college student. Deciding to transfer to a good undergraduate business program, he looked at the list of the top ten in the nation and chose Indiana, the least expensive. He was paying his own way.

IU was a blast. He lost weight, joined the rugby team, started getting dates. "My first two years, my mission was to be the wildest guy on campus who didn't drink," says Cubes. "I wanted to be different, I guess. I wanted to stand out. I'd tell myself, Just pretend you've drunk and do what everybody else does, only I'll be the sober one doing it. I was like the Steve Martin character, one wild and crazy guy."

By junior year, the stamp-and-coin money was gone. Cubes was living on loans and a twenty-dollar-a-week allowance from his folks. Looking to make some extra cash, he began giving dance lessons, then hit upon the idea of throwing big disco parties, late-seventies versions of raves. Eventually, he was renting out the Bloomington National Guard armory, hosting three thousand rowdy students at three bucks a head. His senior year, Cubes bought an off-campus nightclub. He called it Motley's Pub. There were thirty thousand students at IU. Motley's was *the* place to go. Five-dollar all-you-can-drink Wednesdays, quarter-a-drink Thursdays, free kegs at midnight, Cubes spinning the records, dancing like a dervish, buying drinks all around. He'd end the evenings covered in sweat, rolling in dough, a babe on his arm. Everything went great for nine months. Then came the incident with the sixteen-year-old. His bar days were over.

Cubes went home to Pittsburgh after graduation, took a job with Mellon Bank. It turned out to be a key move. Mellon was converting from manual to automated banking systems. Cubes was on the team. Within a year, he was an expert in computers.

Tired of the bank job, Cubes decided to relocate. The year was 1982, and

Dallas was booming. Twenty-somethings from all over the nation were flocking in, looking for opportunity, on the make. He moved into an apartment with six other guys. He got a job selling software.

"I could always sell," Cubes remembers, "and the beautiful thing about the industry was that it was brand-new. Lotus 1-2-3 had just come out. The IBM PC had just been out a little while, you know, with the single and double disk drive. I'd read all the trade magazines, I'd get the manuals and read them, I'd come to work early and just sit on the computer—I didn't have one of my own yet—and I'd teach myself. There was nobody who walked in who could say they knew more than me. I started building up a little customer base. I wanted to do more. I remember asking the guy who owned the place if I could go out and sell to my customers instead of waiting for them to come into the store. And he says, 'As long as you're here by 9:30 to sweep the floor, you can do whatever you want.'"

Cubes left a few months later. Armed with his Rolodex, he set up his own consulting business, MicroSolutions. He taught himself how to write programs, became an expert in connecting computers into local area networks. By the time he sold the company to CompuServe in 1990, he had eighty-five employees, clients such as Neiman Marcus and Zales, a run rate of about $30 million a year. After splitting the proceeds of the sale with his partner and his employees—an eyebrow-raising act at the time—Cubes became a multimillionaire. He decided to retire. He was thirty-one.

His first act of retirement, he says, was to spend $125,000 for a lifetime pass on American Airlines, and his first trip took him to California to visit a friend. Walking down the strand in Manhattan Beach one day, Cubes saw a house for rent, a big five-bedroom place on the beach. He took it. That night at dinner, he ran into two flight attendants. They were honeys. They needed a place to live.

So began the Hollywood years. He lived the life, dated the babes, went to the beach, took advantage of his airline pass, visiting eleven different countries. He enrolled in acting classes, appeared in two movies. One, *Talking About Sex*, starred Kim Wayans. You can catch it now and then on cable. He declines to name the other movie.

While waiting for his star to rise, Cubes began playing the stock market. He'd awaken at 6:30 A.M., turn on CNBC, get on his StairMaster, pick up the phone. "I was popping trades left and right. My roommates were amazed.

Everybody was being a starving actor, but I didn't want to starve. I figured I'd do it backasshalfwards, you know, like always. I was making something like $30,000 to $40,000 a week."

In 1994, Cubes moved back to Dallas to reunite with an old flame, the Safeway-chicken girl. Meanwhile, an acquaintance from college, Dallas attorney Todd Wagner, approached him with an idea: What if you could use the Web to access, say, live IU basketball games from anywhere in the world? Both men had been to parties where big games were broadcast over makeshift speakers via telephone. Why not provide it on demand through the Web, home-team sports for homesick fans—the World Series in Kathmandu; the Final Four in Micronesia; opening day at the local ballpark to your cubicle in the corporate hive. Though early naysayers decried the high-tech idiocy of turning a $3,000 PC into a $6 AM radio, market research showed Cubes and Wagner that fewer than one third of white-collar workers actually had radios on their desks; even fewer had televisions. Almost all of them, however, had PCs, and within a few years, they predicted, almost all of them would have Internet connections as well. A huge, untapped legion of upscale eyes and ears was ripe for the taking. This was where the Web was going—from static text to real-time audio and video. This was where entertainment was going—from network programming to multimedia multiple choice, all of it on demand.

The partners began their venture in the spare bedroom of Cubes's Dallas house, with a Packard Bell computer, an ISDN line, a cheap AM radio tuner, and an agreement with a Dallas radio station that allowed Cubes to broadcast the station's programming over the Web. Though Cubes secured the rights with bold talk of making KLIF into a sort of TBS of the Internet, a radio superstation, things didn't start so auspiciously. One afternoon in the early going, they went off the air when Wagner tripped over a power cord. Within months, however, the bugs were exterminated and the company was occupying a downtown warehouse, having secured agreements with dozens of radio stations and other content providers, adding more every week. Soon, Motorola, Intel, and Yahoo came on as investors. Cubes put in well over a million dollars himself. Within four years, AudioNet—later renamed Broadcast.com—was the leading aggregator and broadcaster of live and on-demand audio and video programs in the world. "It's cable on steroids," Cubes liked to crow as he crisscrossed the country, flying more than half a million miles—the lifetime pass!—to drum up business and buzz, to sell his vision, a whole new way of using the Internet. Early on, a business component was also added to the mix: live, on-demand broadcasts of company-specific programming—conference calls on steroids.

Accessed by half a million users daily, Broadcast.com carried live shows from four hundred radio stations and thirty TV stations around the country. By clicking onto the site from anywhere in the world for the price of a local phone call, users could watch or listen to sports, hometown news, the Super Bowl, the Stanley Cup, police-scanner and air-traffic channels from major cities, the BBC World Service, a jukebox of twenty-one hundred full-length compact discs and four hundred audio books. In September 1998, one million users tuned in to Broadcast.com to see President Clinton's videotaped grand-jury testimony, a record number eclipsed several months later when almost two million people clicked onto its live coverage of a Victoria's Secret fashion show. Though Broadcast.com wasn't yet showing a profit, it was distinguished by a unique strategy. Rather than spend his money on advertising, as did most new Internet companies, Cubes put feet on the street. More than one third of his employees were in sales. Cubes never set year-end goals for his sales force, believing that goals were limiting. In his mind, a good salesman needs to set his sights on only one thing—the next sale.

In July 1998, Broadcast.com went public as BCST. Six months later, when the stock reached 200—it had opened to insiders at fifty cents a share, to the public at 18 dollars—Cubes became a billionaire. Last summer, Broadcast.com was bought by Internet giant Yahoo, in a stock trade worth approximately $6 billion.

"Buying those Pumas, that was the eye-opener," says Cubes, tossing a Wilson football up in the air, lounging on a big sofa in the immense media room of his house. "I got my shoes, I got some money in the bank, and I got my freedom. I could do whatever I damn well pleased.

"I mean, some people can run to freedom. I can sell to freedom. And that's what I learned when I was a kid. Time and freedom. Those are the ultimate assets, absolutely. My self-fulfillment doesn't come from the money. It comes from just knowing that intellectually there are no bounds—that's the number-one thing. Nobody telling me what to do. Just me doing things because I can."

Three guys in a black Lexus SUV, barreling down the rain-swept interstate, a Saturday night on the town, ripe with possibilities. Cubes is driving. Stahl rides shotgun. Kleine is in the back.

Friends since their early days in Dallas, when they used to make dinner out of happy-hour appetizers, Cubes and Stahl and Kleine have been digging it up and tearing it up together for years. Lately, of course, Cubes has been a little busy. The last time they all partied was Halloween. Cubes had just cashed in about $20 million worth of stock, his SEC waiting period having expired at last. To celebrate, he treated a bunch of his buddies to a Las Vegas adventure. Everyone got his own suite and cash for gambling. It was quite the party. Now they are on their way to their first scheduled stop, a Dallas Mavericks basketball game. Cubes has four seats on the floor. The players don't know him, but they know who he is—that loudmouthed guy with season tickets, superfan, always on his feet.

"So what happened with your meeting with Donald Trump?" asks Dave Kleine, forty-five, an insurance agent.

"It went fine, you know. He was Donald," says Cubes.

"How did that come about, anyway?" asks Mark Stahl, forty-two, a flight attendant with Southwest.

"Well," says Cubes, speeding through traffic, settling in to tell the tale, "I got invited down to Mar-a-Lago by this guy named Ray Manzella. You know who he is, chat guru of blonds, that guy Jenny McCarthy dumped? I think he was trying to make points with Donald, so he figured he'd bring me along. So anyway, we get there, and we're sitting by the pool, drinking some drinks. You could see the house up on a higher level, and you could see people eating dinner. I'm there with Ray and his new girlfriend and Jerry Yang, the cofounder of Yahoo, and this other guy, the CEO of Visa, and we're all just hanging out. Then Donald comes by, and Ray introduces everybody. You could tell Donald didn't know any of us from Adam. He was, like, minimally cordial. And he looks around at us and he says, 'It's a shame you guys are down here. All the rich people are up there eating dinner.'"

"Trump for president," laughs Stahl. Many years ago, when Cubes was starting MicroSolutions, the two men were walking down the street one night when Cubes asked him to become his partner in the business. Stuttering at the curveball, Stahl demurred. Cubes turned to him, slapped his cheek.

"What the hell was that for?" asked Stahl. "That's your wake-up call in life, pal," Cubes cold him. "When opportunity presents itself, you need to be prepared to take it." Cubes never asked again.

"So how *did* the meeting happen?" asks Kleine. A handsome guy with a southern drawl, he met Cubes many years ago at the health club. Cubes met Tiffany there, too.

"I guess Ray said something to Donald," says Cubes, "because a few days later I get this call: Donald wants to sit down with me. So I fly up to New York. What the hell, right? And I walk in his office and I just crack up. He's got this huge office, you know, and every square inch is covered with pictures of himself. Like a shrine to Donald, you know? He starts telling me how he's thinking about doing Trump.com, selling Trump this and Trump that, perfume and other stuff, and then he's going to take it public."

"So what did you say?" asks Kleine.

"I told him that it was one of the worst ideas I'd ever heard."

"No shit!" says Stahl, delighted.

"What'd he do?" asks Kleine.

"He looks at me funny for a minute, then he smiles and says, 'You know what? I like you!'"

Though Cubes has been a millionaire for many years, it is nothing like being a billionaire. The toys. The respect. The status. The eau de wallet. Not so long ago, he was flying all over the country, trying to make people listen, trying to make them believe in his company, his vision, trying to get their money. These days, people call him. Wherever he goes, he is accosted by strangers. They act like they know him. They gaze at him reverently. They treat him like he's some kind of oracle. They ask him to autograph their girlfriend's left breast. They regale him with intimate financial details, solicit advice, solicit money. Everybody wants his money. Over the last few months, he's been offered an auto-racing team, a castle in France, a hockey team in rural Texas, dozens of film scripts. One guy wanted him to finance a contest offering $10 million to anyone who could build a rocket to go to another planet and return. Others just want a handout. The pitches can be pitiful: "I have this great idea for a business, but unfortunately I lost all my money gambling." Only this last group pisses him off. Fuckin' losers with excuses. He hates that, people with sorry excuses. If you're gonna do something in this life, you just have to do it.

"The one thing that hopefully I'll never lose track of is that there's no correlation between how smart you are and how much money you have," says Cubes. "Everybody has a different skill set. My skill set is in business. There's just a tune that plays in my head that makes a lot of sense to me. People were always telling me I would be rich from the time I was little. And it always scared the shit out of me. Like when I came to Dallas and I was tending bar, weighing 240 pounds. It was like, All right already, when am I going to be rich?

"The best thing about the money, I guess, is that I don't have to prove myself anymore. There are some guys you talk to, they want to move up the list. They're like, I'm shooting for the top twenty, the top ten, whatever. I don't need to move up the fuckin' list. I'm the first to realize that my success is yesterday's news. But I'm not necessarily concerned about thinking, Can I do it again? What's more important to me is: Can I find something new that consumes me, that entertains me to the same extent, that challenges me in the same way? It's the never-ending question, I guess. What am I going to do when I grow up? What's next?"

The three men drive in silence for a few miles. The lights of Reunion Arena come into view.

"So when are you gonna buy the Mavs?" asks Stahl, joking around, making idle conversation.

"Now, that would be a great toy!" enthuses Kleine. "I want to be in charge of the cheerleaders!"

"You can be the mascot," says Stahl.

"They ain't doin' nothin' with them cheerleaders now," says Kleine. "They're the worst!"

"And you ain't gonna be doin' nothin with them, either," says Cubes, speaking up at last, smirking like a forty-one-year-old billionaire with the world by the tits, a role that is still new to him, a role he is learning to play very well.

On a sunny winter day a few weeks later, you turn on your computer, you check your e-mail. You have a message from Cubes:

"Since I am in the middle of a defining moment, I figured I would e-mail you.

"I am riding the plane back from San Antonio, Texas, to Dallas. The beauty is that I'm sitting here by myself, no fuss, no muss, contemplating whether or not I am going to be able to sign a letter of intent to buy an unnamed sports team this afternoon if the numbers come back like I think they will.

"Then I will go to the gym and work on my jump shot.

"Pretty damn sweet."

A few days later, the *Dallas Morning News* carries a banner headline: BROADCAST.COM FOUNDER PLANS TO BUY MAVERICKS, and a few days after that, Cube—who will own a 70 percent stake in the basketball team when the deal is approved by the NBA—is already at work trying to revive the perennial loser.

Each day brings new reports: Cubes awarded game ball by players. Cubes entertains coach Don Nelson at his house, exacts promise that he will step down following season. Cubes goes online to chat with fans. Cubes runs up and down aisles at Reunion Arena, yelling and clapping like a cheerleader. Cubes offers free drinks to all comers at the arena's bar following games. Cubes plays rousing game of one-on-one with seven-foot German-import forward Dirk Nowitzki. Cubes presides over first home sellout of season. Cubes brings hometown boy Dennis Rodman out of retirement to play for Mavs. Cubes travels with team on the road. Cubes taunts fellow new owner Michael Jordan at a game in Washington, D.C. He tells His Airness: "We're gonna kick your butt."

Because he can.

Esquire, April 2000

Revenge of the Donut Boys

At midday in summer haze the basketballs are bouncing in a playground surrounded by a chain-link fence. From here, on a little hill behind Avon Elementary, Newark, New Jersey, stretches in all directions: the Gothic spires of abandoned churches, the dense brick towers of the projects, the ghost buildings boarded with plywood. Liquor stores, Korean markets, garages, vast tracks of vacant land, acre upon acre of weeds mulched with broken glass and needles and little vials and shell casings, blood dripped and dried brown on chips of brick and concrete, the rubble of housing and commerce and people.

Little kids dart across the asphalt playground, stumbling here and there on tufts of stubborn grass. Bigger kids on corners reach for pockets, shake hands. Women lean out windows, girls gossip on porches, old men hunker at salvaged card tables, drinking from paper bags. Now and then comes a pop-pop-pop and a rolling echo, the crack and thunder of far-off gunplay. No one pays it any mind.

That corner to the north is known for marijuana. Over there you get pills, over there heroin, over there crack, over there powder. The shadow economy working overtime, mutant enterprise blooming amid the ruins of a city that was the leading supplier of manufactured goods to the South before the Civil War. MADE IN NEWARK once meant patent leather and tools. Now it means kids like Raheed.

Raheed isn't his real name. He wants to stay on the super DL, meaning he'll talk, but only with his head down low, incognito. He wears a bandanna on his head folded and tied in the back. His short pants ride low on his hips, hang below his knees. He leans on crutches, eating his breakfast, a bag of chips.

Suddenly from up Avon comes the roar of engines, and two black Mustangs and a Honda crest the hill. People scurry across the street, girls laugh and point. The cars whiz past the schoolyard, each one driven by a boy barely tall enough to see over the steering wheel, each one full of boys, five or six or more, the Honda with two heads in backward baseball caps grinning up through the sunroof. Games cease on the playground. Kids run to the fence. The Mustangs speed through the intersection at sixty, bottom out with a clank, shed sparks, zoom off. The Honda hits the crosswalk, turns hard left, squeals and slides and then spins in the center of the intersection, tires screaming, leaving rubber, raising clouds of thick black smoke that envelop the car, waft off on the humid breeze.

"The Doughnut Boys!" shout the children. They clap and cheer. They do a little dance called the Doughnut, spin round and round and round.

In America's third oldest major city, a new sport has been born. It's called rustling cars. According to auto-theft statistics, Newark has the highest rate of car theft per capita in the nation, more than forty cars each day. Sixty-five percent of the thefts are perpetrated by teens and preteens, known hereabouts as the Doughnut Boys.

The Doughnut Boys steal Hondas, Acuras, Mustangs, Trans Ams, four-wheelers, and minivans: the same models you might see in a high-school parking lot in the nearby suburbs. They use screwdrivers to jack the door and punch the steering column. They override kill switches and alarms. Fifteen seconds, tops. High craft, handed down from brother to friend.

They'll rustle up a car to drive to elementary school, in lieu of bus fare, to get out of the rain, for a date, a purse snatching, a cruise around town, a drug delivery, sometimes an armed robbery. They steal from garages, alleyways, curbs. Not long ago, someone stole the county prosecutor's car from a schoolyard. He was inside addressing an assembly on the subject of stealing cars.

One kid steals a car, picks up some friends, drives to Newark Airport or the suburbs. The friends jump out and steal cars of their own. With the little ones, it takes two to drive. One gets the pedals, the other the wheel. Then it's a race back to the neighborhood, where the fun begins.

Pull up beside a cop, flip him the finger, peel off. The kids know five-o ain't allowed to race: High-speed chase is outlawed. Race them anyway. Turn right, right again, bust the lights, weave the lanes, Mario Andretti. Dick the cops.

That's the object: Smoke 'em. Humiliate 'em. Fuck 'em up. Chicken at sixty miles per hour, stolen Honda heading straight for patrol car. The cops always veer off at the last moment. Pussies. No match. Recently, the Doughnut Boys have added a new wrinkle. Ram a patrol car. See the air bags pop.

"It's a big show," says Raheed. He's seventeen. He's been down to juvenile, but now he's back. He broke his leg the other night fleeing on foot from a stolen car. "It's the most exciting thing going on in the neighborhood. It's like the movies, you know what I'm sayin'? Car chases. Everybody like to see cars spinning and stuff. Everybody want to get in a car.

"When you down in the hood and shit, straight up, preachin' high, we down here trapped off among ourselves. It's like little kids in the hood throw rocks. Then they be stealing cars. Whereas in Short Hills, they might be playing golf. But this is the hood. These are the things that we do for activities. That calms ourselves. It's a recreation-type thing. Like, they got the playground open now. Tomorrow, boom, it's Saturday. It ain't gonna be open. What we gonna do then? You know what I'm sayin'? Fuck it. Let's go get a car. It's like—"

"Shut up, crook!" says a kid on a bicycle. His name is Rico. He's ten.

"Fuck you!" says Raheed. He swings a crutch at Rico's front tire. Rico holds his ground astride his bike, safely out of range. "Fuck yourself," he says. "You ain't got nothin' better to do than try to steal somebody else's car that they done paid for."

"Oh, you a good Samaritan," says Raheed, "you bike stealer little faggot-ass motherfucker. Stop playing me out!"

"Shut up, nigga!"

"Shut up, punk!"

Raheed hops toward the boy, brandishing a crutch. Rico backs off slowly, giggling, taunting. A teacher appears. Ms. Perkins is the drug-education coordinator for Avon Elementary. The city pays her to keep the playground open on summer afternoons. When her car was stolen, she put out the word. Kids from all over were calling the cops with sightings of her white Sunbird. She got it back in a few hours. She puts a hand on Raheed's shoulder. "What's up, gentlemen?"

Over the last year or so, hundreds of kids from Newark have been injured and arrested, and millions of dollars' worth of cars have been stolen. Not long ago, a fourteen-year-old took out half a gas station pulling up to the pump. A pregnant woman was killed when the police fired into a stolen van. In late August, two teenagers on a 4:00 A.M. rustle were shot to death after encountering a pair of off-duty policemen. Cops have been injured, too. Herded to the curbs by teams of unmarked police cars and trucks, the kids have taken to ramming. Back and forth they bang, trying to break a piece of daylight for escape. As the kids become increasingly defiant—most of them are juveniles who will likely be released—the cops grow increasingly frustrated.

So it was this past June when Howard "Bucky" Caesar had the bad fortune to be caught driving a stolen black IROC-Z Camaro belonging to the mother of a Newark police officer. Bucky was doing doughnuts at four in the morning when he lost control of the Camaro and slammed into the curb, breaking an axle. Already there had been reports of Newark cops hiding in the bushes at a local park, throwing rocks and bottles as the Doughnut Boys sped past in stolen cars. Now, when Bucky jumped out of the Camaro on the morning of June 9 to the jeers and catcalls of bystanders at the all-night show, it was gunfire that the police were throwing down. Bucky was hit in the side.

Six cops were on the scene, some of whom weren't assigned to the area. The son of the owner of the stolen Camaro arrived shortly thereafter. The police reported the shooting to headquarters at 4:41 A.M. The car was reported stolen at 4:42. Witnesses reported the police retrieving spent shell casings. In their reports, only one officer admitted firing shots. He and two others have been charged with failing to report the shooting and filing false reports. All six have been suspended. Bucky remains in stable condition after eight operations.

In a city that is a model of urban statistical cliché, Bucky Caesar grew up something of an anomaly, with a mother and father and two siblings at home. His dad was a janitor for the Newark schools. They lived in the ghetto because it was all they could afford, five rooms for $400 a month.

Their neighborhood around Twentieth Street was once known for heroin and pills. Later it would be crack, then guns, then stolen cars. "We didn't need no VCR," says Bucky's mom, Martha Caesar. "Everyone and everything was out there."

"I didn't really feel scared, though," says Caesar, who has since moved. "I like the people down there. I didn't like what they did, but we all stuck together as family. I lived on the third floor, so they couldn't climb through the window, but I had no fear of anyone kickin' in my door or robbin' me, either. I had my husband and my kids. Mr. C. was like a father figure to everyone before he died, rest his soul. He'd get out there in the fire hydrant on hot summer nights with all the kids."

As it was, Mr. C.'s younger son had problems of his own, beginning early on in school. There was the second-grade teacher who smacked him, family counseling, more acting up in class. By the time he got to high school, Bucky was classified as emotionally disturbed. "It made him feel like he was dumb and retarded," says Martha Caesar.

Soon Bucky started stealing cars, and finally he found something he was pretty good at. In fact, he was out of control. One minute he would be out front with his friends. The next he'd be gone. What could Martha Caesar do? When she asked, Bucky said he did it for status, as if stealing the symbols of accomplishment of the middle class raised him up into it. What he couldn't obtain, he just took and used and destroyed.

"You instill in your child what is right and wrong," says Caesar. "But you can't be out there twenty-four seven. The word of God tell us to bring a child up in the right way, and when he get old, he shall not depart from that teaching. But it doesn't say nothing about between the time you train him and the time he get old. He has to get some years on him, some wisdom to know what his parents tell him is true. God help him in the meantime."

"He a car thief," says Rico, spitting out the charge, explaining the sudden flare-up on the playground to Ms. Perkins. "Every time he get locked up, he like 'Pleassse, go get my ma!' "

"That's right, motherfucker," says Raheed. "And you see I be out the next day."

"I ain't never been locked up," says Rico. Standing there astride his bike, between Raheed and Ms. Perkins, he crosses his arms, cocks a hip, assumes a pose of proud defiance.

Ms. Perkins smiles to herself, lets the show run. Rico is one of her favorites. So delicate, with long lashes, yet hardy enough somehow to survive. Ms. Perkins has worked on that boy for four years. He's like so many kids she knows. The children of lost children, little renegades on the loose. His mother's never home, doesn't care where he's at. His brother's a car thief. Rico isn't so much a member of a family as he is a resident of a house. Maybe that's why all these kids use the word *stay* instead of *live* when they talk about home. "I stay over at Clinton Avenue" is how they put it.

Ms. Perkins comes from the neighborhood. She doesn't like what she sees, but that's how it is. She includes in her job description the role of surrogate parent. The government won't do it. The parents won't either. She's spent four years trying to teach Rico things like decision making and refusal skills, responsibilities, goals and directions. She wasn't sure she was getting through. Now, here on the playground, she sees a sprout on one of the seeds she's planted. Just when you think they're not thinking, they're thinking, and you're surprised.

"Why you want to steal those cars anyway?" Ms. Perkins asks Raheed.

"Why?" repeats Raheed, folding his arms across his chest, striking a pose of his own. "Lemme tell you serious. We do it to help society."

"Yeah?"

"Yeah," says Raheed. "Because if it wasn't for us, you wouldn't have no hospitals and police. Word is born. We employ the fuckin' police!" Raheed's voice begins to rise, his words do a dance of rhythmic hip-hop. He hobbles back and forth, a crippled rapper on an asphalt stage. A group of little ones have gathered to see the show, more of Ms. Perkins's kids: Rashonda and Dwane and Hassan, Jennifer and Sade, Aliyah and Tony. They are four, five, ten years old. They hold basketballs and jump-ropes, the sticky hands of younger cousins.

"Word is born!" says Raheed, playing to his Sesame Street crowd. "If it wasn't for niggas like me, a lot of families be starvin' 'cause they husbands'll get laid the fuck off, because it ain't no crime. And what about insurance? The insurance companies be worth, like, billions of dollars and stuff. They wouldn't be nowhere without us."

"You oughta run for president," giggles Rico. The other kids giggle, too.

"I thought of it, but I ain't goin' out like that," says Raheed, talking serious. "I don't even know what the sense of voting in the first place. Ain't none of them crackers for none of us."

"You gotta be about yourself," says Ms. Perkins. "Being about yourself mean getting some education. You sound like you not stupid."

"You got that right," says Raheed. "I got friends that graduated outta high school, and boom, word is born! They working at McDonald's. What's up with that?"

"But they workin'," says Ms. Perkins.

"So what," says Raheed. "I got my equivalency, too. I don't want no job."

"What about a decent job? Maybe like a computer programmer?"

"I don't want no decent job."

"So you to the point where you don't want no job at all," says Ms. Perkins.

"I never did want no job."

Ms. Perkins puts a hand on her hip, gives Raheed a look, part patience and humor, part disgust. "What are you, about seventeen now, boyfriend?" Raheed nods. "Okay. Now I know what seventeen is like, so I ain't gonna press the issue on that. But look. You got maybe sixty more years to live. What you gonna do with that time?"

"I wanna rap," says Raheed.

"You wanna rap," repeats Ms. Perkins.

"You wanna die!" pipes Rico. He giggles. So do the kids.

Ms. Perkins falls quiet. A light turns off in her pleasant, sunny face. She looks around her. Rashonda and Dwane, Hassan and Jennifer, Sade, Aliyah and Tony. Four, five, ten years old, basketballs and jump-ropes and sticky hands. And Rico, posing there astride his bike. "Does he really mean it?" she asks herself. "Have I gotten through?" There are so many kids like Rico. So many more kids than time. In the middle distance, she can hear the piercing rubber squeal of a Doughnut Boy, another lost renegade soul spinning around in circles on a ghetto street in Newark. She wonders what will happen tomorrow. On Saturday the playground is closed.

Rolling Stone, October 1, 1992

Fact: Five Out of Five Kids Who Kill Love Slayer

In red smoke and chaos the demon appears, a spirit in black leather before a field of broken skulls and empty coffins, eyes gleaming, maniacal grin, hair a nimbus of floodlit hellfire. Sweat drips down his tattooed arm, splashes his bass guitar. He steps to the microphone, hocks a fat one center stage. The spots click green. He roars:

"Are you ready to diiiiiiiiiiiiiie!?"

A scream erupts, pandemonium, the primal cheer of six thousand lost young souls from the Heartland, the ticket holders who lined up five hours before showtime to see a concert that wasn't even advertised. (Why bother? None of them read a paper or listen to radio.) Ripped jeans and pimples, bustiers and black spandex minis, cigarettes dangling beneath peach fuzz, metal crosses kissing sweaty virgin skin, mall rats and jail bait and bedroom air guitarists, they are America's future, the fans of a band called Slayer, jammed now, pelvis to buttock, into this civic arena on a full-moon sabbath eve to take dark communion at the head-bangers ball.

The band explodes, a crunching engagement of chain-saw guitars, gutshot bass, thumping drums, feedback thundering from amp stacks two stories high. The drummer beats from a platform in the rafters. Stage left, the rhythm guitarist wears a forearm sheath bristling with tenpenny nails. Stage right, the lead guitarist glares, rakes the strings. There's a hole in the crotch of his leather pants. The demon on the bass bangs his head against the air, furious, down and up, down and up, then switches to figure eights, pounding to the beat of the drum, throwing sweat and musk from his thick, wavy mane. He rolls his eyes back into his head. The spots click red. He sings, hoarse and throaty:

Propaganda death ensemble
Burial to be
Corpses rotting through the night
In blood-laced misery
Scorched earth the policy
The reason for the siege
The pendulum it shaves the blade
The strafing air blood raid

Beneath the stage, just past a buffer manned by bouncers, kids are crammed and jammed and smashed behind a chest-high wooden barricade. Elbows in windpipes, noses in armpits, ears ringing, hearts pounding, heads banging down and up, synapses frying endorphins and kilowatts, bathtub acid and homicidal dreams, fists thrusting toward the stage, index and pinkie fingers extended like horns, the sign of the master of darkness, Hail Satan!

The air hums and buzzes, and in the middle of the floor of this vast, round, seatless auditorium, something called the mosh pit begins to swarm. Shirtless boys and fearless girls—fourteen, sixteen, twenty years old, braces, tattoos, Charlie perfume, half-shaved heads—skip aggressively counterclockwise, cherubs in the inferno, gathering speed, shoulders cocked, elbows crooked like linemen, grinning, grimacing, laughing, crying, bouncing and ricocheting like agitated electrons, like pinballs trapped between bonus bumpers. Here and there one is borne aloft, passed toward the stage on a sea of palms, kicking and screaming and rolling back to front, dumped headfirst over the barricade, to be carried away by a bouncer.

Infiltration push reserves
Encircle the front lines
Supreme art of strategy
Playing on the minds
Bombard till submission
Take all to their graves
Indication of triumph
The number that are dead

Away from the mayhem, all along the perimeter of the arena, every fire door and exit is guarded by a rent-a-cop and two parents with flashlights. They patrol the grim scene with fearful eyes. Outside, near the entrance, a group of Teens for Christ urges leaflets and brimstone upon dopers and metal heads straggling late into the show. Later, two city cops on mountain bikes will ride up hard and adrenalized on a circle of autograph hounds, looking to make a bust. This is Sacramento, California, but it could be any town that Slayer has seen over the ten-week, forty-seven-date cross-country tour called Seasons in the Abyss.

As usual, the sight on the horizon of the four horsemen of Slayer had been cause for panic in cities like Tucson, Milwaukee, Grand Rapids, Poughkeepsie. Newspapers ran foreboding headlines: SLAYER: THEY'RE FROM THE BLOOD, DEATH, BEELZEBUB CAMP. WITH DEADLY LYRICS, SLAYER STALKS FANS. Insurance costs were quoted, editorials were written, past incidents were cited. In New York, fans tear out seat cushions and sail them onstage. In Philadelphia, they pull down the sprinkler system and flood the hall. In Hollywood, tickets sell out and two hundred thrashers riot; one of them is charged with trying to run over a cop with his van.

Everywhere Slayer went, city fathers and mothers slapped palms to foreheads, My Lord, what now? Since the plagues of AIDS and crack had risen up to smite the Me Decade, America had been tripping on guilt. Penitent, confused, afraid, people joined groups and clubs. They started going to church, reciting the pledge, curbing their appetites. They became religious fundamentalists, Meese commissioners, new conservatives, L. Ron Hubbarders, self-helpers, liquid dieters, right-to-lifers. Hollering warnings, they laid their bodies across every alternative exit on the highway of life, trying to detour choice. Reins were tightened. "Do your own thing" was scrapped for "Just say no." Control. Control. Control. That was the answer. Be a community watchdog. Join a health club. Accept the Lord. Eat yogurt instead of ice cream. Drink bubbles instead of beer. Wear a condom, close your eyes, never question authority.

At least that's what grown-up America was thinking. The kids, meanwhile, were in their own world, listening to another kind of music. Called heavy metal, speed metal, death metal, thrash, its focus was devil fantasy, the occult, death, destruction, doom. The groups they idolized had names like

Black Sabbath, Metallica, Anthrax, Suicidal Tendencies, Megadeth. Perverse, contrary, heavy metal was a new soundtrack of protest, a reaction against the reactionaries, a cracked mirror in the haunted house of the modern age. Parents began finding notebooks doodled with pentagrams. They barged through bedroom doors, stood horrified as the stereo blared and little Johnny banged his head against the air.

Soon, lawmakers and experts began their counterassault. A group of political wives led the way, decrying heavy metal for "exposing innocent children to themes of sadomasochism, rape, and suicide." A group called Back in Control demanded a ban on heavy metal concerts and said children who listen to thrash should be "depunked and demetaled before it's too late." William F. Buckley Jr. called for censorship.

Kids who listen to Slayer, said a Los Angeles psychologist, "are violent and heavy drug users, they have no positive orientation." Said a Tennessee psychologist: "The lyrics become their philosophy." An eighteen-year-old boy shoots himself in the head while heavy metal blasts from his car stereo. A fourteen-year-old girl stabs and then bludgeons her mother to death. Seven teens ransack a warehouse, paint SUICIDAL DEATH TRIBE on the wall, jam a dead rat through the plaster. A teenager pleads guilty to mutilating cats and using the blood to scrawl 666 on elementary school walls. Each of the five panel members on a Phil Donahue show titled "Kids Who Kill" name Slayer as their favorite band.

All of which has had a predictable effect on Slayer's popularity. Ten years ago they were playing in high school gyms. Five years ago they were on the road in a rental van and a Camaro. In 1990 the band's sixth album, *Seasons in the Abyss,* made *Billboard* magazine's Top 40 pop chart. In July of that year, Slayer came of age: The cover of the *Rolling Stone.*

Sport the war, war support
The sport is total war
When victory's a massacre
When victory is survival
When the end is a slaughter
The final swing is not a drill
It's how many people I can kill

Back in Sacramento, with "War Ensemble" nearing its final, deafening chords, a young thrasher pushes his way through the crowd, bouncing off bodies like a drunk sailor tacking through a blow. His eyes are bloodshot, one shoe is missing, his hair is matted to his pink forehead. His brand new Slayer concert T-shirt, black with a yellow death head ($22), is shredded. He reaches the cinder-block wall, leans there a moment, dazed.

He stares upward, focusing vaguely on the ceiling, the stroboscopic colored lights, the smoke, the din. What's running through his mind? Maybe a photomontage, quick cuts like MTV, images collected in his brain. A soldier's arms shot away. Cops beating a man with batons. A psycho slicing skin from the back of an attractive blond corpse. An electric chair. A mushroom cloud. A Patriot missile. Burning crude. George Bush. Steven Seagal. Undercover narcs breaking down a door in a ghetto. Kurds rioting for food. A cow bloating in a rice paddy. Protesters smashing windows. Al Sharpton. Elvis. Christina Applegate. Freddy Krueger. A demon thrashing in a fiery quagmire. Whitney Houston singing "The Star-Spangled Banner."

Suddenly, the kid stirs. His brows rise, his mouth contorts, his eyes blaze. He screams, loud, long, piercing . . .

"Ahhhhhhhhhhhhhhhh!"

Then he slams his head, once, hard, into the cinder-block wall.

"Killer, dude!" he says.

"Check this one out, dude," says Tom Araya, waving a piece of fan mail. He sets down the letter, takes a hit off a bong he rigged from a Bart Simpson drinking bottle, free from 7-Eleven when you buy a Big Gulp.

Tom is the demon on the bass, Slayer's leader, home now from the road, catching up on his mail. He sits cross-legged on the sand-colored carpet in his newly acquired stucco rambler, white with baby-blue trim, the same color as his '85 Camaro. The house sits amid the vast sprawling suburbs of the San Fernando Valley. This exit off the 210 Freeway is Santa Anita, the town is Arcadia, though it really could be any exit on this grid-planned, fertile plain of minimalls, stoplights, palm trees, video outlets, frozen-yogurt stores, everything stucco—beige, tan, or cream.

Tom's piece of the lifestyle cost him two and a quarter. It's his first purchase, he's proud of it. Real estate is, like, real, you know? But it also makes him nervous. The payments. Being a Top 40 thrash idol grossed Tom only $90,000 in 1990. He's going to have to wait awhile before buying furniture. For now he's making do with the stuff from his old room at his parents' house. The decor is Early Teenage Suburbanoid, a kind of three-bedroom bed-room—Adults Beware! His pride is his video workshop: a chair, a desk, two monitors, two VCRs. His hobby is homemade music videos. He makes them using Slayer songs and scenes from movies like *Henry, Portrait of a Serial Killer, Platoon,* and *Scarface.* He likes mutilation clips, soldiers, and sexy girls best.

Tom's hair is in a ponytail that stretches midway down his back. On his index finger is a white-gold skull with two ruby eyes, $800, custom-made at a franchise jewelry store in the mall. A little gold ornament dangles from his right ear, some kind of Hebrew blessing, half of it anyway. The other half dangles from the ear of his ex-girlfriend Terry, guitarist in a metal band called Harum Scarum. They were together for three years. Recently they called it quits, which, incidentally, was the name of a disco band that Tom once played in—Quits.

Anyway, Tom's alone now, sort of. There's this one girl begging him to come to Oakland. And another from Dallas who's ready to miss classes and fly out at her own expense. But the one he really likes lives in New Jersey. He doesn't know whether to call her or not. He's always the one who calls. Why is it that when you show someone you like her, she runs the other way? Why don't you get the ones you really want?

Those, of course, are questions with no answers, questions put out of mind right now as Tom exhales his fragrant sinsemilla bong hit and reads a letter. This fan, like Tom, like all four members of Slayer, grew up a little south of here. Tom was born in Chile, moved with his family to Huntington Park, California, when he was five years old. His voice is soft and lilting, a mixture of Valley doper, Teenage Mutant Ninja Turtle, and mambo king.

"Sittin' in the desert, jammin' to 'South of Heaven,' where I'm sixty miles from where the fun will begin. My favorite tune is 'Expendable Youth.' With our jobs and what we do, that's all we actually are. I also like 'Angel of Death' and 'Mandatory Suicide.' I think of that song when I'm firing my Echo 3 M-60 machine gun. Being a grunt is pure motivation—like your music. It puts me in the right state of mind for war. You can count on four dead Iraqis for you guys. Keep kickin' ass, dudes!"

"Cool, huh?" says Tom, giggling. During Desert Storm, 20 percent of Slayer's fan mail came from soldiers.

Tom is twenty-nine, boyish, endearing, handsome in a roguish sort of way, with a good hit of Indian in his cheekbones, and light skin like his mother, a lay minister in the Catholic church, a hairdresser who wears her Slayer jacket to work. When she opened her own beauty shop, Tom and his six brothers and sisters tried to think up a cool name. They suggested the Harem or the Tease, but in the end she settled on her own choice, Cinderella.

"Whoa! Listen to this!" Tom exclaims. He flops down, elbow to carpet, palm to ear, legs stretched out with his shoes off. He reads:

"What's up? I am one of your most devoted fucking fans. You guys are gods in my eyes, I mean, fuck, I'm fucking obsessed with you guys. I'm a hardcore Satanist and I'm also into black magic. I read Tom's interview in the *L.A. Times,* and I don't believe you're a Catholic, I hope you were lying your ass off. I'm fifteen and your music is the only thing that has kept me from losing my mind. Most people go mad with anger and want to go out and kill someone after listening to Slayer. Not me. It soothes my brain."

Tom picks up his Bart pipe, loads a bud, a gift from a fan in Sacramento. The deader the town, it seems, the better the bud. Tom wonders if there's a correlation. He surveys the room, fires up the bowl. He was supposed to paint the living room today, but it's raining, he feels lazy. Maybe tomorrow. He picks up another letter.

"Your music takes me away to a far-off plain, where lies a faithless depth and Hades rapes in clouds. Tom, man, you're really cool. When you sing songs where you hit high notes, it gets me really hyper and glad I'm a head-banger." Two girls from Finland write: "A few days ago we bought Metal Hammer's poster book. There was a picture of you. Tom's balls were so grand (big dick, huge genital, massive gun, sharp sword, manly bar)."

Tom shakes his head and laughs. "This shit scares me sometimes," he says. "The way kids are into us, they way the adults hate us. *Nobody* gets it. It's amazing. Shit, dude! It's all right off TV."

Take "Mandatory Suicide." It's a song about being a soldier, about the draft. Substitute suicide for draft, he says. But it's not antiauthority. It's about informed choice. If you're going to join the army, then know that some general may possibly order your death. That's the duty of a soldier. "And thinking about death," Tom says, "I was wondering what it would be like to get shot. I've seen a lot of people shot in the movies, and I've had dreams where I was shot, so I have an idea, I know that it would burn like hell. I don't think the pain would be as bad as the burning sensation would be."

"Hallowed Point" is about owning guns. If you're gonna have one, it says, be prepared to make a hallowed point. Hallowed point comes from hollow point, as in the kind of bullet. Tom's not against guns. He's thinking of getting one. "Shooting somebody's a lot better than getting your head bashed in," he says.

"Blood Red" was inspired by news footage of a Chinese student playing cat and mouse with a tank in Tiananemen Square. "I read these little news clips about how things are fucked up here, fucked up there, everybody's got a civil war. And the way it goes down, the new guys are just as bad as the old," he says. "Dead Skin Mask" was inspired by mass murderer Ed Gein. "I can't tell you why I'm fascinated with mass murderers," Tom says. "It's like, there are actually all these people out there whose world is murder. They have to pretend to survive in this world with everybody else, but really they're living this hell. That really trips me out."

Tom wrote "War Ensemble" months before Iraq invaded Kuwait. It's not that he was prescient. It's just that he's fascinated with war, or anyway, with movies about war: *Full Metal Jacket, Apocalypse Now, Hamburger Hill.* To write the lyrics he consulted a military textbook.

"Living in the times we do," Tom says, "you don't *have* to make anything up. You got to admit, what goes on in the world is pretty fuckin' bizarre."

Tom pauses a moment, considering his words, reaching into the baggie. He loads another bud into the Bart bong. He's proud of his pipe. With all the head shops gone, a good bong is hard come by, even though it's pretty easy to get drugs. He flicks his Bic, covers the rush hole he bored with his Swiss Army knife, moves the flame slowly toward the bowl, a salvaged piece from a very old pipe. He draws at the convenient plastic straw built into the top of the bottle, making the sound of bubbles.

Mid-hit, he freezes. He tilts his head, listens. "Shit!" he exclaims. "Light a cigarette!"

Tom jumps up from the floor, grabs the Bart bong, the Baggie, the papers, a few loose joints. He scrams into the bedroom.

A knock at the door. A pause. A key.

The door opens. In steps Dad. He looks around, sniffs. Behind him, side by side, are John and Ollie. Tom's younger brother and sister are one year apart, inseparable.

"The whole house smells like pot!" says Dad.

Ollie raises an eyebrow. John smirks.

Dad strolls toward Tom's bedroom. Ollie and John follow.

"Oh! Hey, dad!" says Tom, backing out of his closet.

Dad regards his son a moment. He frowns, shakes his head. "I thought you said you were painting today."

"Mommy, I like that one!" croons the little boy. He's wearing surf shorts and mirrored goggles on a sunny, big-sky day near Phoenix. "The white one, Mom!"

Another subdivision, six hours east on the 10 Freeway, the same mini-malls and yogurt stores, but here the boulevards are wider, the stucco and neon set back from the road, sheep and horses grazing on backyard farms. It's the hometown of the Greenway High School Devils, the Desert Hills Evangelical Free Church, and Kerry King, Slayer's rhythm guitarist.

"I'll tell you," says Kerry, walking over to a white puppy turning excited circles in the last stall of the kennel. "If you're interested in this girl, you should get into showing."

"What does that consist of?" asks Mom, who has yet to convince Dad that the kids need a $1,500 pet. This is her umpteenth visit, but Kerry doesn't mind. He had to feed everybody anyway—twenty Akita sires and bitches and pups, some homebred, some from Illinois, a championship line. "Do you have to take them out of state?"

"The big guns do," says Kerry. "Like, I'm getting into the big-gun area myself."

"Do you show them?"

"I do, ah, I don't. I mean, I don't really have the look," says Kerry, the one who wears the sheath with the tenpenny nails onstage. "You've got to have a more contemporary look. I have a handler who shows them."

"Wouldn't that be discrimination?" asks Mom. "I mean, if your dog is—"

"You know how the world is, ma'am," says Kerry. "People have weird ideas."

Kerry's been living in Phoenix now for about eighteen months. He came here because he needed room to raise his dogs, chickens, and rats, the latter to feed his snakes. He has a collection of two hundred serpents, mostly boas. He also collects vintage Corvettes, horror videos, Slayer memorabilia, sports memorabilia. Kerry has always been a collector. You could say he collected Slayer.

It began in 1981, when he was fourteen. He and Jeff Hanneman met one day when both showed up to audition for a guitar slot in a band. Several days later, Dave Lombardo, a drummer, introduced himself when he was delivering a pizza to Kerry's neighborhood. He'd heard about the spoiled kid in the corner house with the collection of vintage guitars. Kerry was little and skinny then, pretty surfed out for someone who lived so far from the beach. His father was an aircraft-parts inspector who used to plunk "Red River Valley" on an acoustic. The Kings lived in a Mexican neighborhood; Kerry spent his youth running from cholos. After being caught and beaten a few times, he was forbidden by his parents to leave the backyard.

Having collected two guitarists and a drummer, Kerry called Tom for bass and vocals. Tom was working evenings as a respiratory therapist and was back in school to become a nurse. The four convened in Tom's garage. They jammed. Things clicked. They got themselves a manager, a friend trying to break into that side of the business.

And so a band was born. They called it Slayer, you know, like a murderer. Cool. They stole wood from construction sites and hammered together a drum riser and two guitar platforms, made a light frame with floods stolen from different apartment complexes in the neighborhood. Then they rented a high school gym and put on their first show. Tom's little brother John was the only roadie. He worked the lights and sound, and when a guitar string broke he'd run backstage and fix it. Soon they were on the road up and down the West Coast. Tom, the only member over twenty-one, was in charge. The towns had names like Winnipeg, and the crowds were small, but the boys were living their dream, playing in a rock 'n' roll band.

In 1983, Tom and Kerry's father put up $3,000 to cut an album. *Show No Mercy* sold sixty thousand copies, staggering for a band that nobody had heard of. The *Los Angeles Times* would later say that it "codified the gruesome conventions of death metal and became one of the most imitated albums ever made."

The rest, as they say, is show-biz history. More albums, harder lyrics, higher sales for records titled *Hell Awaits, Reign in Blood, South of Heaven, Seasons in the Abyss, Decade of Aggression*.

Mom and her kids are gone, and Kerry is reclining on a patio chaise in his living room. Behind him, on a shelf, is a huge softball trophy. Kerry sponsored the championship team, the Vipers, for two seasons, played third base. Last season, he had to be away on Slayer's European tour, so he decided not to sponsor it again, though he did pay his fee to remain on the roster. He showed up at the fourth game. After warm-ups, Kerry went to take a leak. The team took the field. They never did let him play.

Kerry writes most of Slayer's devil songs: "Skeletons of Society," "Born of Fire," "Temptation." He is about to recite one called "Spirit in Black." In the corner of the room, a trophy of another land, an exotic dancer from Denver, peddles an exercycle. He recites deadpan from the lyric sheet that comes with the *Seasons* CD, looking up now and again for effect:

Welcome to my world
Involve yourself within my dream
Experience a life
Just like your mind thought not to be
Take a look through time
At past or present worlds to be

I rule this inferno
Enthroned for eternity
Spirits damned to rot
Amidst the brimstone fireballs
Eyes of the dead
Watching from their living walls

Broken-glass reflections
Show your flesh eaten away
Listen closely to my voice
Feed me all your hatred
Empty all your thoughts to me
I can fill your emptiness
With immortality

"That one, hmmmm, let me see," says Kerry, tilting his head professorially, one finger to his lip. "Oh, yeah. I was at Blockbuster Video, and there was a video called . . . something about hell. It completely inspired me to write this song about a hell-like world and somebody being in charge of it. It's a fictitious story. It's like, welcome to my fantasy. Everybody would like to have his own world. Like, when you're in my place, you're in my rules, my boundaries, I can make anything happen that I want, 'cause it's my place. I'm the authority. Kind of like a man's home is his castle sort of thing.

"It's like, I try to write songs that are very visual. You can read the lyrics and see what's going on. Like that line, 'Eyes of the dead watching from their living halls.' I got that from *The Sword and the Sorcerer*, that part in the movie where they're conjuring up that guy, and he rises out of this casket of blood and there's this wall of faces, and once he comes to life all the faces come to life.

"That's where I get a lot of my images, from movies. And also stuff I imagine in my mind. Like in 'Spirit,' the first two verses sort of build you a picture of the place. 'Spirits damned to rot,' 'Broken-glass reflections'—you know, you're looking at yourself in a broken mirror or something. It's all visuals, things that are spooky, cool, stuff like that. See, if I had a choice to go to any kind of movie, it would be a horror movie. It's like, *Nightmare on Elm Street.* When that came out, it was just so unique, so well done, I was like, Oh, man, this, like, changes my whole life. *Friday the 13th, The First Power, Leviathan, Night Breed.* All those are really killer movies.

"I describe my songs as horror movies on music," he says. "It's a fantasy world. Tom likes war, serial killers, current-events stuff like that. But I don't know where people get this idea that I worship Satan. I'm not a satanic guy."

Late afternoon in the High Sierras. The land is flat; a snow-capped mountain rises in the distance. Two hours northeast of Los Angeles, the suburbs continue their migration toward the desert and Barstow, a new exit off the freeway, a new development of identical stuccos right next to a new mall. In a cul-de-sac, a family of Asians, Mom, Dad, two kids, stands at the edge of their new cement sidewalk, peering hopefully into manicured dirt, looking for signs of lawn.

"How y'all?!" yells Dave Lombardo, waving from across the street. He pulls a box out of the trunk of his car, a jacked-up Pontiac with a supercharger poked through the hood. "They got a housing committee out here," Dave whispers. "They like you to be friendly."

Dave and Theresa Lombardo have just moved into their first house, an upscale number with a vaulted foyer and neo-Victorian half-moon windows in the front, an expanse of dirt yard enclosed by nine-foot cinder-block walls in back. Dave heads up the sidewalk, checking for signs of his own lawn. He removes his shoes, backs through the front door, pads over the runner on the new white carpet.

"Where do you want this?" he hollers.

Theresa appears at the top of the stairs, floral stretch pants and big hair. She puts her finger to her lips.

"Don't shout!" she whispers. "You'll make the cake fall. Put that stuff in the kitchen. Tiptoe!"

Dave smiles, tiptoes, putting down the box, moving into the living room, where he begins alphabetizing his CD collection across the fireplace mantel. Theresa comes downstairs. They kiss. She goes to the powder room, busies herself arranging a new set of matching mauve bath accessories. She hums.

Dave and Theresa are at their best when they're together, and they're always together, kind of like Barbie and Ken, which is what the other members of Slayer have nicknamed them. During the hours before a concert, while the rest of the band sleeps, Dave and Theresa usually play tourist. In Sacramento they saw the Governor's Mansion, Dave in his long hair and Slayer cap, Theresa in her stretch pants, bobby socks, spike heels, and pancake makeup. As a souvenir they bought a magnet for the new fridge.

At the concerts, Theresa waits at the bottom of Dave's two-story platform. He plays a console of twelve custom-made drums and eight extra-thick cymbals, the largest of which he got because it makes the sound of two trucks colliding. His earliest memories of drums are Tarzan movies and Santeria ceremonies. His parents, who are from Havana, used to bring him. He played along on toy bongos. Now he has his very own roadie and a set worth $15,000.

When Dave plays, high above the crowd, chills run up and down his spine, he gets goose-bumps. It's incredible, he's not good with words, but it's an incredible feeling, the energy, the electricity between him and the kids, it just blows him away. Used to be Slayer was playing and Dave would be watching the kids go crazy, watching them fly all over the room, and it looked like so much fun that he couldn't just sit there on his stool. He'd be like, "I'm gonna jump in too," and he'd climb down off his platform and dive right into the crowd. He'd free fall, and the kids would catch him, and then they'd just, like, hold him up, just, like, floating around, and then they'd throw him back onstage.

It was fun. He did it every show. Then kids started stealing his shoes, ripping his shirt, pulling out locks of hair. Then one night he got punched in the face by a bouncer. Never again, dude.

Now when he's finished, Theresa bundles him up in a robe and takes him around the waist, leads him to the showers. They started dating years ago, while she was a bookkeeper at Sears and he was a security guard at Kmart. These days, they don't really mix much with the band. Dave quit a while back because the guys gave Theresa so much shit, locker-room antics, dick jokes and such. He's back now because after he left, the band never got around to auditioning a new drummer.

Even with the hassles, Dave is thrilled to be in Slayer. Thanks to tours, he and Theresa have seen castles in Scotland, beer factories in Germany, the Imperial Gardens in Japan, a big, humongous church in Milano. They try to make the most of things as they are right now. They don't know how long stardom is gonna last. Nothing lasts forever. (Within nine months, in fact, Dave and Theresa would split up.)

"It's still an incredible thing," says Dave, slotting a Slayer CD into the machine. "I can't believe this. Is this really happening? I still am a fan. I'm more of a fan than I am a player in the band. I'm just like the kids I play for, I guess. I mean, I enjoy listening to the music. I get into it so much. The energy. The energy. There's no weak point. It's just, the music, the way I feel it. When I play, I give it everything. I know every kid in that arena would love to be doing the exact same thing if they could. I'm just one of the lucky ones."

"I'll tell you honest," Eddie is saying as the burgers are served in a greasy spoon on the Sunset Strip. "One time when Kerry called me, my phone went flying off the bed. It really did. You know, the cord was sticking straight up and the phone was, like, swinging around the room, and I'm just, like, sitting there watching my phone go crazy. I was totally straight. I didn't even know what drugs were about at the time. Finally, I caught the phone and I pulled it down and like, 'Hello?' And it was Kerry. He was like, 'What the hell are you doing?' "

Eddie's real name is Laura. She's the assistant to a regional sales rep for a large national firm. She's also Slayer's biggest fan. It started years ago in Houston, when she was in ninth grade, living in the suburbs with her parents. Her father was the manager of a dry-cleaning plant. Her mother, a former big-band singer, had been reborn as a strict Baptist.

Laura was going through a kind of rebellious stage when she found heavy metal. She learned about it from a guy named Venom at a concert given by a Christian band called the Ethereals. Venom listened to Iron Maiden and Motörhead. And he listened to Venom. That was his favorite band. Venom wore leather and chains and safety pins. He was very cute.

Laura started calling herself Eddie. She dyed her hair jet black, wore leather, metal studs, skull rings. She liked her new music, but kept thinking, *There's got to be something heavier.* Then she heard Slayer's song, "Chapel of Sin." There was this solo on it by Hanneman that made her feel like she was underwater and she couldn't catch her breath. She was just like, Oh, my God, this is incredible! And the words. She doesn't know why—*Harlots of hell/ Spread your wings as I penetrate your soul,* you wouldn't think she'd dig something like that—but damn, it was good. It just went right through her, just made her go wooooooooow! It was like, she could listen to it, and then she was in a really good mood. Hearing "Chapel of Sin," that was it. She vowed right then and there, Slayer was her band.

See, weird things had always happened in her life. Like her Mom would walk in and find her levitating near the ceiling. She'd call out *Laura!* and the girl would just drop down to the bed. And there were the visitors. They were hooded people, she doesn't know who. She called them the Council. The members of the Council never spoke, but they showed her things, pictures. To this day she'll see something, like a déjà vu, and remember that it was something they showed her. And one time, when she was seventeen or eighteen, she had troops marching through her house. Her dad was asleep on the couch. She was like, "Daddy, wake up, we got to get a priest in here." Daddy wouldn't wake up. She called her girlfriend. The friend asked, "What's all that rumbling in the background?"

Eddie joined the Doom Society, a kind of fan club that brought heavy metal bands to Houston. They got some press when they sacrificed a stack of Mötley Crüe albums to Slayer in an occult ceremony outside a radio station. It was a majorly outfreakish event, way cool. They drew a crowd. Eddie loved Slayer because they were fast, and there was just such power behind their music. It assaulted her. She could feel it. There was nothing like it. She got a buzz from it. She and her friends would have thrash sessions; they'd put on Slayer and pile on top of each other and just let it all out.

What were they letting out? She doesn't know exactly. Something about being a teenager. Something about living on this planet in these times. It's like, sometimes you want to scream, you know? It just feels great, great and free. They can put on an album and just slam into each other, just totally have fun in the privacy of their own rooms.

To Eddie's thinking, Slayer has become more and more popular because of what she calls "the slayerness of it all," the majorly fucked up state of the world. At home, at school, on television, one thing is clear: Life sucks. Slayer commiserates. The demon on the stage recites truths that the kids in the audience already know inside themselves. Only when someone else says it do they know they aren't alone. And once that sinks in, and they see how hopeless everything is, the music and the buzz and the head-banging and all the rest helps them let it out, purge, a joyous, unified, tearless, savage good cry.

"It's like that song, 'Temptation,'" says Eddie, dipping a french fry in ketchup. "It gets to me because it says, 'Have you ever wondered why it's evil you're attracted to?' You know, I do wonder why. There's just so many people out there that are supposed to be on the good side, but they're not for real. Politicians, teachers, parents, ministers, Christians, everybody. They're hypocrites. The whole society. All the adults. They're so phony."

Eddie pauses a moment, lets her emotions run past. She looks over toward the door. In profile, the bright California sunlight makes her hazel eyes look yellow.

"I get frustrated," she says. "I try to keep things fine and wonderful, but, shit, talk about an angry sleeper. I wake up and my blanket is ripped to shreds, and oh, my God, my head will be inside a hole in the blanket, strangling me. I don't know how I do these things. In my sleep. Strangling myself. Just a majorly outfreakish event. Weird, huh?"

Almost Famous

After you've cried enough, you go for a walk.

That's what Lynn does. It's a little ritual she's evolved over the years for times like this, when she's feeling rejected, anonymous, totally freaking worthless. She begins to raise her abject self from the sofa, making mental note of her loathsomeness, her breach of faith. She has broken her own cardinal rule: Never let this damn town get you down.

Buck up, she resonates to the four corners of her soul, managing to achieve a seated position. The sofa was among the splurges occasioned by the long national run of her husband's Mercury Sable commercial. "Make it a red one, Gordo," said Steve, playing an upstart yuppie exec. People still recognize him on the street. "Do I know you from college?" they ask.

Lynn fingers a wispy lock of chestnut hair behind her ear, wipes the moisture from her cheeks. She is beautiful when she cries. That's what Steve thinks. Lynn doesn't like to think about it. She hates makeup, carrying a purse, looking in the mirror. She refuses to bleach her hair back to its childhood blonde. When someone admires her dress, she'll say that she's wearing the wrong slip. When people scrutinize her, take her picture, roll a camera, she gets extremely uncomfortable. For years she kept herself camouflaged underneath fifteen extra pounds.

Right now, however, the issue she's grappling with isn't beauty. Nor is it the paradox of someone so painfully shy, so self-conscious, yearning to be twelve feet high on a movie screen. There are thousands of beautiful women in Hollywood; many, no doubt, have a very strange and special relationship with their looks. Right now the issue is sanity. Lynn must concentrate. Pull things into perspective. Remember to breathe. She flicks the remote, kills the tube, mumbles something to Steve, up in his loft, clicking away on the computer.

Lynn hits the elevator—three, two, lobby. She waits for the shudder: the mechanical one at the bottom of the shaft; the biological one at the bottom of the tears. Appointment. Disappointment. Only three little letters of difference.

Ding, the elevator door slides open. She ventures forth, wearing shades and tennies, a trace of lipstick left from this morning's audition, for the role of yet another wisecracking but earnest young sitcom mom. It is spring in Hollywood, pilot season, a time when the earth is blooming and television shows are being born. Dozens of actors will be auditioned to play a sitcom sidekick. Hundreds will read for an hour-long drama with an ensemble cast. One thousand will be seen to find the perfect guy to run a Weedwacker for a nanomoment in a thirty-second commercial. Thousands more won't ever get in the door. To land a job, you have to get an audition. To get an audition, you pretty much have to have an agent. To get an agent, you have to have a job; they want to see you perform before they take you on. The agent who handles Steve's work for commercials receives fifty unsolicited photos every day. In eighteen years, Lynn's theatrical agent has signed only one person on the strength of an unsolicited photo; you wouldn't recognize his name. According to the Screen Actors Guild, 40 percent of its 80,000 members make less than $3,000 a year pursuing their chosen field. There is no accounting of unpaid hopefuls. Though you've never heard of them, Lynn Clark and Steve Bean are among the lucky few. Over the past few years, they've grossed a combined $100,000 annually. Of course, Ted Danson used to make that much in about five minutes of an episode of *Cheers.*

So the calls go out, and the actors do their hair, change and rechange their clothes, try to look the part as described in the character breakdowns that come grinding out of special wireless printers in the agencies: "affable wise guy," "Chris Elliot type," "feisty young mom," "the kind of woman who jogs and eats granola every morning." They read a few lines, smile, try to act as if they don't really need this job. Then they go home, wait, try to forget it even happened.

It's been a little dry lately for Lynn.

Well, very dry.

She didn't think it was going to be like this. Last February she did *Friends*, and she was sure a breakthrough was at hand. Then . . . nothing.

This morning, on a sunny day in mid-May, almost three months since *Friends*, Lynn took out her calendar and counted exactly how many auditions she'd done this season. How many jobs she didn't get. She knew it was a bad idea, but she did it anyway. When you choose to be an actor, you start a war inside yourself, and everything after that just serves to escalate the hostilities. It is a battle between reality and fantasy, work and unemployment, fame and obscurity; between the affirming exhilaration of applause and the paralyzing fear of failure. Sixty-eight auditions: zero jobs. She could kick herself. Why count?

Lynn cuts her eyes to the rows of gleaming brass mailboxes. She stands a moment in the marshmallow pink glow of the open foyer, leaning in her mind first toward the mail, then toward the front gate. In the air is a familiar scent of laundry lint, chlorine, sun-baked stucco, smog. Birds chirp, palms rustle, a car alarm bleats. Once Lynn looked in her mailbox and found a thick envelope. *Santa Barbara* had made it to Europe in syndication. Lynn had appeared on the soap as Lily Light, teenage evangelist. There were forty-eight checks inside, each for $167. It felt like hitting the lottery.

She chooses the gate, scuffles double time down the steps. As always, she looks for her Honda Civic, making sure it's still there. The Civic replaced her '64 Dart, assembled the year she was born. Lynn still has the Dart, a sort of monument to feast and famine. The Honda was purchased after her last pilot, for *Banner Times*. Retooled and recast, the show was called *Hearts Afire* and had a regular prime-time slot. The star of *Banner Times*, Jeff Foxworthy, has his own new show.

To date Lynn has done four pilots, three movies of the week (two starring Raquel Welch), a Columbo movie, recurring roles on Santa Barbara and *Days of Our Lives* and an episode of *Murder, She Wrote* (with Steve, playing a couple). In '92 she starred in *Grapevine*, an ensemble-cast twenty-something sitcom on CBS that paved the way for shows like *Friends*. She has done a handful of stage plays in L.A. She's been called "beguiling and sensual" by *Daily Variety*. She was once the answer to 71 Across in the crossword puzzle of the *Los Angeles Times* TV-listings supplement. Also in her credits are long stints as a waitress. If you add up the hours . . . well, it's best not to get into that.

Lynn hits the pavement, turns left, arms levering into a power walk. Heel, toe, elbows and fists, one foot in front of the other. Lynn got into power walking at the suggestion of a personal trainer when she finally decided to lose the extra weight. Fifteen pounds later, she got *Seinfeld.* In her first episode, she met Jerry at a dinner party. In her second, they went away together for a weekend. Then the producers decided it would be better if Jerry played the field.

The *Seinfeld* stint raised her profile, however, and Lynn eventually landed the part on *Grapevine.* Set in Miami, written and directed by David Frankel (*Miami Rhapsody*), the show suffered the mixed blessing of critical acclaim. After four episodes, it was history.

Heel, toes, elbows and fists, one foot in front of the other. Lynn keeps her eyes straight ahead, focusing on the fuzzy distance. A little past two in the afternoon in North Hollywood, California, means a little past five on the East Coast. That's where the producers of a pilot for an hour-long political drama called *The Monroes* are holed up at this moment. On location outside Richmond, Virginia, in the final days before shooting the show—a sort of *Dynasty*-goes-to-Washington, starring William Devane—the producers have decided to replace an actress. The character has three lines; she's the faithful wife of a philandering congressman. Lynn was at the studio for a different audition when she happened to bump into the casting director. She put Lynn on the tape of prospective replacements.

Now it is two days later, and Lynn still hasn't heard anything. When you're an actor, no news is not good news. If Lynn had been chosen, someone would have called by now. It was this realization that drove her to her sofa, her calendar, this walk.

Heel, toes, elbows and fists, one foot in front of the other. Just to the south, Lynn can see the Santa Monica Mountains. On the other side is the land of Hollywood. The metaphor is hackneyed but inescapable. Thousands of aspiring actors like Lynn and Steve live here in the San Fernando Valley, a traffic-choked suburban sprawl of stucco apartment complexes and cookie-cutter strip malls, incorporated into patches called Studio City, North Hollywood, Burbank and Toluca Lake, the rents lower the farther you get from the mountains.

Sometimes, when Lynn looks to the mountains, she imagines herself as a character in the Felliniesque movie of her career quest, a tiny figure in a panoramic shot, halfway up the face. The rocks are slippery. She clings and claws. Steve is off to one side, as are many, many others, some higher, some lower, all of them dangling by threads.

She has another audition at five, so Lynn makes two quick circuits around a nearby park. She loves the park, all the green; it reminds her of her home, the tiny burg of La Plata, Maryland. But it also holds bad memories. Lynn arrived in town nine years ago, on the same day as her graduation from the drama department at Carnegie Mellon University. Though she had been flown out for a screen test, she didn't get the part. Two months later, the same folks gave her Lily Light. Six months later, Lily walked out the door after Christmas dinner and never returned to *Santa Barbara*. Lynn's sudden termination by the new writers caught her by surprise. She was twenty-two and nearly broke. She had to get a job. One afternoon, cutting through this park with her new green waitress apron and a Hamburger Hamlet manual in her arms, she ran into the makeup woman from *Santa Barbara*. Had Lynn owned a sofa at the time, she surely would have gone to it.

Quick shower, change clothes, another audition in Burbank, another performance of her life: I don't really need this job. Then back home. Lynn dons her favorite ratty T-shirt, slumps into the sofa. Steve arrives two hours later.

"How're you feeling, hon?" he calls out tentatively, treading down the short hallway toward the living room. He too has had his ups and downs in the past eight years. Steve Bean has been a guest star on *Cheers, Coach, Married . . . With Children, Dave's World, Burke's Law* and many others. He's been a stand-up comic; an MTV veejay; a regular and a staff writer on *Tim Conway's Funny America* and *Not Necessarily the News;* a member of the comedy troupe the Groundlings, a proving ground for *Saturday Night Live.* He's performed a Kabuki-Hasidic adaptation of *Macbeth* in an empty swimming pool. He's done more than fifty national commercials. As only 1 percent of actors get about 80 percent of the work in commercials, he's pretty successful. His agent credits his improvability, his rubber face, his "fun-time, talk-fast, real-guy, Everyman look."

Several years ago, Steve won a part as a regular on *Ann Jillian*. Before the series hit NBC, however, he was replaced. So deep was his funk that he considered quitting.

For maybe five seconds. More than anything else, Steve wants to perform. He must perform. He is compelled to perform. To be watched, photographed, filmed. What a job! You say your lines and people clap.

Instead of quitting, Steve got a therapist and an audition coach. Lynn has the same complement of professional help. Both of them worry about telling this to people outside Hollywood, lest you think they're fruitcakes or whiners. But the fact is, they're playing a rough game in a rough town. Nothing makes sense; nothing is real; the rules change as you go along. You walk into a room; they dismiss you. They don't know you, and they don't know what they want. All they know is what they don't want. It's usually you. For each role awarded, says Lynn's agent, there are probably twenty other actors who could do it just as well. A search for the words *aspiring actor* in the *Los Angeles Times* database gives some idea of the toll: Sexually abused by agent. Bilked by phony talent agency. Files suit against Oprah for not including her in segment on "Hollywood Hopefuls." Guns down three to avenge rent dispute. Shoots self in mouth with pistol while rehearsing *Lethal Weapon* scene in acting class.

Like Lynn, Steve looks at the Santa Monica Mountains and registers the metaphor. But as he is the kind of guy who thinks of the glass as half full, he sees that he and Lynn are better off than most. They seem to be making progress. Getting there. Almost there. Almost famous. They just have to stick it out. Someday, he hopes, he *believes*, all their years of struggle will be reduced to one amusing paragraph in a magazine cover story occasioned by some fabulous success.

"Hi, hon," says Lynn, basking in the eerie light of the tube. She is screening a favorite tape, William Shatner doing a dramatic recitation of Elton John's song "Rocket Man." Because of her business, Lynn prefers watching documentaries, movies—anything but regular TV. Watching those shows is like revisiting her failures, seeing someone else performing roles she auditioned for. She was almost Jennifer Aniston in *Friends*. She was almost Julia Duffy in a number of shows. The Shatner tape, on the other hand, is a hoot. Split images of three Shatners, posing, overacting. "I'm a rocket, man," he recites in a beatnik voice. So rich and famous is Shatner, so bad is his performance, it has a weird calming effect on Lynn, proof of the madness of her world.

Steve peers through the dark at his wife. "What's wrong with your face?"

They hustle to the bathroom. The vanity lights over the mirror are harsh. Lynn's face is mottled. Her eyes are beginning to swell shut. She felt a little itchy, but . . . She checks her arms, her legs, her butt. Hives!

The waterworks begin anew. Steve hugs her, holding himself back a little, lest she be contagious. He too is up for a pilot, *Cleghorne!*, starring Ellen Cleghorne from *Saturday Night Live*.

The phone rings; they let the machine pick up. Then they hear a familiar voice. It's Lynn's agent. She got the part in *The Monroes*. "You're going to Richmond tomorrow, sweetheart," he says.

"Look at that pile of beef!" announces Steve Bean, indicating with both hands a corned-beef sandwich that has to be six inches high. Steve speaks like a guy in a commercial, narrating his life as it goes, or maybe like a guy who has a very strange and special relationship with his voice, wrapping his mouth quickly but carefully around each syllable, pausing a millisecond between words, projecting to the back of the house, even at close range.

It's late in June now; the Valley is arid. Steve is on a stool at the Formica counter overlooking the kitchen sink, which is stacked with dishes, orderly but unwashed. Lynn is running around the apartment, a few degrees below frantic, gathering props and costumes, making a pile by the door. The Onstage Company, a North Hollywood theater group of which she is president, is in final rehearsals for a showcase. She wrote her piece, called "The Working Actor," with two other women, based on their experiences in the food-service industry.

"Have some of this nice protein, hon," intones Steve.

"I don't know," says Lynn. She's smoking a Marlboro Light, from the first pack she's bought in two years.

"Come on, it's from Jerry's," he coaxes, separating the halves, picking up one, mugging. "Protein and a good ol' dose of Jewish self-esteem," he announces, opening his rubber mouth extra wide, going in for a bite.

Lynn grimaces. "I'm gonna put this in my car."

Believe it or not, things are rosy around here today, the expectant butterflies of impending performances having replaced the angst of freaking worthlessness. Besides the showcase this weekend, Lynn starts filming *The Monroes* later this month. Not only was the pilot picked up but her part was upgraded from recurring role to regular. For the next twelve weeks, she will be a prime-time network star.

Steve goes on this weekend for the first time with the main company at Acme Comedy Theatre. And, at least for now, he is back in the running for

Cleghorne! It's been a long haul. First he did the audition, then four callbacks. Then the producers gave him the role in the pilot. Then they axed him. Then they hired him back. Then the pilot was picked up by Warner Bros., but Steve wasn't. The network auditioned every semiknown comedian in town. Then they decided to invite Steve back for a screen test. He's waiting for that call now.

In the meantime, Steve's trying his best not to think about it, focusing instead on his writing—the stuff for Acme and also a spoof feature film, *T3: Terminate Her Too.*

Steve climbs upstairs to his loft, a five-by-ten-foot nook overlooking the living room. He sits at the computer, surrounded by his collection of kitsch. Gumby, Bullwinkle, Donnie from New Kids on the Block. A Gene Autry lunch box, a bumper sticker from his dad's race for town councilman: ELECT IRWIN LEVY.

Steve Bean's real name is Levy. Steve explains that he changed it because people constantly mispronounced it. And then there's a long story about a guy who found a bean in his apple-peach cobbler. Suffice it to say that the first time he did stand-up, at the beginning of the comedy-club wave of the early '80s, he used Steve Bean, and he killed them, and that has been his stage name ever since.

Steve is the middle child of Irwin and Dottie Levy—an industrial engineer and a schoolteacher—of Providence, Rhode Island. Lynn is the eldest of four born to Randy and Janice Clark—a retired postal worker and a real estate agent—of La Plata. They describe similar upbringings: loving parents, extended families, high achievement, early feelings of specialness, a knack or a yen for being the center of attention.

Steve likes to say that his desire for the spotlight was the result of his very birth: As the only son and first grandson in a close Jewish family, he was put on a pedestal. For years, at home and at temple, when everyone toasted *L'Chaim,* young Steve, whose Hebrew name is Chaim, thought they were toasting him. "It's very difficult to try and live up to all that unconditional praise heaped upon you as a child," says Steve. "If you're in a position where the understanding is that you are already the best simply because you exist, then how do you live up to that feeling of specialness as years go by?"

Lynn was a shy, quiet kid, a bookworm, reading Nancy Drew on Gram's sofa while her brothers romped outside. She took piano and singing lessons and joined 4-H, which sponsored public-speaking contests and demonstration days. Each time she was to perform, Lynn suffered nausea, tremors, stomachaches, such dread that she was always just shy of too sick to go on.

Steve found the answer to his special need for recognition in a high school production of *The Crucible*. Soon he was playing lead roles, and all the girls had a crush on him. In the eleventh grade, he won an award for best actor at the New England Drama Festival.

Lynn's first high school play was also *The Crucible*. When she read for the part, her teacher remembers, "it was phenomenal; it was like the air around her changed the minute she started speaking." In her senior year, Lynn was one of thirty students to win the National Foundation for the Advancement in the Arts' national talent search.

For Lynn acting wasn't so much a matter of gaining attention. "I loved the release," she says. "I always got these fiery characters. Abigail in *The Crucible* is constantly screaming and hallucinating. And I played Louise in *Gypsy*, and I got to slap my mother in the face. I guess I was always so self-conscious and so insecure about expressing my opinions or feelings about things that I needed an outlet.

"I think a lot of it has to do with Catholicism, just feeling the fear of God and shaming you about your individuality so you'll behave. I guess it's the same thing with my looks. It's shameful to dwell on beauty. So I don't. But when I'm acting, I can be someone else. I feel free."

Both Lynn and Steve attended Carnegie Mellon, though not at the same time. One of the oldest drama schools in America, Carnegie's is a notch below Yale's and Juilliard's. Alumni include Jack Klugman, Laura San Giacomo, Ted Danson, Steven Bochco and Holly Hunter.

Enrollment in Carnegie amounts to being chosen, recognized, treated like a member of the company, like a working actor as opposed to an aspiring one. When you graduate, you leave feeling like you've paid your dues, earned a shot at the big time. The problem is, no one else knows. Entering the real world, you have to start all over again.

Steve lasted only two years at Carnegie. A few days after he left, he landed in the Pittsburgh Metropolitan Stage Company.

After two seasons (performing in *Waiting for Godot* and *A Midsummer Night's Dream*, among other productions), Steve started doing stand-up with a fellow Carnegie dropout, Chris Zito. For the next six years, Zito and Bean, based first in Pittsburgh, then in Boston, worked regularly in fifteen states. They used props and costumes, wore fake noses, sang send-up songs. Skits included "Night of the Bill Bixby Clones" and "Attack of the Headless Barbies." *The Boston Globe* described them as "provocatively original . . . among Boston's top comics."

Eventually, Zito and Bean went their separate ways. Steve drove to Hollywood to seek his fortune in August 1987, the year after Lynn arrived. The couple met the following April at a showcase mounted by Carnegie alumni. Steve was performing. Lynn had come with another alum, who was by now an agent.

"That was a night to remember," says Steve. "I got an agent and a wife."

"Of course, it took a while before we actually dated," says Steve, sitting poolside, wearing shades.

"Maybe this should be off the record," says Lynn. She is also in shades, stretched out on a chaise longue.

"It's all true," says Steve.

"Maybe we could tone down the heavy-drinking aspect."

"Everyone will understand," says Steve. "You were nervous. You were on your first date with me."

"Hey, you! You Hollywood stars!" It is Lynn's brother Donnie calling out from the house. "Can I interrupt your exclusive poolside interview a minute? We're going to get steamed crabs. You guys gonna eat some?"

"Are you kidding?" Lynn says, laughing. "Get a bushel for just me!"

It's late in July, and Lynn and Steve are visiting the Clarks in La Plata. Just an hour south of Washington, D.C., it's a place George F. Will once called "that village of a few thousand souls, [where] folks raise tobacco and soybeans and children." Lynn tries to make it back at least four times a year.

As it looks right now, barring acts of God—or of producers, directors or studio execs—Lynn and Steve will be returning to Los Angeles in a few days, both to begin work on new television series for the fall lineup.

Just before he left, the network called once again about the *Cleghorne!* part. Arriving at the studio, figuring they were going to give him the job, Steve found five other candidates. They all sat together in a small room. It was obvious to Steve that the network still had no idea what it wanted for the part. The casting people had collected a handsome guy, a bordering-oneffeminate guy, a Jewish character-looking guy and another affable wise-guy type like Steve.

The actors read, then waited. At 5:30 they were told to go home.

Saturday, Sunday, Monday: no word. Steve stayed in bed for half a day, then cried on Lynn's shoulder, the little ritual *he's* evolved over the years. Then, on Tuesday, his agent called. None of the guys had been chosen. The network wanted a "name" for the part.

OK, fine! Steve thought. *That's it. Over. Done with.* He could finally let it go. He had gotten the pilot on his thirty-fifth birthday. He'd been jerked around for almost four months now. The network wanted a name. That was it. Another of the many decisions in his life that were completely out of his control. He decided to go to the movies. He chose *Under Siege,* had a grand time watching lots of people—every single one of them an actor—get blown away.

He returned to the apartment at six. The phone rang. It was his agent: "They're considering you again. You'll have an answer tomorrow morning at eleven."

"You know something?" Steve said, everything welling up, his voice catching. "I don't care anymore. I don't give a shit. I have let it go. If it happens, great; if it doesn't, great. I just don't care."

There was a moment of silence. Then Steve spoke again. "What time did you say you'd call?"

His agent phoned at ten of eleven the next day. "You have it. Be there at eleven."

Steve got to the studio about a half hour later, driving at breakneck speed over the mountain to Hollywood. The whole cast was sitting around a table, reading the script, and Steve rushed in when they were on the page before his scene.

He took the empty seat at the table, out of breath. He turned to his part, spoke his first line.

And then everyone in the room—Ellen Cleghorne, the producer, the director, the rest of the cast—everyone looked up, registered who was reading. There in the chair was Steve Bean, the guy they had started with, who'd done the pilot, who'd been screwed around so famously, so typically, by a bunch of suits who never, ever knew what they wanted in the first place.

Spontaneously, everyone at the table began to clap. It was long, sustained, heavenly applause. And it was all just for Steve.

Now, in the waning days of their summer vacation, Lynn and Steve are kicking back in La Plata. This, to Lynn, is the purest drug, being home in the embrace of her family. Her Hollywood pipe dream is to leave Hollywood. To do a series for a couple of years and make enough to buy a house on the water in Maryland, close to her family. She'd buy a piano. Read. And when she and Steve had kids, she'd be home as much as possible. Of course, they'd have a second place in Hollywood.

"Perhaps we can skip this first-date story," says Lynn, sitting by the pool. "The producers of *The Monroes* are going to think I'm a drunk."

"*Tsk, tsk*, oh, Lynn," says Steve. "Whatever you wish, hon."

At one point, around the time of her funk last fall, Lynn didn't know if she wanted to act anymore. She didn't know if she even *liked* acting. She had such bad stage fright, she was messing up her auditions. She always felt sick before going on. And when she was actually acting, she felt totally incompetent. It was just painful. She felt so judged, so ineffectual, so loathsome and, when she wasn't working, totally freaking worthless.

Then something happened that had nothing to do with Hollywood or acting or fame. It had to do with her little sister.

Christy was 18 at the time, had a wonderful fiancé. They'd been together since high school. Larry was 21, a great guy. Then, one night, he was leaving a bar. There was an electric sign outside and a puddle on the ground beneath it. Larry slipped and fell against the sign. He was electrocuted.

When that happened, Lynn says, "suddenly, I began to think, like, what does all this matter? Hollywood is meaningless. It's all about exterior and status and how people see you, and it's a big freaking popularity contest. Who needs that?"

So it was that Lynn set about changing her priorities. She read *Zen and the Art of Motorcycle Maintenance, The Artist's Way*, any book that seemed in sync with her mood. She bought pots of flowers for her balcony, became president of the Onstage Company, started writing some stuff she could perform herself. Once upon a time, when she didn't have an audition, she would fill her days with tasks and errands. She'd go to the dry cleaner, recycle the papers, wash the car. Now she is trying hard to remember that life is something you do, not something you watch or wait for. If nothing's happening, she'll go down to Santa Monica and ride her bike along the beach. Or she'll go to a museum or drive up to Mulholland, just sit there for a half hour, admiring the view.

"Before, it was like I was sitting there on the sofa, waiting for my life to happen, thinking, If I only get this job, then I will be a worthy human being. But you know what? I'm finally starting to see that life is all about the process, not the product."

"I'm very impatient with myself," adds Steve. "There's always that big question: When am I going to be famous? When am I going to be rich? When am I going to be happy? When am I going to be satisfied? When, when, when, when? It can be toxic."

So this is the idea," says the exec from TBS, sitting behind her big desk, looking up at Steve and his audition partner, an actress he's never met. "A guy and a gal, dinner and a movie, OK?"

"OK," Steve says tentatively. The actress says nothing.

"Look," says the exec. "You know the show *Friends?* Well this is like *Friends*, but with a movie in it. In other words, you're kind of cooking dinner, hosting a movie, but after a while, people won't just tune in to the movie; they'll be tuning in to see your relationship."

"I see," says Steve.

"But I don't want comedians for this job. What I'm looking for is a comedy team like Abbott and Costello."

"Ummm-hmmm," says Steve. He smiles even wider. Then, hoping to showcase his talent for improv, he says, "So, how *are* Abbott and Costello doing? I heard they had a very busy pilot season. Maybe you could get *them* for this gig."

The executive's face darkens. A deep, black thundercloud of ire. "You got a problem with Abbott and Costello? Lou Costello was my grandfather."

It's October now. Steve is gone from *Cleghorne!* From the beginning, he'd felt out of place. The lone white guy in a *Jeffersons*-like sitcom, he played Ellen's business partner. With each week of his six-week stint, he had fewer lines. Finally, the network decided to ax the office setting entirely. In the meantime, he's gone back to auditioning for commercials. His first shot was an Alpo ad. The gist of the message was that changing your pooch's brand of dog food might give him diarrhea. Steve didn't get that. But he did land two voice-overs for a cell-phone company and a Sparkle paper-towel commercial.

He's happy for the work, but, well, need he explain? Two weeks ago, he was a series regular. It was a horrible show, but it was a show. He's trying to be philosophical.

"One of the weird things in the aftermath of *Cleghorne!* was that here I had worked with these people for three months, and when my part was canceled, only one person in the cast called me.

"I let that slide. Because that's the way it is. And then, three weeks later, I get an autographed cast photo in the mail—'To Steve, Best Wishes.' And I was like, this is really insulting. You don't have time to call me, but you'll send me a glossy photo as if I'm a fan or something. I feel that it was a nice gesture. But the reality of it . . . well, it hurt.

"My feeling is that when you have a success or victory in your career, everybody is very willing and able to share in that, to call you up and say, 'How wonderful.' But when you have a loss, then it's like a disease, and that disease is contagious, and they don't want to touch it because they might get it. The next time I do a show, I'm going to be the boss of it myself. I'm going to write, produce and act in it. There's no way I can live without performing, so I'm just gonna do it myself."

Joining Steve in the ranks of the newly unemployed is Lynn. *The Monroes*, airing Thursday night on ABC, opposite *Seinfeld*, had been touted by the *Los Angeles Times* as "a smartly written *Dallas* on the Potomac that packs enough melodrama in its premiere to nourish an entire season." Though Lynn's character, Ann, had only three lines in the first episode, her part became more and more substantial. In a family full of misfits and demigods, Ann was a smart, pretty, upstanding young mother. People began to recognize Lynn on the street. She started getting fan mail.

During the week the seventh episode was shooting, Lynn got her best scenes to date. She found her husband with another woman and shouted him down, and then she got to drink too much and tell each and every Monroe what she thought of them.

Not ten minutes after Lynn finished her second emotional scene, the executive producer gathered together the cast and crew and said the show had been canceled. Out of 116 prime-time shows, *The Monroes* was floundering in ninety-sixth place. Even ABC's other turkey, *Charlie Grace*, was ranked at eighty-four.

"I'm really quite disappointed," says Lynn. "That's probably an understatement. Because this was the first time I was really enjoying the work I was doing. Kind of feeling like an actress. It wasn't a dumb sitcom. I was getting some fun scenes to work on, and I felt like I was really facing the challenge.

"When I told my friend Liz that we were canceled, she said, 'Do you feel relieved that it's over?' And I said, 'Not at all.' When other jobs have ended, I have felt a certain sense of relief. But I did not feel one iota of relief this time.

"I think what this has taught me is that I know I can do it now. I feel competent. I know I can act. I really wasn't there this time last year. Career-wise and personally and artistically, I feel like I've grown. I can stick it out. I'll make it. I'm almost there."

GQ, February 1996

The Marine

Dragon Six is Oscar Mike, on the move to link up with Bandit.

Foot mobile along Axis Kim, he is leading a detachment of ten U.S. Marines across a stretch of desert scrub in the notional, oil-rich nation of Blueland. He walks at a steady rate of three klicks per hour, three kilometers, muscle memory after twenty-three years of similar forced humps through the toolies, his small powerful body canted slightly forward, his ankles and knees a little sore, his dusty black Danner combat boots, size 8, crunching over branches and rocks and coarse sand.

His pale-blue eyes are bloodshot from lack of sleep. His face is camouflaged with stripes and splotches of greasepaint—green, brown, and black to match his woodland-style utilities, fifty-six dollars a set, worn in the field without skivvies underneath, a personal wardrobe preference known as going commando. Atop his Kevlar helmet rides a pair of goggles sheathed in an old sock. Around his neck hangs a heavy pair of rubberized binoculars. From his left hip dangles an olive-drab pouch. With every step, the pouch swings and hits his thigh, adding another faint, percussive thunk to the quiet symphony of his gear, the total weight of which is not taught and seldom discussed. Inside the pouch is a gas mask for NBC attacks—nuclear, biological, or chemical weapons. Following an attack, when field gauges show the air to be safe once again for breathing, regulations call for the senior marine to choose one man to remove his mask and hood. After ten minutes, if the man shows no ill effects, the rest of the marines can begin removing theirs.

The temperature is 82 degrees. The air is thick and humid. Sounds of distant fire travel on the wan breeze: the boom and rumble of artillery, the pop and crackle of small arms. He is leading his men in a northwesterly direction, headed for an unimproved road designated Phase Line Rich. There, he will rendezvous with Bravo Company, radio call sign Bandit, one of five companies under his command, nearly nine hundred men, armed with weapons ranging from M16A2 rifles to Humvee-mounted TOW missile launchers. In his gloved right hand he carries a map case fashioned from cardboard and duct tape—the cardboard scavenged from a box of MREs, meals ready-to-eat, high-tech field rations that cook themselves when water is added. Clipped to the map case is a rainbow assortment of felt-tip pens, the colors oddly garish against the setting. His 9mm Beretta side arm is worn just beneath his right chest, high on his abdomen. The holster is secured onto his H harness, a pair of mesh suspenders anchored to the war belt around his waist—which itself holds magazine pouches with spare ammo and twin canteens. Altogether, this load-bearing apparatus is known as deuce gear, as in U.S. Government Form No. 782, the receipt a marine was once required to sign upon issuance. These days, the corps is computerized.

Near his left clavicle, also secured to his H harness—which is worn atop his flak vest—is another small pouch. Inside he keeps his Leatherman utility tool, his government-issue New Testament, a bag of Skittles left over from an MRE, and a tin of Copenhagen snuff, a medium-sized dip of which is evident at this moment in the bulge of his bottom lip, oddly pink in contrast to his thick camo makeup, and in the bottom lips of most of the men in his detachment, a forward-command element known as the Jump. They march slue-footed in a double-file formation through California sage and coyote bush and fennel, the smell pungent and spicy, like something roasting in a gourmet oven, each man silent and serious, deliberate in movement, eyes tracking left and right, as trained, each man taking a moment now and then, without breaking stride, to purse his lips and spit a stream of brownish liquid onto the ground, the varied styles of their expectorations somehow befitting, a metaphor for each personality, a metaphor, seemingly, for the Marine Corps itself: a tribe of like minds in different bodies, a range of shapes and sizes and colors, all wearing the same haircut and uniform, all hewing to the same standards and customs, yet still a collection of individuals, each with his own particular style of spitting tobacco juice, each with his own particular life to give for his country.

In the center of his flak vest—hot and heavy, designed to stop shrapnel but not bullets or knives—is a metal pin about the size of a dime, his insignia of rank, a silver oak leaf. Ever since he was young, growing up on the outskirts of Seattle, the second of four sons born to a department-store manager and a missionary's daughter, Robert O. Sinclair always wanted to be a marine. Now, at age forty, he has reached the rank of lieutenant colonel. He has what many consider to be the ultimate job for an infantry officer in the corps, the command of his own battalion, in this case BN One-Four—the 1st Battalion, 4th Marine Regiment. A proud unit with a distinguished history, the One-Four saw its first action in 1916, during the Banana Wars in the Dominican Republic. In the late twenties, the 4th Marines became known as the China Regiment when it was sent to Shanghai to protect American interests. During World War II, the One-Four was part of a larger force that surrendered to the Japanese at Corregidor. Its colors were burned; the survivors became POWs, forced to endure the infamous Bataan Death March. Re-formed two years later, the unit avenged itself in the first wave of landings on Guam. It has since fought in Vietnam, Desert Storm, and Somalia.

Come January, Sinclair and the One-Four—expanded to include tanks, artillery, amphibious and light armored vehicles, engineers, and 350 additional troops—will ship out on three Navy amphibious assault vessels as the 13th MEU (SOC), Marine Expeditionary Unit (Special Operations Capable), bound for the western Pacific and the Persian Gulf, ready for immediate action, fully equipped to wage combat for fifteen days without resupply or reinforcement, a unit precisely suited to a war against terrorism. "We specialize in conducting raids," says Sinclair. "We're tailor-made for special ops. We're trained to get in, hit a target, kill the enemy, and friggin' pull back to our ships again. We can go by helo. We can infiltrate by land. We can go ashore conventionally. We can put together anything. We're ready to do whatever it takes."

At the moment, in marine lingo, it is twenty-four sixteen thirty uniform May zero one, 4:30 in the afternoon on May 24, 2001, well before the prospect of going to war suddenly became real and imminent this fall. It is the fourth day of something called the Battalion FEX—a field exercise, on-the-job training for Sinclair and his marines. Truth be told, this is the first chance Sinclair has ever had to take his entire battalion out for a spin. Eight months ago, he had a lower rank and a different job in another unit somewhere else. Eight months ago, 90 percent of the men in his battalion were somewhere else; a good percentage of them had only recently graduated from high school. All told, between the time he took the flag of the One-Four—a dragon wrapped around a dagger on a blue diamond; the motto: Whatever It Takes—and the day this January or sooner when he and his men and all their equipment steam out of San Diego Harbor—wives and families and a brass band left behind on the dock—Sinclair will have had only eighteen months to build from scratch a crack fighting force, trained for every contingency from humanitarian aid to police action to strategic guerrilla raids to full-scale invasion. He has seven more months to get the bugs out. There is much to be done.

And so it is that Bob Sinclair is Oscar Mike across a stretch of desert scrub in the notional country of Blueland, which is actually in the state of California at Camp Pendleton, the largest amphibious training base in the world, spread across 125,000 rugged and breathtaking acres along the Pacific coastline. In ten mikes or so, ten minutes, over the next rise, Sinclair will link up with Bandit, the main effort in this five-phase operation. From there, Sinclair will lead his marines into the mountains, toward a BP, a battle position, high atop a steep, no-name hill. At zero four hundred hours, with the pop and arc of a white double-star-burst flare, the battle will commence: a nonsupported, nonilluminated night attack against the invading enemy forces of Orangeland, dug in at a critical crossroads, eyes on the Jesara oil fields.

Or that is the plan, anyway. Like the bubbas say: A plan is only good until the first shot is fired. Sometimes not even until then.

At Phase Line Rich, Sinclair and his men take cover in a stand of high weeds. The four young grunts who form his security element—a corporal and three privates, pimples showing through camo paint—employ along a tight circular perimeter. They assume prone positions on the deck, in the rocky sand, cheeks resting against the stocks of their weapons, three M16A2 rifles and an M249 SAW, Squad Automatic Weapon, a 5.56mm light machine gun with a removable bipod.

The ground is riddled with gopher mounds, busy with ants, bugs, and small lizards. Three types of rattlesnakes inhabit the area, along with scorpions, coyotes, roadrunners, and mountain lions. Overhead, against a backdrop of rugged mountains and gray sky, a red-tailed hawk backpedals its wings, suspended in flight, talons flexed, fixing a target far below.

THE MARINE   145

Sinclair sits with his legs crossed Indian-style. A fly buzzes around his head; bees alight upon the intricate yellow flowers of the black mustard weeds. Filled to capacity, his assault pack and his ass pack form a backrest, a comfortable pillow on which to lounge. Inside the packs, among other items, he keeps a roll of toilet paper; extra socks; reserve tins of Copenhagen; map templates; his NVGs, night-vision goggles; his CamelBak, a one-gallon water reservoir with a long drinking tube attached; and his MOPP suit and booties, Mission Oriented Protective Posture, marine lingo for the overclothes worn with the gas mask in case of NBC attack.

Five feet six inches tall, Sinclair has a quick, high-pitched giggle and bulging biceps, a Marine Corps tattoo on each shoulder. He is, in the words of one of his officers, "a good human being who's able to be a taskmaster." He has a pretty wife, his second, and a baby son and partial custody of his eleven-year-old stepson. They live among civilians on a cul-de-sac in a cookie-cutter subdivision about thirty minutes from the base, a black Isuzu Trooper and a black Volvo station wagon parked side by side in the driveway. He loves fishing, prays before eating his MREs in the field.

Though Sinclair was once lampooned in a skit as the Angry Little Man, he is known to his marines as a teacher and a father figure. Above all, he is known as a bubba, a fellow grunt. Unlike most marine officers, Sinclair joined the corps right out of high school. He spent the summer in boot camp in San Diego, then went off to Western Washington University. Following graduation (he majored in political science), upon completion of his basic officers' training, Sinclair was asked to list three career choices. He wrote *infantry* three times. He was chewed out by his CO for disobeying orders—if the Marine Corps says three choices, it damn well means three—but it was worth it to him to make the point.

At twenty-two, as a lieutenant, Sinclair became a rifle platoon commander. At twenty-nine, as a captain, he was a company commander in an infantry battalion similar to the One-Four and saw action in Somalia and Rwanda. In his early thirties, as a major, he served time as both a key member of a general's staff and as the director of the Infantry Officer Course in Quantico, Virginia. Today, as CO of the One-Four, he is known for his attention to detail, his almost wonkish expertise in battlefield tactics and techniques. Important also is his reputation for pushing down power to the NCOs, for delegating authority to the noncommissioned officers, the sergeants and the corporals, an essential managerial concept in this bottom-heavy organization. The smallest of all the services—about 170,000 compared with the Army's 480,000 (800,000 including reserves)—the Marines also have the lowest officer-to-enlisted ratio, one-to-nine, compared with the Army's one-to-five. More than half of the corps is composed of the three lowest pay grades—lance corporals, Pfc.'s, and privates. Every year, more than 30 percent of the enlisted ranks muster out and return to civilian life. Discounting career officers and NCOs, that means a complete recycling of bodies about every three years.

Now, as Sinclair sits in the weeds near Phase Line Rich, dark clouds gather ominously over the mountains. "Guess we're in for a nice little hike," he says, flashing his trademark smile, toothy and overlarge.

"Yes, sir!" sings out Sergeant Major, sitting to his right. John Hamby, forty, is the ranking noncommissioned officer in the One-Four, the most senior of all the enlisted, though still junior to the greenest second lieutenant. A good ol' boy from Georgia with a booming gravel voice, he is always at Sinclair's side, offering advice and support, implementing orders, watchdogging the interests of his men. Asked about his favorite marine memories, he thinks a moment, names three: the day, at age twenty-nine, that he received his high school diploma, the 4.0 valedictorian of his class; the day his father pinned his sergeant major chevrons to his collar; the day, when he was stationed in Vienna as an embassy guard, that his son was born by emergency C-section.

"Those peaks behind Basilone Road are gonna be a ball buster," Sinclair says. "Holy Moses!"

"Been there many times," Sergeant Major says. He spits a stream of brownish liquid into the weeds. "Character builder, sir."

"It won't be as steep as yesterday, but it's a lot friggin' higher," Sinclair says, his flat northwestern accent flavored with a bit of southern drawl, affected to a greater or lesser extent by most marine officers, no matter what their regional origins—homage, perhaps, to the antebellum notion of the southern gentleman, upon whom the patriotic ideal of a young American military leader was modeled. He spits a stream of juice, then kicks some dirt over the wet spot on the ground, covering it up.

"You would think there'd be a limit as to how much character you can build, sir. But I ain't reached it yet."

"Oo-rah, Sergeant Major."

"Ain't that right, Colón?" Sergeant Major cuffs the shoulder of the nervous young radio operator sitting behind Sinclair, nearly knocking him over. Pfc. Mike Colón is twenty years old, a slight youth just this side of pretty: five feet four with long curly lashes. The twelve-pound radio he's carrying—a one nineteen foxtrot SINCGARS, a single-channel ground-and-airborne radio system—fits with some difficulty into his assault pack. The ten-foot whip-style antenna makes balance difficult. Thirty minutes into the hump, he has already slapped Sinclair on the helmet several times with the thick rod of rubber-coated steel.

Born in Puerto Rico, raised in the ghetto of Holyoke, Massachusetts, Colón speaks English with the singsong rhythms of his home island. Both of his earlobes are pierced, a remnant of his days with the Latin Kings. Six months ago, Colón was breaking rocks with a ten-pound sledge in the CCU, the Correctional Custody Unit at Camp Pendleton, busted down to private for drinking in the barracks. It was his third offense; the Old Man could have run him out of the corps. But Sinclair prides himself on being able to judge his marines, to see into their souls. As he likes to say: "You can't friggin' command from behind a damn desk." In battle, you have to know what to expect from your men. That's the whole reason they practice everything so many times. That's the whole reason he's out here on the Jump rather than back in the rear, commanding from a camp chair in the relative comfort of the COC, the Combat Operations Center, a big black tent with a generator, lights, computers, and a banquet-sized coffee urn.

Sinclair saw something in Colón, and Colón responded: He was down but he never dropped his pack, as the bubbas say. Now he has found himself assigned as the Old Man's radio operator. He darts a look at Sergeant Major. Privilege in the Marine Corps is often a two-edged sword. Had he not been so honored by this assignment, he'd be back at the COC himself, pulling radio watch. He aims a stream of brownish juice toward the ground. A little bit dribbles down his chin, onto his flak vest. "A definite character builder, Sergeant Major."

Sinclair twists around, flashes Colón his smile. "There ya go, stud," he sings encouragingly.

"Here comes Bandit right now," announces the OpsO, the operations officer, indicating the lead element of Bravo Company, coming around a bend double file.

Major Minter Bailey Ralston IV—Uncle Minty to his friends—is Dragon Three to Sinclair's Dragon Six. He plans and coordinates, all battalion movements in the field. Thirty-two years old, a strapping six feet two, he's a graduate of the Virginia Military Institute. Since 1856, every Minter Bailey Ralston before him had been a pharmacist. Growing up in the tiny town of Westin, West Virginia, the only boy of four children, he set his sights early on the Marines. "John Wayne and comic books took me to the dark side at a very early age," he says.

Blond and blue-eyed, with circles under his eyes, Ralston was up all last night on the laptop computer in the COC, pecking out Battalion Frag Order zero one tach four, the detailed, six-page battle plan for tonight's movement. Grimacing, he pops two large pills without water. Three weeks ago, he underwent surgery on his right calf muscle. He is not yet cleared for exercise of any kind.

Sitting next to Major Ralston is the FSC, the fire-support coordinator, Major Randy Page. Six feet four with green eyes, thirty-four years old, Page hails from Wagon Wheel, New Mexico, population fifty. His job is coordinating artillery and other weapons fire to support the grunts on the ground. Married with no kids, a foreign-film buff, a self-professed computer geek, Page loves being in the field. His favorite marine moment is a snapshot: "You're in the rain, you're on a knee, and everyone's just miserable. And you just kinda look around and it feels like—you feel like crap because you're cold or hot or wet or whatever—but it just feels good."

Now Page hoists himself off the deck. He scans the horizon, taking a deep draft of the spicy air. "Looks like that fog is comin' in a little early, sir."

"Roger that, Major Page," Sinclair says, grunting a bit as he rises, as men of a certain age begin to do.

"On your feet, marines," growls Sergeant Major. He kicks playfully at the boot of Lance Corporal Joseph Gray, the other radio operator on the Jump. Gray has been dragging lately. He's newly married to a very young Cuban girl. There are troubles at home, a baby on the way. Sergeant Major reaches down and offers Gray a helping hand. "Move it, Devil Dog," he barks.

After a long, steep climb—the last bit a 70-degree slope through sharp thistles—Dragon Jump and Bandit are in place on the summit of No Name

Hill, looking down upon Battalion Objectives Four and Five. Huddled together in the pitch-dark, Sinclair and his men are totally assed out. They sit in rocky sand, on a firebreak cut across the topographical crest of the hill. A cloud bank has settled over them. Visibility is nil; their NVGs, which use ambient light, are inoperable. It is cold and wet and quiet, the silence broken only by the beep and crackle of the SINCGARS radios.

The time is zero one thirty hours. According to intelligence, there is a company-minus, about 150 men, of Orangeland forces dug in around the two key crossroads in the valley below, just to the northeast of No Name Hill, fifteen hundred meters away as the crow flies. Scout/sniper reports have the enemy armed with AK-47 rifles, light and medium machine guns, and 82mm mortars. Based upon documents taken from the body of a notionally dead officer (members of the One-Four's H&S company, headquarters and service, are playing the role of the enemy), there is reason to believe that the Orangeland forces, members of the dictator's elite Revolutionary Guard, will attempt to hold their positions at all costs.

Though the original frag order tasked Bravo Company as the main effort of the attack, it has become clear that the plan is no longer viable. Not apparent on the contour map was the fact that the northeast face of No Name Hill is a sheer cliff. There is no way Sinclair is going to order a company of green marines down the side without rappelling systems. Likewise, the firebreak is useless as an avenue of approach; cut by giant bulldozers, one hundred feet wide, that piece of terrain is completely exposed—the face sloping down gradually onto the objective like a ski run.

Because they're here to learn how to think on the fly, Sinclair has ordered Ralston to recast the attack, a laborious process that began with Ralston—owing to the blackout conditions in effect—lying for a time beneath his rain poncho, his red-lensed flashlight in one hand, a pen in the other, writing up formal orders for the new attack, composing sentences such as: O/O ATK TO DESTROY EN VIC BN OBJ 4. Once completed, the orders were disseminated via radio down the chain of command. Upon receiving his orders, each marine made a few notes for himself in his olive-drab journal, part of his required gear.

The new play goes like this: Charlie Company, down in the valley, formerly the supporting effort, becomes the main effort in the attack. It will move across the desert floor, around the bottom of No Name Hill, then turn left in a bent-L formation. Upon seeing the signal flare—a green double star burst—it will attack the enemy's flank. Bravo Company will remain on No Name Hill in a support-by-fire position. In addition, Sinclair has called up the CAAT platoon, the Combined Anti-Armor Team, a motorized unit comprising Humvee-mounted .50-caliber machine guns and wire-guided TOW missile launchers.

While Charlie Company moves into its new position—difficult in the dark without NVGs, foot mobile at the excruciatingly slow rate of five hundred meters an hour through the difficult terrain—Sinclair and his men hunker down on the firebreak atop No Name Hill, a dark circle of faceless shadows enveloped in a fine, cold mist.

Lounging against his assault pack, Sinclair's camies beneath his flak vest are sopping with sweat. He's cold and tired, and his knees ache. He's "dawg-gone friggin' miserable"; he's happy as he can be. This is what he signed up for. He's glad he chose to go out on the Jump tonight, down and dirty with the men, the more miserable the better, commanding with his eyes instead of a radio handset. There's a purity to being in the field. It helps you keep your edge. It helps you keep your sense of perspective. You learn not to take your lifestyle and your freedoms for granted. You learn not to care so much about what year the wine was bottled, what brand of clothing you wear, all that horseshit that people think is oh-so-civilized. Being out here, you learn to appreciate the simple things, like just how great it is to sit on a toilet to take a dump.

Over the years, Sinclair has endured conditions much worse than these. He's been in the desert in Kuwait, 130 degrees. He's looked into the eyes of starving infants in Somalia. He's rescued civilians from the American embassy in Rwanda. And he's seen men die; he's written impotent letters home to inconsolable mothers after a firefight with Somali thugs in pickup trucks. It's bad out here tonight on No Name Hill, but it's not so bad. In real-world time, he's a thirty-minute drive from home. Come tomorrow evening, he'll be in his living room with Jessie for their fifth wedding anniversary—the first such celebration he's ever been able to attend.

"I read the other day that gas prices have gone up 149 percent in the last year," Sinclair says, trying to pass the time.

"The cost of living here has gotten to be more expensive than Hawaii," says Page, seated to Sinclair's left. His words come out a little slurry. He chides himself for not sleeping last night. He shakes his head, trying to rid the cobwebs.

"Guess there's no chance we're gettin' a raise anytime soon," Ralston says. Though no one can see it, he has his boot off, an instant ice pack on his badly swollen calf. He missed the last big exercise because of his surgery—if you can't do your job, the Marines will replace you. Someday Ralston would like to be in Sinclair's boots; this is too good a billet to let go because of a little pain. Or that's what he thought. Now the calf is throbbing. *Could I be happy as a civilian?* he asks himself, only half kidding.

"The president has already submitted his supplemental budget this year, so we're looking at zero three at the earliest for any kind of COLA," Sinclair says, meaning cost-of-living adjustment, his wonkish side still apparent through his own physical exhaustion. Oddly missing from his encyclopedia of knowledge is the exact amount of his salary. For that information, you must see Jessie. He draws $72,000 a year, plus an additional $1,700 a month for food and housing.

"That's just peachy," Sergeant Major says. He pulls down about $45,000 a year, plus $1,500 a month for food and housing. "Maybe I'll trade in my car and get a beat-up old Volkswagen. Put the wife on the street corner."

"We won't quote you on that, Sergeant Major," Sinclair says.

"Definitely not," says Page.

"Even *I* don't go *that* far," Sergeant Major says. His voice softens, grows sentimental, like a guy talking to the bartender late at night. "There ain't none like her. She's mine. We have our times, but it wouldn't be no fun if there wasn't a little challenge."

"Damn," says Ralston. "The wind's kickin' up."

"I'm kinda hoping that stink is you and not me," Sergeant Major drawls. "You know it's time to take a shower when you can smell your own ass."

"Jeez-*Louise*, Sergeant Major!" Sinclair says. "Thanks for sharin'."

At zero three fifty atop No Name Hill, the rain has subsided; the clouds remain.

Sinclair and his men are on their feet now, helmeted shadows milling between two Humvees. Parked on the firebreak, on the crest of the hill, each of the four-wheel-drive vehicles is fitted with a TOW missile launcher and an infrared sight. In a few minutes, when the liquid nitrogen in the mechanism reaches a temperature of -318 degrees, Sinclair will be able to look through a rubber-capped eyepiece and see the heat signatures of his otherwise-invisible foes, tiny red human forms in the valley far below. Mounted to turrets atop the roofs of the vehicles, the TOW sights emit a loudish ticking noise, a strangely familiar sound, like the timer on a heat lamp in a hotel bathroom.

"Spare a dip, Sergeant Major?"

"Sorry, Major Page, I'm plum out."

"What about you, OpsO?"

"I was just gonna ask you."

"Well, isn't this a fine damn thing," Sergeant Major says. He pauses a beat, thinking. A few days ago, back at Camp Horno—the One-Four's compound at Pendleton—Sergeant Major needed a sleeping bag for a reporter to take on the FEX. Informed by supply that the battalion was fresh out of sleeping bags, Sergeant Major ordered the lance corporal on the other end of the line to *shit* a sleeping bag *posthaste*. The bag was delivered in ten minutes.

Now, five days into the FEX, twelve hours into this movement, what Sergeant Major needs—what they all need—is a good whack of nicotine. He turns to Sinclair. "What about you, sir?"

Sinclair pulls off his right glove with his teeth, reaches into the pouch secured over the left side of his chest. He takes out his tin of Copenhagen, opens it. "A few dregs," he says, disappointed. Then he brightens. "Criminy! Check my assault pack!"

Sinclair turns his back and Sergeant Major unzips him, rummages carefully through his gear. Though entirely offhand, it is an intimate act. He comes out with a fresh tin. "You ain't been holdin' out on us now, sir, have you?"

"Pass it around, by all means!"

"An officer and a gentleman," Sergeant Major declares.

"Anything for my marines," Sinclair says. He looks around the loose circle of his men, the faceless shadowy figures so distinctly recognizable, even in the murky gloom. In boot camp there are no walls between the shitters in the latrine—that's how close you get to the other guys. And when you have to lead them, when your word is literally their command, well . . . it's hard to find a way to express it. Eight months into his tenure as the CO of the One-Four, Sinclair finds himself stepping back every now and then and thinking, *Dawggone, I still can't believe I have this authority!* You go through the years, gaining experience, working hard, moving up. And then one day *you're* the Old Man. But you still feel like you; you're the same as always—a little bit afraid of fucking up. It makes you want to be careful. Not cautious, just more careful to consider things from every imaginable side. Bottom line is a most awesome fact: He has lives in his hands.

When he looks at one of *his* marines, Sinclair doesn't care what age or color he is, what MOS or billet he occupies. He doesn't care if he's a wrench turner down in the motor pool or one of his company commanders. If he didn't need that man in the One-Four, the Marine Corps wouldn't have assigned him. Every truck driver hauling water and chow to the grunts in the field; the comm guys running wire and maintaining the nets; the eighteen-year-old rifleman toting a 60mm mortar launcher over his shoulders, sucking on his water tube like a pacifier as he humps up a hill— they're all important to him as a commander. They all need to know that Sinclair's thinking, *Hey, stud, I know that job may not seem fun or exciting, but I need your skills to make this whole thing work.*

"So what do we do now?" asks Sergeant Major. He takes a pinch and passes it on. He's feeling better already.

"We could fight this little battle," says Ralston.

"I make it zero three fifty nine," says Page, taking the tin from Ralston.

"I know," Sinclair says. He rubs his hands together greedily. "Who can we meritoriously promote?"

"Excellent idea, sir!" Sergeant Major says.

"How about Rivers?" suggests Page.

"He's ready?" asks Sinclair. "Definitely, sir."

"What do you think, Colón?"

"Definitely, sir," says the radio operator, taking a dip, passing the tin.

"All right, good to go," Sinclair says, inserting his own pinch of dip between lip and gum. He steps up onto the fat tire of the Humvee, swings himself into the turret. "We'll just take care of business here," he calls down from his perch, "and then—"

Now there comes the distinct explosive pop of a flare, and everyone turns to see. A green double star burst, lovely and bright and sparkling, it floats down toward earth on its invisible parachute, as languid as an autumn leaf falling from a tree, illuminating the target below in surreal shades of magnesium green.

Down in the valley, Charlie Company opens fire. There is the crackle of small arms shooting blank rounds, clusters of bright muzzle flashes against the dark, the loud cacophony of voices that accompanies a firefight—men on both sides shouting orders and epithets as the battle is waged at close quarters.

Atop No Name Hill, fore and aft of the vehicles, platoons from Bravo Company are set along different elevations of the firebreak. As this is only an exercise, the budget for the FEX is limited. The men of Bravo Company have been told not to expend their blank rounds. They have humped ten difficult miles in the last twelve hours to get into position for this attack, through fields of cactus and thistles, up steep slopes and through ravines, weighted with myriad weapon systems and gear. They have shivered in their own sweat in the fine, cold rain, faces in the sand with the insects and the weeds, fighting boredom, dehydration, fatigue. They have done everything the Old Man has asked, and they have done it without question or excuse or complaint. On order, they open fire.

"Bang bang bang bang BANG!" they shout into the darkness, two hundred strong, every shape and color, all wearing the same haircuts and uniforms, their voices echoing across the valley, a shitstorm of simulated plunging fire raining down death upon Orangeland's elite Revolutionary Guard: "Bang bang bang bang BANG!"

By zero seven thirty, the enemy has been vanquished.

Dragon Jump and Bandit have humped down the firebreak, consolidated with Charlie Company. Together, they occupy Battalion Objectives Four and Five.

It is cool and overcast. The two key crossroads are little more than dirt trails etched through the valley. Sinclair and his men mill about. No Name Hill looms above them, impossibly high from this vantage point, a scrubby, humpbacked ridge stippled with boulders, the firebreak running like a raw scar over the crest. Colón and Gray and the other enlisted are circled up, passing a rumpled menthol cigarette that Colón has found in his pack. Sinclair and Sergeant Major lean against a Humvee, shooting the shit with the battalion XO, the executive officer, Major Rich Weede. Thirty-seven years old, a graduate of VMI, Weede is Dragon Five to Sinclair's Dragon Six, responsible for many of the nuts-and-bolts issues of command. Since 1935, there has continuously been a Weede on active duty in the Marine Corps. His grandfather retired as a lieutenant general. His father retired as a colonel. His brother is a captain.

Sinclair has logged only about six hours of sleep over the last five days. His eyelids are sprung like window shades. His smile seems plastered onto his face. His knees feel disjointed, as if he's walking on eggshells. He feels thready and insubstantial, oddly gelatinous, a little queasy, as if he's treading water in a vitreous sea of adrenaline and dopamine, nicotine, and excess stomach acid. Now the drifting conversation has turned toward a mutual friend of Weede and Sinclair's, a retired officer.

"So he's got a beer distributorship?" Sinclair asks, his voice tight and forced.

"Every day he's gettin' invitations to fuckin' golf tournaments," Weede says, breaking out a couple of cheroot cigars.

"That's like the time I met this guy through my father-in-law," says Sergeant Major, accepting a cheroot, taking a bite. "He flies me down to Texas to play golf at his country club, and we played a round, and then he takes me over to his warehouse. He tells me how he's having problems with his employees, how he can't get them motivated. And then he says, 'Your father-in-law seems to think you're pretty good at that shit. You want a job? I'll make it well worth your while.'"

"I'da friggin' asked how well," Sinclair says, taking a bite of his cheroot, working it down to his gum.

"That's like Gunner Montoya," Weede says, blowing a smoke ring. "He said he told the guy, 'I'm a marine gunner, I don't know a friggin' thing about this business.' And the guy tells him, 'You're a marine, you can manage this shit, trust me.'"

"The salary kicks up to a hundred grand after a year," Sergeant Major says. "He put in his papers this month."

"I can't even fathom that kinda money," Sinclair says. He looks off toward No Name Hill, shaking his head.

OpsO Ralston limps over, and Weede offers him a cheroot. "Time to head back to the barn, sir," Ralston says to Sinclair. It's a three-hour hump back to Camp Horno.

"We goin' up Sheepshit Hill, sir?" asks Sergeant Major.

"Only the best for my Devil Dogs!" Sinclair sings.

"They'll be back by this afternoon and too tired to bitch," drawls Sergeant Major. "Then they'll get up tomorrow all sore and thinking, *Fuuu-uuuuck!* But come Sunday, their tune'll change. It'll be: *That wasn't shit!*"

"Twenty-four hours from now they'll be bragging about how tough it was," Sinclair says. He spits a stream, kicks some dirt over the wet spot.

"You know," Sergeant Major says. "I didn't sign up for infantry. I was gonna be a mechanic."

"Well, I did. All I ever wanted to be was a grunt."

"Then I guess all your dreams have come true, sir."

"Oo-rah, Sergeant Major."

On a sunny Sunday afternoon a few weeks later, Sinclair is sitting beneath a striped umbrella on the patio behind his house. He is barefoot, dressed in a tank top and surfer shorts. His face and neck are deeply tanned; his shoulders and legs are milky white. Even on his day off, he sports a fresh shave. In his mind, he's never off duty; he's a marine every hour of every day. He doesn't even go to Home Depot without shaving first. He has his whitewall-style haircut trimmed weekly, seven dollars a pop.

Sinclair was up early today, ripping out the roots of a tree in the front yard that had begun to encroach upon the sidewalk. For a tool he used an old bolo knife he bought in the Philippines when he was a second lieutenant. A short machete made from dense steel, the thing hasn't been sharpened in twenty years and it's still the best dawggone piece of cuttin' gear he's got. Now that the tree roots have been vanquished, Sinclair needs to repipe the irrigation in that area. Not to mention all the other chores. His tidy two-story house, decorated in earth tones, is filled with projects not yet completed: a partially painted wall, a set of dining-room chairs only half reupholstered. An epic list maker, he has yellow Post-its everywhere at home and at work. He's got a lot to do before January.

At home, Jessie is the idea guy; the Old Man is the grunt. When he comes through the front door, he always says, "Just tell me what to do. I don't want to make *any* decisions." Jessie and Bob met on a blind date eight years ago. He was a captain then, a company commander; her sister was dating his radio operator. They went to a Japanese restaurant. When he returned home that night, Bob looked in the mirror and told himself he had found the woman he was going to marry. Two days after their date, Jessie came down with the flu. Bob drove an hour to bring her some medicine. "I could tell right then he was a keeper," she says.

Jessie sees Bob as being tough in his professional life, yet very tender in his personal life. He is honest and sincere, a mature man with a lot of integrity, very different from other men, a grownup in every way. When she was laid up in the hospital before their son, Seth, was born, he took off work and camped out in the room with her for an entire week. Five years into their marriage, he still refers to her as "my bride."

Soon after they began dating, Bob went off on a six-month deployment. Jessie sent him care packages filled with Gummi Bears and pistachio nuts. They wrote letters every day. She didn't know where he was, exactly. Somewhere out on a ship. Bob is an awesome letter writer. He would write about what he did that day and how he was feeling about stuff. And then there were the romantic parts. Those were her favorite.

One night when he was on the float, Jessie's phone rang. It was Bob. "I just wanted to tell you I love you," he said casually, and Jessie thought, *Uh-oh, I don't like the sound of this.* Before he hung up, he mentioned that she should watch CNN the next day. Sure enough, there were the Marines, evacuating civilians from the embassy in Rwanda.

Following his deployment, Bob was transferred to Quantico, Virginia, for three years. The couple maintained a long-distance relationship, getting married along the way, holding their reception at the Japanese restaurant where they'd had their first date. Though she doesn't want to say it in so many words, Jessie is not looking forward to this deployment. Bob's been home now for a long stretch. She's used to having him around. He's funny, he's good company, he has sexy arms and a nice smile. He doesn't mind doing the vacuuming. He thinks everything she cooks is delicious. And though he's not much into television—not even sports—he's happy to sit with her and watch her shows: *Friends, Ed, The West Wing, ER, Malcolm in the Middle.* When he goes away, it's always hardest in the beginning. Then she bucks up and gets in the groove; she just kind of goes about her business. In time, she even starts to enjoy being on her own—pretty much, anyway. It's funny, but having Bob gone so much has taught her just how secure a person she really is. In that way, the Marine Corps has been good for her as well.

This time the float will be a little different for the Sinclairs. They'll have e-mail. And because he's the battalion commander and she's the Key Volunteer Adviser—informally in charge of overseeing all the dependents—he'll be calling her by telephone weekly.

The biggest difference, of course, is Seth, eighteen months old, a towhead like his mom. The first time Bob left for two weeks in the field, he came home and Seth wouldn't go to him. You could see it really crushed Bob. And now he'll be gone six months. He's seen kids hide from their dads when they return from a float; he's seen kids cower in fear. And Luke, her son by her first marriage, has grown close to Bob as well. Luke likes to tell the story of how Bob took him fishing for the first time. Luke caught a catfish that was *this* long. Actually, Bob helped. "But he told everyone I caught it myself," Luke says proudly.

With everyone out of the house for a while, Sinclair is taking some time to reflect, a little reluctantly, on his career. He rocks back and forth gently in his chair. "This is probably going to sound like propaganda," he says, taking the opportunity, in his family's absence, to indulge himself in a dip, "but my primary motivation for being a marine is that I love this country. I feel that being born in this country is a privilege. Right, wrong, or indifferent, this is still the greatest country in the world. All you have to do is travel to figure that one out. I thank the good Lord that we have a lot of great men and women in this country who feel the same way as I feel, who are willing to make that ultimate sacrifice for what they believe in. None of us wants to die. But we know if we have to, it's for the greatest reasons.

"I have to admit that becoming a dad, especially this late in life, has completely changed me. When you're younger, it was like, Okay, if you die, you can leave your parents behind, or your brothers. That would be sad, but you know, you can kind of accept that. Once you get married, you're kinda like, Hmmm. But you can justify that, too. The wife's an adult, she's intelligent, she's beautiful, she can get on with life. But then all of a sudden you've got that child. I never understood it until Seth was born and lying there in the hospital weighing two pounds, not knowing whether he was going to live or die. And I just looked at him and said, 'This is a life that we've created and that I'm responsible for.' His entire hand could grab around the knuckle of my little finger when he squeezed."

He rocks in his chair; he is a man who is seldom at rest, who wakes up at full speed and doesn't stop until he shuts his eyes, whereupon he falls instantly into a deep, untroubled sleep, as he did on the couch after the FEX, on the night of his anniversary. At least he made it through dinner.

Birds sing in the trees. A lawn mower drones, echoing through the cul-de-sac. The grass in his backyard is lush and green; the fence line is planted with riotous bougainvillea, rich shades of red and purple and pink. An old dog naps at his feet. A small fountain gurgles at the back corner of the lot. "I know this float is going to be tough," Sinclair says. "But it's like anything else. We'll get on that ship, we'll do what we have to do, and then we'll come back, and life will continue to move on. That'll be six months you can never make up, but what we do as marines is that important. Nobody wrenches your arm to sign that contract. These men do this on their own. They all know the risks. That's why leading them is just an honor beyond belief.

"I am loyal to the corps, but my family is more important to me. If you take it in order, I'd say it's God, country, family, and then way down at number four on the list is the Marine Corps. That's not insulting the corps; it's just that the bottom line is that someday the corps is gonna kick every one of us out. Even the commandant of the Marine Corps is gonna retire, and they're gonna say, 'Thank you very much for all your years of service, General, but it's time to move on.' They're gonna do the same to me. They always say we're here to train our own replacements. There will always be plenty of great people to take my place. But my family will always be there for me. I mean, I'll probably be up for colonel soon. But with our family situation—the fact that, you know, Jessie can't leave the state to share custody of Luke . . ." His voice trails off. "I'd hate to leave the corps, but I can't leave my family and become a geographical bachelor again."

He spits a stream of brownish juice onto the lawn. "The bottom line comes down to this: It's hard to put into words. It's more like a feeling. You feel it, and you know it's right. It's like trying to explain morals or religion or love. The Marine Corps exists to fight and win America's battles, to help keep our country free. It sounds corny, I suppose. But like they say, somebody's got to do it. I guess one of those somebodies is me."

September 2001: Sinclair is at his desk at Camp Horno. There is a heightened security aboard the base, but training continues as normal. Sinclair's deuce gear and his flak vest and his helmet lie in a heap in the corner of the small room. His M9 side arm, holstered, is atop his desk.

On September 11, upon waking to the horrific news from the East Coast, Sinclair called his XO, Major Weede, and told him he was going to stay put for a while and watch the events unfold on television. He felt a need to be home with his family. He also knew he didn't have to hurry to the base; it takes a long time to plan military action, Sinclair points out. The Japanese bombed Pearl Harbor on December 7, 1941. The first ground offensive by U S. forces against the Japanese didn't occur until August 7, 1942, when the 1st Marine Division—the division that includes Sinclair's One-Four—invaded Guadalcanal.

Come January, however, or whenever Sinclair and his 13th MEU (SOC) steam out into the WestPac, things will probably be much different. The kind of campaign they're talking about is the kind the One-Four has been trained to undertake. With the threat of war, perhaps a sustained one, Bob and Jessie Sinclair must put their worries about career and future and geographical bachelorhood aside. There is no doubt about the order of his priorities at a time like this.

"It's one of those things where you train your whole life for something you hope you never actually have to execute. But I think there's something primal about each one of us marines. If we're at war, you want to be in the operating forces. You don't want to be sitting on the sidelines. This is what we do. This is what we're trained for.

"The initial thing I felt, seeing that plane fly into the tower, seeing the pictures of the Pentagon, was absolute anger. You realize that your country has been attacked. That is a deep, deep wound, a sharp slap to the face. You wanna strike back. But at the same time you have to keep your head. You know that you've got this whole system in place. There are politicians and diplomats. In a way, you're angry deep down inside your gut, but you're also in realization that, okay, there are people who are much smarter than me, and they are in charge, and I completely trust their leadership. As a member of the military, I'm here to support and implement whatever decision they make.

"Like the president said, 'Get ready.' Well, we are ready. This battalion is ready right now. We'll do what needs to be done."

Esquire, December 2001

The World According to Amerikkka's Most-Wanted Rapper

Three in the morning, soft light in a sound booth, downtown, underground. Ice Cube in the house, on the mike. Headphones, knit cap, arched brow and a scowl, a spiral notebook on the music stand, CUBE'S MONEY scrawled across the cover, dope rhymes ink-penned inside. He clears his throat, adjusts the spit screen. Head up to rip shit, you know what I mean? Yo. To flow and throw and show. Drop an old school beat, homeboy. Kick it, Cube:

> *I heard pay-bucks a muthafuckin' nigga, that's wild*
> *I'm sick of gettin' treated like a goddamn stepchild*
> *Fuck a punk 'cause I ain't him*
> *You got to deal with the nine double m*
> *The day is come that you all hate*
> *Just think if nights decide to retaliate*
> *They try to keep me from runnin' up*
> *I never tell you to get down, it's all about coming up*
> *So what they do—go an' ban the AK*
> *My shit wasn't registered any fuckin' way*
> *So you better duck away, run and hide out*
> *When I'm rollin' real slow and the lights out*
> *'Cause I'm about to fuck up the program*
> *Shooting out the window of a drop-top brougham*
> *While I'm shootin' let's see who drop*
> *The police, the media, the suckers that went pop*

And muthafuckas that say they too black
Put 'em overseas, they be begging to come back
They say we promote gangs and drugs
You wanna sweep a nigga like me up under the rug
Kickin' shit called street knowledge
Why more niggas in the pen than in college?
And 'cause of that line I might be your cellmate
that's why I'm the nigga ya love to hate.

O'Shea "Ice Cube" Jackson is the Nigga Ya Love to Hate, the 1990s Nigga, check him out. Twenty-one years old, dark and chunky, wearing Nikes, Levi's, Swatch and Gap, Cube is a product and a prototype, a dissident and an entrepreneur, a beat reporter, a writer of Rhythmic American Poetry, also known as rap. His apocalyptic baritone riffs are the hocked-up anthems of his age—primitive, phlegmatic spewings from the underclass fester, an infection of attitude, restlessness, contempt. His field is street knowledge, and his images are his world, the naked, obscene facts. Cube comin' from the block, kickin' reality: gang bangers and dope men, homeboys and hoes, AKs and 9mms, Jeeps and Alpines, a runny-nosed kid with a load in his pants.

Cube is an MC of the hard-core school of rap. Like Ice-T, Luther Campbell, the members of Public Enemy and Niggas With Attitude, Cube is a young black man riding the wave of rap-mania, using America's newest musical obsession as a forum and a cash box, working his perverse magic on the nation. Even as parents and police groups and national publications condemn Cube and his ilk, *Billboard* and the Grammys have added rap categories, and the black album and singles charts are filled with rap. Rap language is spoken on street corners from Watts to Bensonhurst; rap clothes are sold in every mall. There's a rap movie, a rap comedy show, a rap video show, rap commercials. Even the Pillsbury Doughboy has a rap. He says his little rhyme, then does a little flip. And nobody pokes him in the stomach with a finger.

Cube first surfaced as a member of Niggas With Attitude, one of the boyz from the lowdown dirty 'hood of South-Central, in Los Angeles. He wrote most of the songs on N.W.A.'s first album, *Straight Outta Compton*, featuring the hit "Fuck tha Police." After that, he wrote most of a solo album for N.W.A.'s founder, Eazy-E. Cube's work, so far, has been panned by critics, banned by MTV, ignored by radio, investigated by the FBI, cited by police in Cincinnati.

Yet over the last two years, his songs have sold nearly 4 million units. His first solo album, *AmeriKKKa's Most Wanted*, went gold in ten days, platinum in three months.

"Fuck all y'all," says Cube.

Late in the afternoon, the homeboys begin to stir. April in New York, a one-bedroom loft in a trendy co-op on Greenwich Street. Black leather, blue neon, technotronic toys. And on the walls, life-size, anatomically perfect bas-relief bronzes of naked white girls. Cube is subletting. He's in town for five weeks to work with Chuck D and Public Enemy on *AmeriKKKa's Most Wanted*. Staying in the apartment with him are several of his posse, members of the Lench Mob, spelled like it sounds.

Rap being a tribal thing, a rapper needs his crew, so Cube has paid airfare to rotate his homies in and out of town. They fly in on the red-eye, chill in the Large Apple for a few days, do guest spots, fill-ins, and choruses on his songs. A rapper's posse is kind of like his gang, only instead of being down for territory or drugs, Cube's gang is down for Cube. Since his break with NWA, Cube has learned that he needs to surround himself with niggas that ain't gonna be frontin' on him, that got his back, that ain't no punks. In turn, what he's gonna do is see that they get crazy paid, 'cause yo, he's into robbin' these record companies, cause they robbin' him.

Sir Jinx, nineteen, is Cube's producer, DJ, and right-hand homes. Before he got into rap, Jinx was into graffiti and break-dancing, an expert in windmills and headspins. Ironically, Jinx learned producing behind his cousin, the famous Dr. Dre of NWA, who would have been producing this album if Cube's first manager hadn't treated him like a young nigga from the hood who didn't know how to get himself a lawyer. Jinx wears four gold rings and a sort of modified Gumby haircut that works down to a steel wool pony tail, and a pair of high-priced hiking boots with the tag left dangling for effect. He quit high school in twelfth grade, has a passing knowledge of the King's English. He was always the guy in the back of the class asking: "How this shit gonna help what I do?" When Jinx gets rich off rap, he says, he'll fill his life's ambition to open a hair salon.

T-Bone is Cube's partner; he go wherever Cube go. Small but powerful, he wears a close-cropped, scissored fade. He serves as Cube's Greek chorus: "Word 'em up!" "I heard dat!" "Um-humm!" "Tell it Cube!" The two grew up in the same South-Central neighborhood, met on the bus that took them each morning from their ghetto to a mostly-white junior high school in the San Fernando Valley. Like Cube, T-Bone is twenty-one. He's been working as a printer since the day after graduation from high school. Currently he makes $12 an hour; he's in line for a promotion. But when Cube tour bust a move, he says, he outtie.

J. Dee is also from the 'hood. He's a little older than Cube at twenty-three, a big guy with a scissored close crop. Four years ago, his father was killed in a neighborhood cross-fire, but even before that, since he was four-teen, J. Dee has pretty much fended for himself, bouncing between neighbors, relatives and his grandma. Back in the day, J. Dee, which is short for Junkie D, was a gangbanger and a dope man: the tattoo on his hand labels him N-HOOD, meaning the Neighborhood Crips, which control the territory between 108th, Western, Imperial and Van Ness. If Cube had joined a gang, he'd have been N-Hood too. J. Dee has been trained by GM in automotive robotics and has worked as a maintenance man and as a security guard in a jewelry store in Beverly Hills. He got fired from the guard detail for his atti-tude. The owner was always ordering him to trail the black customers through the store. This offended J. Dee, so he started following the white customers around, too. At the moment, J. Dee is between jobs. The other day he needed $500 to pay his car insurance. He earned it on a curb in three hours.

With them too this afternoon is Rob. A New York native, Rob is Cube's driver and man Friday, on loan from Public Enemy. He wears his Levi's hanging and cuffed up high, his baseball cap cocked to the side. He picks the hat not on the basis of team allegiance but for its colors. If you shit right, you hat match you kicks, your tennis shoes. The boyz from Cali make fun of Rob's style. The major differences are the cuff and the cock, but that's enough. The way they see it, anything different from they shit is wack.

Rob has his uses, though. He's shown Cube and the boyz how to order-in hamburgers, fried fish and other covered plates. Previously, Cube was living on Häagen-Dazs vanilla and Chips Ahoy. On this unfamiliar turf, McDonald's is the only restaurant he'll venture into. That and one other place, a trendy SoHo eatery across the street from the recording studio.

When Cube and his posse go, they sit at the bar, drink White Russians through a straw, eat buffalo chicken wings. The first time J. Dee was there, he looked around the room, noticed that his was the only black face, contemplated his wings, then commenced eating with a fork. Rob has also shown the homies to a mall in Queens. Jinx alone has spent two grand on tennis shoes, corduroys, a diamond and gold jinx ring and remote-controlled racing cars.

Now, after a late night in the studio, Cube comes down from his loft, turns toward the kitchen. From head on, he looks evil, all eyebrow and stare, wearing a T-shirt with a happy face with a bullet hole between its eyes. But see him in profile, pudgy, face creased with sleep, his hair on top a little nappy, and he's just a boy. Sometimes, in a rare moment, he'll be watching TV, maybe an ad for the movie *Teenage Mutant Ninja Turtles*, and suddenly his devil eyes will dance and his thick lips will turn up smiling, and he'll say, "Wow, I got to catch that shit!"

The homeboys mutter good mornings. They move about slowly, dressing from piles of clothes scattered around the parquet floor. The place has one bed. Cube gets that. Jinx gets the big sofa in the living room. J. Dee and T-Bone make do with the love seat and the chair. Rob gets the floor.

Suddenly, from the kitchen, a roar—hoarse and urgent and cataclysmic.

"Where my juice go!?!" Cube hollers.

All activity stops. The members of the posse eye one another nervously.

"I didn't drink no juice," T-Bone ventures.

Cube walks into the room, palms up, shaking his head. "So can I take up a collection?" he asks.

"A collection for what?" Jinx asks.

"A collection for juice, cookies and potato chips," Cube says. "You eat up every fuckin' thing that set foot in here."

"I didn't eat no cookies," J. Dee says.

"You better talk to this mothafucka over here," says Jinx, pointing to Rob.

"You the one had some juice," Rob protests.

"I ain't ate shit," Jinx says.

"I don't give a fuck," J. Dee declares. Though Cube has paid for his homies flights, no per diem is provided. J. Dee is to the curb, not a dime in his pocket. "Niggas can get mad, niggas can go outside and fight. But I'm eatin' everything in this muthafucka!"

"Word!" says T-Bone.

"Goddamn!" Cube says. "I had four mothafuckin' cookies, and one drink of juice. All y'all niggas on my dick!"

Cube peels a twenty off a thick roll, dispatches Rob for supplies. Rob goes grudgingly, hitch-stepping out the door, hat cocked.

Cube and the others settle around the television. In the 'hood, in the home, the electronic hearth is always on, warming the room with subliminals and worldview. Much of Cube's imagery comes from the tube. Cube's rap "A Gangsta's Fairytale" begins with *Mr. Rogers* theme played on a toy piano. Jack gets the clap and goes to see Dr. Bombay, the warlock doctor on *Bewitched*. The old lady who lives in the shoe sells drugs to an important guy who stays in an Air Jordan. In other raps, Cube's got the 411. He gets sucked up like Bounty, the paper towel. He changes like a Decepticon, the car-robot toy.

Right now, though, Cube can't find shit to watch. He flips through the channels, waiting for his cookies and juice. When Cube was growing up, he watched a lot of TV. His favorites were sports, action movies and black sit-coms. Then one day he was watching *Good Times*. In the episode, the father found a lot of money. Here was a family man from the projects. He was per-manently looking for work. At the end of the show, the father returned the cash. At that moment, Cube decided: "TV is bullshit."

"Yo. Check it out," he says now, and he holds up the remote. "Let's see if we can find a black face."

Cube punches through the channels. "No . . . no . . . no," he chants. "There go one. A basketball game." He punches all the way through, 1 to 43. He counts four black faces: a basketball coach; an ad for the black movie *House Party*, an extra in another movie, playing a soldier; JJ from *Good Times*. "See what I mean?" Cube asks. "I'd rather see a muthafuckin' cartoon. It's bullshit to me. The shit ain't real. I can only look at things one way. I'm black. When you younger, you don't worry about that shit. Only thing you worry about is when you gonna get that dirt bike. Only shit you worry about is muthafuckin' Christmas and your birthday. You know what I'm sayin'? Every-thing else is just shit you got to go through. Livin'. But then you start gettin' older. You start lookin' around and you like, *Yo! This is bullshit!*"

He flips channels some more. Some more. Click. Click. Click. The posse sits quietly. Rob comes in with the supplies. Click. Click. Click. Finally, something interesting. A very tight close up of Minister Louis Farrakahan, leader of the Nation of Islam. He's on *Donahue!*

"Yo! Look at Phil sweat!" laughs J. Dee.

Phil *is* sweating. The talk show host's usually-perfect gray hair is mussed, his glasses have fallen to the tip of his nose. The knot in his tie is skewed to the left, his lips are visibly trembling. Black people in the audience hurl epithets, demanding respect. The white people, attempting to hurl, are jeered back down into their seats. Through it all, Farrakhan sits serenely in his chair, knees crossed, hands folded in his lap. His bow tie, like his God's-on-my-side smile, is in perfect arrangement. He speaks with a certain possessed calm, enunciating carefully, as if what he's saying isn't as important as the way he's saying it.

Cube watches, eyes glued to the drama, as the show comes to a crashing end. As the credits roll, Cube's brows arched, his jaw is set. Inspired, he stands and begins pacing the room. "I wanna talk about the word nigga," he announces.

"People say. 'Why you use the word nigga?' Well, it like this. Back in the day, when you call somebody a nigger, that meant they were stupid and inferior, right? But now, I'm slapping the muthafuckas in they face with they own shit. You know what I'm sayin'? Yo. If every nigga was like me, you'd have a problem on your hands. This is the 1990 Nigga. When you say nigga today, you gonna say it in a different light, 'cause this is the 1990 version of the old shit.

"What fucks with the white people is when you kick 'em out your muthafuckin' pockets. When they can't make no money off Ice Cube and NWA, them muthafuckas are furious. You know what I mean? When I got a muthafuckin' black lawyer, a black manager, black folk to do my T-shirts, black folk to do my videos—if everybody who I work with is black, and the white corporate muthafuckas can't find no way to get in my goddam pocket, *that's* when you hurt em. That's the 1990s nigga, the nigga you love to hate. You know what I'm sayin'? They can pray to God that every so-called nigga ain't like this one. 'Cause if they were they'd have a muthafuckin' problem on they hands."

Cube's pace picks up as he circles the room, riffing, beating the air with a fist, lecturing like a Latin American dictator, stopping here and there to perch on the back of the sofa, the arm of a chair, the edge of a table.

"I think they should just have a black music industry," he continues. "Like if you got R&B and you got a black artist, you let this artist deal with these black people, and let them produce 'em, let 'em write, and all that. Minister Farrakan say that the white people owe us fuckin' liabilities for the shit they put us through 400 years ago. He say they liable for that shit so they have to pay it—like Germany paid the Jewish people from the Holocaust. But them muthafuckas ain't giving up no ass. *Ain't nobody given' up no ass.* Gimme my 40 acres and a mule. Right. So you got to take the shit. You can't depend on nobody, white or black, to give you shit. You gotta get your muthafuckin' own, you know what I'm sayin'? You gotta help your mothafuckin' own self. You gotta take what's yours. Not physically or in a muthafuckin' way to steal, but you gotta take what's yours though the actions of your mind. You can't wait on no otha muthafucka. If you at home and you ain't got no car, you do not wait for a muthafucka to pick you up. You find your way there. You know what I'm sayin'?

"It's like welfare. I'm not totally against the welfare, but I think the shit need to be conditioned. Instead of having muthafuckas sit on they ass and wait for a check, you say, 'Yo. You muthafuckas want to get your check? Then you gotta do community service. You wanna get this check? Then you gotta help the elderly.' Muthafuckas wouldn't go for that shit. They'd go find jobs. They'd *take* jobs. They'd get up off they asses and do some positive shit.

"It's like those nature films you see on TV, you know, when the mother bird brings food to the baby birds in the nest? Those muthafuckas scramblin'. Now, you can't live your life that way, for the simple fact that you don't want to step on no otha muthafucka to get what yours, but at the same time, you know what I'm sayin', you gotta do what you gotta do. It all boils down to how much muthafuckin' food you can put on the table, 'cause everything else is bullshit."

"**Money,** where you get that shirt!" laughs Jinx, incredulous.

"That shit ancient!" says Rob.

"That shit so old, it got history!" says Chuck D, and then he cups his ear, strains forward. "Listen! You can hear it: Mets Win the Pennant!"

"Wilt Chamberlain Scores 100!"

"Slaves Freed!"

"Jesus Born!"

Al "Purple" Hayes is gettin' faded. He's gettin' sweated, cuffed, rolled, dissed, fitted fo' he panic cap. Lench Mob is in the house, Public Enemy in effect too, late night in the SoHo basement that is Greene Street Studios. A track from Cube's album plays in the adjacent studio, pounding through an open door. Lined along an L-shaped sofa are PE producer Hank Shocklee, Chuck D, J. Dee, Jinx, Rob, Cube and Run of Run-D.M.C., one of rap's original superstars.

Cube came to Chuck in January, when he was sure things were over with N.W.A., and asked if Chuck would produce his album. Now, after a few false starts, its happening, a seditious East-meets-West congress of hard-core rappers. Funny thing about this scene: Except for Jinx—who is wearing a green pajama suit decorated with white and yellow golf balls and tees, and, over his shoulders, an ankle-length, acid-washed-denim, sheepskin-lined coat—you'd look at this group and figure it was just another crew of homies down on the block. Loose cords or black Levi's, oversize sweatshirts, a leather Africa pendant or two, baseball caps, Nikes, an assortment of creative haircuts. Cube has the least flash in the bunch. Just his black Gap wears and his ever-present L.A. Raiders knit cap. As Cube says, "Stars in the sky, you know what I mean?" The tube is on, as usual, everyone sort of half-watching the Grammys.

Al Hayes stands against a wall, trying to smile. The subject of all this dissin' is his clothes. They old. They tight. They wack. While Jinx stands to make something like $20,000 for his five weeks here, and Cube's "advancement" from Priority Records is about a quarter million, Hayes, who will show up each night for all five weeks of recording, will end up making about $600.

Hayes is a musician from Harlem. He plays guitar, bass, keyboards, drums, harmonica and a little sax. Hayes started playing at age eight, on a cardboard-box guitar purchased at a five-and-dime. At twenty-nine, he has studied classical and jazz guitar and has received a BA in music from Five Towns College, in Seaford, Long Island. Now he works days as a casher in a twenty-four-hour convenience store in Harlem. Every night, he comes to the studio. He sits until somebody needs the seat, then he stands, and he waits, word-upping and uh-humming, being agreeable, hoping that sometime, somewhere on all these yards of recording rope being filled, there will be a little track for live music, a little piece for him. He has had a few chances. One night, they needed a funky wah-wah for a few bars of "Once Upon a Time in the Projects." Another night, he did a bass line for "I'm

Only Out for One Thang." In "The Nigga Ya Love to Hate" he got a guitar solo. Two bars.

"Man!" says Shocklee. "Why don't you get some new clothes?"

"That shit so tight the Statue of Liberty have her arm down by her side!" says Cube.

"The twin towers all stuck together!" says J. Dee, talking about the World Trade Center.

"Everything getting all close together. The whole country like two feet across!" says Chuck.

"Hey, I'm going across the street to Cali," Jinx announces. "Anybody need anything?"

"I'm jumpin' to London," yells Cube, getting up, hopping back and forth, jumping the big pond. "New York to London, New York to London," and then, stopping, railing, laughing: "The year getting all stuck together. Short! It just Christmas then New Year's, Christmas, New Year's. I'm twenty-five years old, Christmas, New Year's. I'm forty-six! Christmas, New Year's! I got fourteen platinum albums!"

Over by the wall, Hayes shrugs his shoulders, keeps his mouth shut. This is the wave of the future. Twenty-four tracks, nary a musician in sight. He'll take what he can get.

The instruments for this recording session include computers, voices, old albums, CDs, movie and TV soundtracks. It begins with Jinx. He starts on a drum machine, laying down the bottom beats and the snare. Cube matches in a rhyme, then Jinx adds the samples, scratches and sound effects. The music is rooted on old soul—little snatches of Aretha Franklin, Marvin Gaye, James Brown, the Ohio Players—pieced together through the magic of computers and imagination. Jinx will hear in his head a sound he'd like to put on a record—a two-bar guitar thrum, a three-word refrain—then he'll try to find it on an old album. He gets the albums from his friends' parents, digging around in dusty stacks. Everything is rehearsed, perfected. The posse crowds around the mike to make the sounds of a crap game. They shout, "Fuck you, Ice Cube!" for a chorus. T-Bone takes half an hour to perfect "Roll the mothafuckas up like a fat-ass joint!" A nine-year-old boy is brought in for "A Gangsta's Fairytale." Cube closes the studio and takes the boy, little Lester with a high top fade, into the sound booth. He coaches patiently, teaching him to say, "Yo, Ice Cube, why you always kickin' the shit about the bitches and the niggas? Why don't you kick some shit about the kids, man, the fuckin' kids?" For the intro to "Rollin' Wit the Lench Mob," Cube uses tape from a live television broadcast about gang violence in L.A. Says NBC's Tom Brokaw: "Outside the South-Central area, few cared about the violence, because it didn't affect them." The announcer on "A Gangsta's Fairytale" is a walk-on, the white guy who answers the phones at night for Greene Street, another musician.

"The Drive-By," is a little skit between two songs, a you-are-there rendering of a drive-by homicide. For this one minute radio drama, Jinx and another producer record a speaking script, then Jinx spends hours searching through a CD sound effects library: A car door shutting; two different calibers of bullets firing; an engine racing; rubber peeling; dogs barking; women screaming. When the gangbangers walk to the car for the drive-by, Jinx pans the sounds so that the listener hears their footsteps move from his left ear to his right. "Better off Dead" is another skit. In this one, Cube is taken from his prison cell and electrocuted in front of a gallery of witnesses, but not before he tells his guard: "I never liked you anyway," and speaks his last words: "Fuck all y'all!" The electrocution was conceived to demonstrate the theme of the album: "Every muthafucka with a color is AmeriKKKa's most wanted."

Jinx is at his finest on "It's a Man's World," an argumentative duet between Cube and Yo-Yo, a girl rapper Cube drafted because someone has to give the ladies' point of view. Jinx goes through every musical and comedy album he can find, searching out the word *bitch*. He samples each *bitch* onto the E-MU SP1200 sequencer, manipulating the sound electronically until the pitch and sustain are to his liking. He assigns each different *bitch* to a different key on a keyboard. Then, a two-fingered pianist, he plays a bitch song, sixty straight seconds of *bitch*, all of it dedicated to the girls out there who wouldn't give them any play before the album came out. All of this for a little break in the cut.

There's been a lot of talk and litigation about rap sampling, the practice of using pieces of other people's copyrighted work. Cube's feelings on the matter seem to sum up the rap community's sentiment: "Say you take some shit from Sly Stone. When the last time he had a hit record? Yo. He gonna get some money, but the muthafucka can't get more than he deserve. If I didn't take they shit, they shit would be older than the muthafuckin' garbage."

Cube and the rappers are the latest evolution in a musical chain that links disco; go-go; funk; street corner doo-wop; be-bop; blues; ring games; skip-rope rhymes; prison and slave songs; military marching call-and-response; gospel call and response; Jamaican toasting; a ghetto boasting game called the Dozens; close harmony; vaudeville . . . all the way back to the groits of Nigeria and Gambia.

Like other musical forms, rap is not just about notes and rhythms combined in a signature fashion; it is a reflection of its times, of larger doings and ideas. Rap is part of a culture called hip-hop, the expression of an ever-growing young black underclass, a sort of born-again black-movement. If hip-hop is the nation, and the homies are the tribe, then rap is the anthem. Hip-hop is a style of dress, talk, attitude, action. Hip-hop brought us graffiti and break dancing. And once again, hip-hop is showing how America appropriates so much of its popular culture not from its marble towers but from its asphalt jungles. Whence came jazz and blues and rock & roll? Cornrows? Stacked platform shoes? McDonald's rapping potato? In the last ten years, hip-hop has worked its way from the West Bronx to Madison Avenue and into America's homes. Funny how new expression comes from the bottom in America. The lower classes are taught to emulate the uppers, to buckle down and learn the accredited route to success. Yet, when it comes to the fun stuff, the music, the dance, the style, the things that have nothing to do with success, the uppers are always emulating the lowers. Perhaps the qualities that lead some groups to racial and political domination are just the qualities that make them less inclined to create new kinds of fun. Perhaps the opposite is true as well.

Rap began not with rappers but with disc jockeys. Back in the late sixties, early seventies, the vogue in the West Bronx became parties with DJs spinning the music. Equipped with two turntables, a mixer, headphones, a "coffin" full of records, and the largest speakers they could find, DJs hosted block parties, school dances, or big outdoor throwdowns in the parks, the latter powered illegally with juice from the street lamps, usually shut down pretty quick by police.

Kool DJ Herc is generally credited with being the first DJ virtuoso. Though he was born in Jamaica, Herc found his sound in Latin-tinged funk. He'd pick out fragments of songs that were popular with the dancers—a conga or bongo solo, a timbales break, a drum beat, a brass or guitar riff, ten seconds, thirty seconds, a couple of minutes. Using the two turntables, switching back and forth, clicking and changing, Herc developed the basic music of Hip Hop—an endless, cacophonous, disharmonic loop of hot dance beat. What's known as "scratching"—dragging the turntable needle back and forth across the wax surface of the album, using the effect as another form of percussion—was born out of the cueing process. To find the part of record he wanted, the DJ would listen through the headphones, spin the record slowly with his fingertips. If he scratched the needle quickly back and forth, he got a new sound, another rhythm to work with, something else for the mix.

It was only natural that the DJs had mics: Soon, Herc and others began rapping. At first it was mostly boasts: money, pussy, who's in the house. In truth, rap was really nothing new. The team of music and talk is as old as religion. And just prior to Herc and his b-boyz were the jazz talkers of the sixties—Amiri Baraka and his "Black Dada Nihilismus"; The Last Poets and "White Man's Got a God Complex"; Gil Scott-Heron and "The Revolution Will Not be Televised."

Rap went public in 1979, with two singles, released in quick succession. The first was by Fatback, a waning street funk group from Brooklyn that put out a record with an unknown DJ named King Tim III. The rap was called "King Tim III (Personality Jock)." The second, more important, was "Rapper's Delight," by the Sugarhill Gang. Though Fatback's record was a success of sorts, it's style was more reminiscent what you might hear on a radio, a sort of disc jockey jive. "Rappers Delight" not only used rapping but also mixing and sampling. Part of its appeal was its appropriation of the music from Chic's huge disco hit, "Good Times," for its backing track.

On the heels of "Delight" came Kurtis Blow, Afrika Bambaataa, and Grandmaster Flash and the Furious Five. Flash's 1982 song, "The Message," a stark and ugly tale from the ghetto, was hailed as the single of the year by both the *Los Angeles Times* and the *New York Times*. It demonstrated, according to one critic, that "rap was not simply an echo of the fluffy disco era," but a new genre unto itself.

In 1983, when the Simmons brothers of Queens entered the scene, rap started its journey toward the mainstream. Russell Simmons was the businessman. Joseph Simmons was the rapper. While a student at a mortuary college in New York, Joseph wrote "It's Like That." The record sold 500,000 and pushed his group, Run-DMC—with their gangsta hats, gold chains and oversize glasses—into the forefront of rap. Crossover success came with their next release, a remake of Aerosmith's rock and roll classic, "Walk this Way." Now, the white kids began listening. The single climbed to number 4 on the charts; it was named Record of the Year by the *Village Voice* annual critics' poll. When forty-one fans were injured during an outbreak of gang violence at a Run-DMC concert in Long Beach, California, rap's gangsta glamour became legend. Soon, rap was playing out of boom boxes everywhere from New Jersey to Idaho; boyz and girlz were going into garages and basements and recording their own demos, signing contracts with hood-spun record labels like Def Jam and Delicious Vinyl. Soon came *Licensed to Ill* by the Beastie Boys, a trio of raunchy white rappers from Long Island. The rock singer Blondie weighed in with a rap as well. In 1988, the Grammies added a category for "Best Rap Performance." The first winner was DJ Jazzy Jeff and the Fresh Prince, the latter also known as Will Smith, who would go on to become the first of many rappers to cross over into acting and mainstream superstardom. The era of the rap superstar was born.

Another day, outside his trendy New York digs, Cube sits in the passenger seat of his rental car, door open, one foot in, one out, waiting for Rob to drive him eight blocks to the studio.

Cube thrums his fingers on the dashboard, groans, sighs, shifts around, checks under the seat. A can of black spray paint! Jinx must have used it to finish one of the plastic bodies for his model cars. Cube shakes the can, the little ball inside bounces back and forth. He finds a rhythm, shake shake shake, a beat to pass the time.

Across the street, upscale hipsters with money in their pockets parade past a gormet market, carrying flowers and bagettes, jogging, walking designer dogs. He shakes his head sadly, a crooked grin on his face. "When you black," he says, voice philosophical, spray paint spelling out LENCH MOB on the sidewalk, "white people seem so corny."

White people. That who been fadin' him about his songs. Parents' groups, police groups, the federal government, the Tennessee judge who ruled him obscene. All these white people listening to his records. The problem is, they don't understand what they're hearing. The language of Hip Hop is imaginative, imperfect, vague, tenseless, primitive, impressionistic, onomatopoeic—

perhaps the reason why the two most oft used phrases are: "You know what I mean?" and "You know what I'm sayin?" When Cube raps about doing a drive-by shooting, he says, he's not talking about actually killing people with Uzis. He's talking about cappin' society in they ass with fact, about murderin' ignorance and oppression. It's poetry. It's metaphor. It's based loosely on the King's English, like creole or pidgin.

Down on the block, of course, they understand Cube insists that he makes his music for the boyz and girlz in the 'hood. Just them and him talkin'. And when it was only homies buying Cube's records, nobody was giving him any grief. Sure, they weren't playing his songs on the radio, too many dirty words. But Cube and N.W.A. didn't need the radio. Their shit sold through word of mouth. Back then, the only media interested were fanzines like *Right On!*, *Word Up!* and *Yo!* Now, however, white kids in the suburbs are buying his records, millions of dollars' worth, and a lot of grown-ups are complaining that Cube has no right to put out albums that say the things his say. That's another meaning of "AmeriKKKa's Most Wanted." Most wanted by the authorities, yes, but also most wanted by the kids. Cube knows that a lot of people wouldn't mind seeing rap pass quickly into fad purgatory. But as he tells a reporter from *People* magazine on the phone: "If I'm more of an influence to your son as a rapper than you are as a father, you know, you got to look at yourself as a parent."

Cube doesn't understand what everyone's so scared about. What's all the fuss? What could be so horrible that milquetoast *Newsweek* unleashes a racist diatribe of a cover story detailing the horrors of rap? True, Cube's album with N.W.A. was produced with a guy's drug profits. And true, Cube was arrested once. He's had his nose ground into concrete, a police officer's knee pressed between his shoulder blades. He's been in fights, he's been shot at, he's held a semi-automatic pistol in his hand. And though he's from a nice neighborhood in South-Central, it's still the hood, Sowetto south of Pico, they like to call it. Even Cube's block has its open-air drug markets and its gang. Cube raps about what he knows, what he's seen, learned, grown up with. How black kids are killing each other. How police are killing black kids. How drugs, money, clothes, and pussy are the icons of the young men of his day. How people live in the projects on county checks. How black men are always playin' the Mack—Manipulatin' And Connin' for Kash. How black women are always playin' the hoe—givin' away what they got only if you got the price. How the white man thinks he knows what's best for the black man. How the white man don't know shit about the black man. Turn off the radio, Cube says in one of his songs, program your own shit. He talkin' to the brothers. Why the white man so faded?

"I feel like this," says Cube. "Yo. White people, they got their own complex with theyself. They know we been fucked over, and they know that—to be honest man, I don't see why the fuck they scared. If something go down where there's a muthafuckin' confrontation, the brothers ain't got no muthafuckin' chance. We don't make no muthafuckin' guns, no bullets, no muthafuckin' missiles, *nothin'*. Them muthafuckas can wipe us out like that. You know what I'm sayin'?

"I don't know what the fuck they scared of. They say we use profanity. Fuck that. All we doing is tellin' the real deal. You can watch Disneyland all muthafuckin' day. You can watch Mickey Mouse. But when you go outside on the street, yo, it ain't no Mickey Mouse. That shit real.

"The white people say brothers all racists. How the fuck we gonna be racist? White people prejudiced. Black people angry. White people control all the shit. How can we be prejudiced against them? It ain't us holding back jobs from them. The only thing we are is muthafuckin' angry for the shit we had to go through and we ain't havin' it. Muthafuckas ain't backing down no more. Yo. You the bully of the muthafuckin' school, but when the muthafucka you beatin' up on say, 'Fuck it, we gonna fight!' you get kind of nervous. You say 'Wait a minute, this muthafucka might got somethin' we don't know about.' And that's what they scared of, us having something they don't know about, us havin' rap music. Bottom line is this: Rap music is a muthafuckin' metaphor. Rap is the biggest muthafuckin' black media, and it's takin' over the country. Pretty soon muthafuckas gonna be listening to rap records instead of watching *60 Minutes.*

"When we have something of our own, we have rap, the whites say 'Oh, wait a minute now. You can't talk among each other. You just supposed to be hating us. You supposed to focus everything on hating us.' Cause if we keep hating them, that keeps them superior. I tell you. Ain't no brothers planning to take over no white people. Period. And I don't think white people are assholes. I figure it's just ignorance. I want muthafuckas to listen to my shit. This is all I want. I want them to say 'Damn, that shit true!' I ain't just muthafuckin' nigga this, bitch that. I think carefully about everything I say in my songs and how muthafuckas gonna react."

Like Abbie Hoffman or Jerry Rubin or Malcolm X, Cube is a herald, standing at the mike, saying what he sees. He's not running for office, he's reporting. Outside the castle walls, the Eurocentric standards of life as America has known it for 200 years are changing. And even though the white man has a particular penchant for leaving all the bad stuff left unsaid, for "sweeping niggas like Cube up under the rug," Cube is putting the white man on notice. According to U.S. Census projections, by 2056, the "average" American will trace his or her descent to Africa, Asia, the Hispanic world, the Pacific Islands or Arabia. As they say in democracy, majority rules.

Deep in South-Central, in the dark of night, a prim brick bungalow illuminated with colored spots. Inside the house, a lady in a church dress. The eyes, the brows, the cheekbones, the nose. It's Cube's moms, Doris Jackson.

Cube lived here full time with Moms and Pops until a few months ago. He'd be here still but he couldn't get no rest. People would find out where he lived and come over all the time; he was getting all these headaches. Now he's got a nice new two-bedroom apartment a couple of miles away in Culver City. It is furnished almost entirely in black leather. Whether or not he lives with a girlfriend is off the record. Either way, he still spends a lot of time at Moms' place. He gets mail here, has his own keys to the front door.

O'Shea Jackson was a Father's Day baby, a surprise, eight years since the last. The fourth child, second boy, he was named after Moms' favorite football player, OJ Simpson. O'Shea was a cute little kid. When he was five, Moms signed him up with a modeling agency. One gig he got was posing with a little girl for a calendar—for every month, a different pose: Building a sand castle, eating ice cream, down on their knees in church.

O'Shea went to Hawthorn Christian school for his first three years, then asked to change because he didn't like the uniform and the tie. Doris, who had moved here from Columbia, South Carolina, and her husband Hosea, from Chatham, Louisiana, had come west to find a better way of life. At the time of Cube's birth, Hosea was a machinist, employed at a brass works in downtown L.A. As a youth, O'Shea played Y-league basketball and Pop Warner football (outside linebacker, fullback, kickoff return, not so much fast but quick). A solid-B student, he was well-liked and well-behaved. "I never did have to go to school for anything for him," says Moms, in her thick drawl. "I really appreciated that. He was a very nice young man. Every time someone would take him places, a field trip or something, they always had something good to say about him. I remember when he was playing football, and the team went to San Jose. He stayed with this couple which was blind. They wrote a little note saying how wonderful he was."

Mom's house is on the west side of South Central, near Inglewood, not very far from Watts, the scene in 1965 of a drunk driving arrest that became a milestone riot. With thirty-four killed, more than 1,000 injured, and 600 buildings destroyed, burned or looted, the riot ignited a racial conflagration that roiled across the nation like a carpet bomb, credited by historians as the beginnings of a momentous chapter in the American movement for black civil rights. Since then, of course, Watts has been rebuilt; the people of South-Central have been preoccupied fighting another kind of battle, this one against gangs and drugs. Though more than half of the city's estimated 90,000 gang members live here, South-Central looks at first glance like a nice place to live. There are neighborhoods on hills with big houses, shopping centers and malls, the usual low-slung business sprawl. Even the poorest and most drug-infested neighborhoods have lawns and palm trees, the smell of flowers in the air. Compared to the ghettos of the East Coast—the Bronx, North Philadelphia, Anacostia in D.C.—South-Central appears to be a suburban idyll.

O'Shea discovered rap when he was in fourth grade. He'd chipped his tooth and his moms, who was working as a clerk at UCLA hospital, asked his uncle to drive him to the dentist. At that point in his life, says Cube, "I was into basketball. I was into football. It was Magic Johnson and Marcus Allen. Period. Everyone else was bullshit. Everybody else was just, I could care less." Then his uncle put a new tape in the deck. It was called "Rapper's Delight" by the Sugarhill Gang. Little O'Shea was mesmerized.

Growing into his early teens, which are for many the prime gangbanging years, O'Shea hung out a little, got into a few fights, done a little bullshit like breaking into cars. But he wasn't no gangsta. "I couldn't figure no money in the shit," says Cube. "I was usually down at Jinx's house, trying to hook up some music."

O'Shea wrote his first rhyme at the end of ninth grade, in a typing class at a junior high in the mostly-white San Fernando Valley high school, where he and a bunch of others from his hood were bussed an hour each way. One day, he and his homeboy in the next seat had finished a typing test early. They'd recently seen Ice T perform at Magic Mountain, and "muthafucka wrecked shit," they were real impressed. So they're sitting there and homie say to O'Shea, "Yo man, let's write a rap." Homie wrote one he'd heard before, one of Ice T's raps, only changed to include his own name. But O'Shea—he typed up some new shit. He wrote a whole page, folded it, stuck it in his pocket. Later, on the bus, he kicked the shit, recited it for his friends, and everybody liked it, and he *really* liked doing it. It made him feel large.

As it turned out, Jinx's cousin was a guy named Dr. Dre. He was in the Wrecking Crew at the time, one of the early L.A. rap groups, and he was DJing at a club called Doto's. Cube recruited another friend, and with Jinx formed the Stereo Crew. They kicked for Dre, and he liked some of they shit, but he told the youngsters: "Y'all can't rap like y'all rappin', y'all got to say somethin' funny. If y'all don't be funny, them people in the club gonna fool you."

Cube and them thought about it for a while. At the time, West Coast rap was down like that—it was funny and gimmicky in the style of rappers like Fresh Prince and MC Hammer. Cube didn't like being funny. He wanted to be different. They wracked their brains for something to do. "There was this song by UTFO out at the time called 'Roxanne, Roxanne,'" says Cube, "so we was like, fuck it, we gonna change the words and call the shit 'Diane, Diane,' talkin' about this bitch we trying to fuck instead of beating around the bush. And we did that shit in the club, and we wrecked shit, you know what I'm sayin? We did better than the even the Wreckin' Crew that night. And all the guys in the Wrecking Crew was like, 'Yo, man, y'all wanna make some records?' And we was like, '*Yeah.*' So we went into the studio. Shit didn't come out so hot, though. The lyrics, they were cool, but they wasn't no exciting type of mind-boggling shit. And we didn't have the voice and the delivery to deliver the shit right. I was only fifteen, you know."

But Cube continued rapping, battling with other rappers on the corners, playing Skate Land and talent contests and even getting into the finals of a radio station rap battle in the Hollywood Palladium. Soon he formed his next group, CIA. A guy named Lonzo put them down on Crew Cut Records, but they didn't get paid. "Lonzo said the record didn't do so hot," says Cube, "but muthafuckas still to this day comin' up and axin' me about the record, you know what I mean? So he dicked me on that."

In 1986, through Dre, Cube met Eric "Eazy-E" Wright, a runty former dope dealer who'd made a small fortune selling crack in Compton, then used his profits to start his own label, Ruthless Records, pronounced roof-less. Eazy had signed a group called HBO, and he wanted Cube to write something for them. Cube was getting pretty good at writing by then. You could give him a scenario and he's write some dope shit. In exchange for the song, Eazy promised he'd buy Cube a Volkswagen Beetle, something Cube had always wanted.

Dre and Cube took a meeting on the song. What they needed, they decided, was a whole new style. The regular shit wasn't selling. "We decided we gonna just curse, fuck it," says Cube. "So Dre say, 'Yo Eazy! Why don't you do it?' and Eazy was like, 'I ain't never rapped before.'"

And so it was that Eazy released "Boyz in the Hood" to great sales and acclaim. He, Cube and Dre formed Niggaz Wit Attitude. Cube wrote most of the songs and rapped on them, too. And they were selling. They'd hit on something big. The future looked assured. Cube was going to be a star.

Then came the voice of Moms.

"Wait a minute, O'Shea. You need an education first."

Doris Jackson didn't have anything against rap, not really. She remembers proudly the first time her daughter came into the kitchen and said, "Listen at O'Shea rhyming. He pretty good!" O'Shea, she agreed, *was* pretty good. He'd played "Dope Man" for her and she'd liked it. How could she not? It was her son's song on a real tape. What her son had neglected to mention, however, was that the version she heard had been vacuumed, the cussing removed. Somebody else played the real one for her, at a party at her work. "Doris, is that your son doing all that cussing?"

"Oh, my Lord," said Moms.

O'Shea wasn't allowed to curse at home. "You never know what they're doing behind your back," says Moms, "but before the record, I never knew O'Shea to cuss. I kind of sat him down and I said, 'Do you have to do quite that much cussing?' And O'Shea said, 'Well Moms, this is what the kids want to listen to. We're talking about what's going on out in the street today.'

"I really don't think rap is that bad," says Moms, who has raised a groundskeeper, a nurse's aide, a new moms, and a rap star on the streets of South-Central. "The way I look at it is this. Usually kids pick a lot of stuff up outside the home. And they learn a lot inside the home too. I think parents forget a lot of time that their kids are around, and maybe Daddy and Mom aren't getting along or have some words, and the kids are sitting there. Things come out. In the end, kids are going to learn anyway. It's the real world out there. I don't care how much raising you will do, they have to have their own mind. You have to kind of instill things into them. They still remember a lot."

And so it was that Cube's career was put on hold. Off he went, in a Volkswagen Bug his parents bought for his eighteenth birthday (Eazy had never come through on his own offer) bound for the Phoenix Institute of Technology, a one year course in drafting.

Street Knowledge Productions, in Culver City, is a walk-up over a machine shop in the industrial flats, just across the railroad tracks from a truck yard, where a score of young male Hispanics play soccer at lunchtime on the fenced-in asphalt. We are in the office of the vice president, Pat Charbonnet. She's conferring on the start-up with the president of the firm, Ice Cube.

Outside the window, Cube can see three Mexican women pushing an old Chevy down the littered street, past his brand new Honda Accord—four door, black. Cube figures he don't need no Mercedes. The way he sees it, "Some people gotta be known by what they own. You ask, 'Yo, you know Joe?' And muthafucka don't know who you're talking about. Then you say 'You know, dude with the Cadillac?' And *then* you know who he talking about." Cube wants people to know him for his name. An Accord is a good enough car, and it cost him only about twenty grand. Cube doesn't like to spend too much money. As his manager, he pays Pat 10 percent instead of the standard 15. Everybody gets paid, but only what's fair. Since he's the one making the money, he decides what's fair. No niggas gonna ride his dick for free.

Cube gives himself an allowance of $1500 a month in cash. If he spends more than that on buying things, the way he see it, "I'm robbin' myself, my savings account leavin'." He writes his own checks for rent, electric, telephone and other expenses. He likes to know where his money is going. He hasn't been doing this long: He's on check number 132 in his checkbook.

At the moment, Cube and Pat are discussing corporate finances. Street

Knowledge Productions is a brand new entity. They've just moved into the building. Pat's mother-in-law is helping out, answering the telephones. There are a million details to discuss. Pat sits at her desk, Cube stands over her. Each one holds a pen. Because there is a reporter present, when they have to mention a dollar amount, they write the numbers on a pad of paper.

"I have to have a fax machine and a chair," Pat is saying. "It's like maybe another. . . ." and she writes five figures with her pen.

"I can deal with that," Cube says.

"And also, does anybody get any more of this amount that you got in that deal?" Pat asks, scribbling five more. "Is Jinx okay right now?"

"He should be. I gave him some from my half. The thing you got to work on is Yo-Yo."

"But she's not entitled to anything until the album's completed. See here?" she points to a ledger. "I'm paying her rent right now. It's this much," says Pat, scribbling three figures, smiling up at Cube.

Pat is a self-described "African Princess," dark and pretty and "thirty-something," the great granddaughter of an English Jew. She's wearing dope shades, black leather pants, ankle boots with fake leopard trim. The daughter of a businessman and a nurse, Pat grew up in the suburbs of New York, attended Pace University. After college, she lived in the Bahamas for a while, then moved to Los Angeles, where she soon became National press director for United Artists. In 1985, while working for CBS Records she was named national Publicist of the Year.

After winning the award, Pat had left the game to have babies. She is married to a black man named Mike. His father began years ago as a contractor, specializing in fire insurance work. Over time, he'd bought large chunks of South-Central; now he owns, among other things, the shopping center in Compton. Mike and his posse are surfers. Not long ago, they were kickin' it at Laguna Beach when a bunch of white guys yelled "Nigger Go Home."

Pat got back in the business last year, going to work for Priority Records to handle N.W.A. and several other rap acts. To her, working with Cube and other rappers is a lot more than just flacking music. What they're doing is political, she says. Maybe even historical.

"In every time, there are young voices like Cube," Pat says. "People call them rebels or radicals, but really what they are voices that articulate the sentiment of the time that they live in. Look at a Public Enemy—'It Takes a

Nation of Millions to Hold Us Back.' For kids buying their records, this is probably the first time they're hearing stuff about black power and black pride. The people I heard, growing up, like Martin Luther King and Malcolm X and Stokley Carmichael and Rap Brown aren't real for them. Every year during black history month, all they hear is the same regurgitated stuff all about the peanut guy, Washington Carver. And by the way: Has anybody ever noticed that Black History Month is February, the shortest month of the year?

"Everyone has been saying that this generation is apathetic. That all they care about is drugs and gold. I say differently. I think the handwriting is on the wall. We've always been told as black people that we have to know everything about white culture. See, one thing that white people don't understand is that there's a feeling in the hood that what's going on in white society is not important anymore. That's over there, that's them. This is here. We're directing ourselves to each other. Look at the whole history of communications. When the slaves were brought over, they were separated so they couldn't communicate. People were put together whose languages were different. Now look. There's a national rap network. Black people are talking to each other through rap."

And through rap, they are doing business.

"You need to work on those credit cards," Cube is saying.

"That's why I'm going to see Irl," Pat says. "And that's why we wanted you to go over there take him a lump sum."

"Ok, 'cause I need them cards, like, yesterday so I can go get the equipment for the studio. Either that, or I gotta go get money orders for the shit."

"Lemme see if Irl can see us tomorrow," Pat says. "These kinds of people—"

"And I don't want no five dollar limit," Cube interrupts.

"Don't worry. We'll do it." She turns to another page of business. "Now, I have to ask you about—"

"Damn!" Cube says, shaking his head. "This shit ain't just funky beats and rhymes no more, is it?"

The Lench Mob is meeting at Cube's crib one evening. There's Cube, T-Bone, Jinx, Chill and Yo-Yo, all of them in the dining room around a glass table. Cube and his girlfriend have been out all day buying furnishings for Cube's first apartment. A week ago it was pretty empty. Now it's filling up. For the study they've gotten a black Italian coffee table, black leather sofas, a black desk. Over the fireplace, they've hung a print of a woman, a neon tube incorporated in the design. The telephone is one of those clear acrylic numbers with a neon tube inside—there was a similar one in the sublet in the Large Apple.

The meeting tonight concerns Yo-Yo's first album. They're going into production soon. At the moment, Yo-Yo is reading from her spiral notebook, telling the Lench Mob the names of her songs:

"There's 'Sisterland,' 'Enuf is Enuf,' 'I Got Played,' 'Talking Hip Hop,' and um, oh yeah, 'Who Needs a Man,' " she enumerates.

"You gonna do eleven songs," says Cube, munching on a chicken leg from KFC.

"I think 'Who Needs a Man' might be outtie," says Jinx. "The music hype, but it too slow. It just like a story rap, but that's something you do after you make it. Right now we gotta—"

Yo-Yo is eighteen, drives a school bus during the day. She's big and beautiful with bronze-colored skin, green eyes, and long bronze hair extensions—in her spare time she also braids hair. Tireless, gregarious and husky-voiced, Yo-Yo grew up in South-Central, a cheerleader and a member of the drill team who was popular for her raps—she won her school's Star Search four years in a row. Later, she'd win rap battles at World of Wheels and Skateland so many times that they wouldn't let her win no more; they made her a special guest instead. Not long ago, she was attending to her first semester of college while working thirty hours a week at McDonalds. Now, through Cube, she's got six-figure deal with Atlantic Records.

Sitting at the table in the living room, Cube is looking a bit tired. He's got so many things on his mind—today he's thinking about tomorrow, you know what I'm sayin'? He's thinking his record coming out in late May, coming out right and on time. The songs, the mix, the art, the copy, the distribution, the money. He's thinking about Yo-Yo's project, from songs to cover design. He's thinking about the studio he's building downstairs from Street Knowledge, about buying the equipment, about getting that plastic from Irl. About his Lench Mob T-shirts. His long form video. A director for his video. When it will be done. How much money Priority Records will put up. Taking his new car to the shop to have a telephone installed. Putting his tour together. Paying his taxes—for the first time in his life.

Only two years ago, in September 1988, Cube himself was just graduating from the Phoenix Institute of Technology. When he returned to Cali, N.W.A. went to work. They did Eazy's album, then they did *Straight Outta Compton.* Cube wrote or co-wrote nine of the eleven songs on *Straight* with MC Ren. During this time, Cube says, "I was happy as a muthafucka." He loved N.W.A. He felt as though he was an integral part of the crew. He thought everyone in the crew was integral—that's what made it so great. "I kind of figured if anybody left, the group would be hurt. If I left, it would be weak. If Ren left it would be weak. If Dre left it would be totally weak. And Eazy, you know, he had the money."

Unbeknownst to Cube, however, he had never actually signed a contract with N.W.A. He signed a lot of stuff—he's still not sure what all of that was. It seemed that while they were recording, there was a different piece of paper to sign every day. Who knew what they said? Who cared? "Everybody was broke, and if muthafucka show you where you can make some money, you gonna rush it. First of all, I didn't have the money to pay for a lawyer, and I didn't know the way to go about finding a lawyer. I was really into makin' the music, you know what I mean? Getting back into the swing of things 'cause I was gone for a year. And I wanted everybody to feel that I was back, without coming in and you know, stirring up things."

Straight Outta Compton dropped in February of 1989 and hit big. By the time N.W.A. left Cali for a fifty city tour, the album had sold 750,000, and the media was beginning to make noise. Their hit song, after all, was called "Fuck tha Police." In 1989, obscenity was not allowed on the radio. Somehow, though, everyone found out about it.

Out on tour, before playing any of the dates, N.W.A. had to agree not to perform "Fuck," or another song called "Gangsta Gangsta." Despite these assurances, police in Milwaukee refused to work security for the concert. Police in several other cities followed suit. The Mayor of Kansas City tried unsuccessfully to block their show. The University of Tennessee was successful. Cincinnati was a particularly difficult stop. First, the members of the group were questioned by federal agents, who said they believed that Cube and them were Los Angeles gang members trying to infiltrate the Midwest. Then, the band couldn't get a hotel room—no establishment in the city would let them in. After their show, the group was ticketed for disorderly conduct; that evening, the chief of police faxed N.W.A.'s lyrics to other chiefs along the route of their tour. In Toledo, expectations of violence ran so high that local TV channels interrupted prime-time programming for updates from the concert hall. No violence was reported. In other cities, local black ministers were encouraged to tell their parishioners not to go see N.W.A. The FBI also sent N.W.A. a letter, saying they could not condone songs like "Fuck." In Detroit, angered by their low placement on the bill, N.W.A. went ahead and sang "Fuck" anyway. The audience went wild. Plain clothes police rushed the stage. Shots were fired. Cube and the boyz ducked out the back door of the auditorium, into their waiting bus.

It was in Phoenix, midway through the tour, that things between Cube and N.W.A. went south. Jerry Heller was the group's manager. An industry veteran, he'd been involved in the careers of Elton John, Pink Floyd, Journey, The Guess Who and others during the seventies. Heller met Eazy in a studio, the kind of place where you pay to have your own records pressed. At the time they met, Heller has said, Eazy didn't have a bank account—he was paying for everything in cash, small bills in a paper bag. Heller has refused to be interviewed for this article, as have the other members of N.W.A.

In Phoenix, Heller came to each member of the group with a contract to sign and a check for $75,000. "He said, if you sign the contract you get the check," Cube remembers. "I'd been talking to Pat and she had asked me a lot of questions I didn't know the answers to about publishing, royalties, how much I got on Eazy's album, all that kind of shit. And I was like, 'I don't know.' I felt like an asshole 'cause I didn't know.

"So Heller give me this contract, and I said I want a lawyer to see it. He almost fell out his chair. I guess he figure, 'How this young muthafucka turn down this money? How dare you turn down this money.' It felt fine, 'cause I knew I was gonna get my money sooner or later. I just wanted things done the right way. I saw everybody else in the crew all happy and shit. Everybody else signed. But I wouldn't. I told them, 'I wanna make sure my shit right.' I remember them niggas laughin' at me. They was like, 'Yo! $75,000! If that shit ain't right ain't nothing right!'

Cube got an accountant and a lawyer. Figures showed that the tour grossed $650,000, and that Heller kept $130,000 for himself. Cube went home with $23,000. By fall of 1989, the group's two albums had sold 3 million. Cube either wrote or co-wrote about half the raps on those albums. He earned $32,000.

Next, Cube's representatives asked Heller for copies of Cube's contracts. After repeated calls—the last one from Cube's Moms, Heller finally complied.

"Turned out there was only one problem," Cube says. "Muthafucka forgot something—my muthafuckin' signature!"

Cube's people entered into negotiations with Heller for compensations due, and eventually a settlement was reached. Cube told the boyz no hard feelings. He loved N.W.A. like a muthafucka. He would have stayed. He just couldn't work for Heller, not after this, no more.

Heller painted it differently. "The real reason that Ice Cube left NWA was that he was incredibly jealous of the notoriety and success of Eazy-E," Heller has said. "He wanted to be Eazy-E. He was jealous because not only is Eazy a key member of N.W.A., with a successful solo career, he's also the president of his own record company. Eazy-E is a major star and a successful businessman. Ice Cube isn't."

Cube's response: "How can I be jealous of a muthafucka with no talent? He got money. I'm gonna have talent *and* money."

And now he has Street Knowledge, his own record label. At the moment, he's producing Yo-Yo. Next comes Del. "Me and Pat decided, yo, let's produce groups, sign them to our production company, sign the rights over to major labels and basically get paid. Find some good talent, and everybody get money. I want to see everybody get paid, 'cause there's enough out there for everyone. We gonna do ours the right way."

After Street Knowledge gets off the ground, he says, he wants to invest in real estate. "I want an apartment complex, muthafuckin' shopping centers. I want all kind of shit. I want houses that I can rent out, or you know, fix up. I can take a house that need some paint, some work, put ten grand in the house, and make forty or fifty off it. Yo. That's what I'm into. I don't want to rap forever. I'll rap for as long as people like me. I'd rather go out as a champ than as a loser.

"Right now I'm working hard, struggling to take care my shit, make sure my shit together. I figure I'll do this from like twenty to twenty-five, so that from twenty-five to the graveyard, I'm taken care of, you know what I'm sayin'? Won't have nothing to worry about. I could travel. Hire a muthafucka to have my headache. So, you know, it's no problem for me right now. You got to take care of business. Everyday, I get something done, so I don't have to think of that shit no more. Man, nobody can take care of me better than me. Nobody. Not even my Moms."

Saturday night, 80 mph in the right-hand lane, Cube on the fly to Anaheim, T-Bone riding shotgun, J. Dee in a car following behind. Show tonight. Showdown.

The clouds began gathering yesterday. A reporter from the *Los Angeles Times* had been interviewing a new group, Above the Law. Fare of the Ruthless posse, another Jerry Heller production, the members of ATL are from Pomona, the suburbs, but they used to come to South-Central to go to rap clubs. The leader of the crew is Cold 187um. His DJ is Go-Mack. Their first album, *Livin' Like Hustlers,* has sold 140,000 in its first week. "Murder Rap," the single, is Number Two on the *Billboard* rap chart after one month.

The reporter had interviewed ATL, then called for a comment from Cube. This morning, the *Times,* page F8:

GO-MACK: Ice Cube? How he going to write about somethin' he never been through? Ice Cube had a good house, he had both a mother and a father with him, he got bussed to a good school. The only rowdy people he knew was us. He was writing about us. What you hear on N.W.A.'s album, we was in it while he was only writin' about it.

ICE CUBE: New jacks from Pomona should only talk about the 10 Freeway.

This afternoon, after Cube read the article, you couldn't tell whether he was upset or not. His face rarely makes a move. But Cube had gone over to Tone-L[o]c's house to talk it out. He visits Tone sometimes, Ice T too. They older, he says, they know shit he don't. One thing he doesn't know, or maybe it doesn't occur to him, is that if the L.A. *Times* guy hadn't stirred things up by asking Go-Mack what he thought of Cube, hadn't asked Cube for a retaliatory comment, none of this would have come to the surface. At any rate, there's some serious dissin' goin' on in the 'hood, and Cube needs some advice. As Cube sees it, Jerry Heller's in control of some people's minds. Cube's got no cause with the members of N.W.A. or any of its posse. They go back to the days. Where these new boyz come off talkin' that trash?

As it happened, ATL's manager, LayLaw, was over to Tone-L[o]c's. He's an old friend of Cube's, one of N.W.A.'s posse. They shot some hoops, talked. Cube said, "Yo, man, what up with your boyz? We have to talk this shit out."

"Come backstage at the show," said LayLaw.

Now Cube pulls up behind the Celebrity Theater, pays the white money taker, parks. On the bill tonight are ATL, Low Profile, Compton's Most Wanted. Joining ATL for a few numbers, giving it a little push, will be several members of N.W.A.

Cube has gotten tickets for Yo-Yo, Chill, DEL, Jinx, a few others. He wants the Lench Mob in effect in Anaheim tonight.

Cube collects his backstage pass, goes through security. T-Bone comes in with him. J. Dee gets left outside with two dozen other unluckies. The bouncer has never heard of the Lench Mob. All he knows is J. Dee don't have a green pass, so he ain't getting in.

Backstage is thick with homeboys—everybody got a pass. Different posses, different gangs, girls in tight dresses, the rapper Michele'le with her tits and squeaky voice. Two Gs in leather jackets have shown up with some tired white hoes. Another G noses around the hallway with a video cam. Instamatics flash. Homeboys strut and flare, throw hand signs. Once upon a time, gangs fought for turf. Then there were gangs for drugs. Now there is the posse, suckin' on a nigga's ass, down for they boy, they meal ticket. Every few moments a beef erupts and homies are holdin' other homies back. The security guys put out the brush fires. They throw people out; they get back in. One moment, a guy laughin'. The next moment, he's coppin' a war pose. Everyone wants to fight. Everyone's having fun.

Cube sends T-Bone to find J. Dee a pass. He stands alone a few minutes, surveying the scene. He spots Go-Mack, the rapper who dissed him in the newspaper.

"Yo man, what up?" Cube says.

"You got something to say to me?" Go-Mack says.

Suddenly, backstage goes silent. All eyes are on Cube.

"Yeah, man, I do," Cube says. "Let's go in your dressing room and talk it out, man to man."

Back in the hood, everybody knows: no one goes into hostile territory himself. Wherever you go, you take a partner. If there's a beef in the air, you take your whole crew. Even if you don't plan to get physical, even if there's the slightest possibility of trouble, you take backup.

Unfortunately, at the moment, Cube is solo. J. Dee is stuck outside. T-Bone off somewhere trying to get J. Dee in. The rest of the Lench Mob hasn't finagled its way backstage either. The only one left is a little Jewish guy, the reporter who has been shadowing Cube on and off now for several weeks on both coasts. Cube had earlier complained that the reporter was following him everywhere, even to the bathroom. And now, as Cube follows Go-Mack into ATL's dressing room, the reporter attempts to do the same. This time he's stopped at the door by a bouncer. Cube goes in alone with Go-Mack. The door closes with a resounding click.

Cold 187um jumps Cube first, a sucker shot to the head. Then Go-Mack piles on, as do the others, a hail of fists. Cube starts swingin' and wind-millin', trying to back up outta there with his life. Somehow he manages to stay on his feet. He bursts out of the door like an animal chased, disappears into the crowd.

Much later, Cube is found in the back of the theatre. T-Bone is with him, as are J. Dee, Jinx, Del, Chill and the others, all of them sitting around him in two protective rows. At rough count, there are 500 paying customers in the 2,000 seat auditorium. Cube wants to see ATL perform.

He sits through a couple of numbers, watches while Ren and Dre and his other old homies from NWA come on and do guest spots for their new boyz. They march and skip across the stage; they spew and hurl and rhyme. They pump their fists in the air. The crowd roars.

Then the sirens sound the beginning of ATL's Number 2 hit, "Murder Rap," and the crowd goes wild. Cube stands. It is time to go. His posse stands too.

Cube lingers a moment, scanning the small, centralized mayhem down in front of the nearly-empty house. His bottom lip is still oozing blood—a chunk of skin has been taken out, most likely by an oversized gold ring. His eyes are bloodshot, his knit cap is skewed to one side, a button is missing from his shirt. He thinks about his album, soon to drop, and about his tour, soon to bust a move. He thinks about Street Knowledge, about Pat and Yo-Yo and Del, about being 46 years old with fourteen platinum albums, about owning apartment complexes and shopping centers, about taking what you want, 'cause nobody giving up no ass.

"Fuck all y'all," he says.

Rolling Stone, October 4, 1990

My Man Desmond

"Desmond? Desmond!"

"Sir?"

"Is the cook on strike?"

"I don't believe so, sir."

"Well, find out, will you?"

"Very well, sir."

Desmond, the butler, replaces the wine in the silver bucket, covers it properly, takes one step back from his place near the elbow of the chairman of the board. He stands straight, stares ahead. For one brief moment, he looks as if he'll faint.

His eyes bulge, his face goes white. His lunch of sushi rises on a tide of bile, and he feels the way he felt the time he turned on the gas oven, forgot about it a while, then struck a match. He was found semiconscious on the floor by His Excellency, the boss, who asked, "Will you be all right to serve the *poulet?*"

That time, Desmond excused himself, changed his shirt, shaved what remained of his mustache, cooked and served the meal. This time, things are not so simple, and as the sushi subsides, as the one brief moment becomes the next, Desmond regains his hold on the situation, on this dinner without food, and his eyebrow, his left one, arches an eighth of an inch, and the little broken vessels around his nose crawl to the surface and rage. *Willie!* he thinks. *You bloody toothless Frenchman! You arse! You . . .*

Desmond snaps, pivots, glides slew-footed across the priceless Oriental rug in this grand dining room of the house, barely disturbing the air.

The chairman's inquiry having been registered, the room fills once again with the nonchalant syntax of empire building, the intraplanetary arbitrage that occasioned the chairman's flight this day on the Concorde and his delivery straight here, to the upper seventies and Park Avenue, to this eight-story Stanford White town house, to this Regency-period dining table. . . .

"—representation," the chairman is saying. "I think we need a name or two from the United States and—"

"What names do we need?"

"Well, if we're going to do a newspaper-related deal—"

Reaching the other end of the table and then the end of the room, Desmond pauses, turns, bows. He is a handsome Anglo-Irishman of Swords, North County Dublin. Aristocratic cheekbones, middle-class broken nose, white hair, mustache, a bit of extra girth. Frozen there midbow, he is the picture of the perfect butler, composed and invisible, a Victorian android in a black coat, black tie, striped pants, silent and serene, totally without attitude, exuding not a hint of the foment in his brain, his absolute ire, his homicidal thoughts about Willie, the cook.

He completes his bow, backs through the door to the serving kitchen, erupts.

"Bloody effing hell! What is that fool doing? Where are the string beans? Where are the chops? Where is Willie?"

He grabs the telephone, one of thirty-one in the house, and buzzes the main kitchen, one of three. No answer.

"Oh, Christ!" exclaims Desmond to the temporary houseboy. "Do something!"

Desmond Gorges doesn't need this. Doesn't need this at all. Just this morning he nearly fell off a ladder changing the light bulb in the entryway. Just this afternoon he had a row with Wendell, that southern midget who used to be the houseboy. Wendell's coming back to town. He wants to stay in the house. The man actually used to call the pay phone on the corner and invite whomever answered to come home. Until Desmond found out and fired him.

And just this moment, with Willie in absentia and the chairman, a prominent British banker, getting hungry, the central air conditioner is leaking from the ceiling, sending drops of water along the length of frayed wire that powers the bare bulb in the back stairway. The repairman has been called; he's coming quick as he can. He told Desmond to cut off the juice.

Desmond, of course, couldn't do that. The chairman, the Concorde, the chops.

In theory, this house could blow at any moment.

Desmond buzzes the kitchen again.

Willie answers.

"Where have you been?" Desmond hisses into the phone, his voice rising in pitch from butler to scullery maid. "What have you been doing? Gumming the neck of your Haitian girlfriend? Come on, Willie! The dinner!"

After a time, a long time, a time long enough for Desmond to pour a spot of eighteen-year-old Macallan scotch, knock it back, and pour another, the dumbwaiter squeaks slowly upward. Desmond stands, transfixed.

A solitary drop of sweat splashes his collar. It is a handmade shirt, white cotton. On the left side of the chest is stitched the Gorges family shield, a blue whirlpool on a silver background. *What sort of life is this for a Gorges?*

Desmond is one of the last of the Gorges, descendant of a "great family whose members played distinguished roles as courtiers, soldiers, colonizers, and men of affairs, friends of poets and counselors of kings," according to *The Story of a Family through Eleven Centuries,* a history of the Gorges written by one, Sir Raymond.

Here he is, sixty-one years old, Desmond Patrick Hamilton Gorges, a man with two university degrees and three languages, a former journalist, PR man, bon vivant, and Tunisian hotelier, who traveled the world on his family name for fifty years until the luck and the money finally ran out. Desmond P.H. Gorges, butler. A man descended from Sir Ferdinando Gorges, founder of the Plymouth Company, lord proprietor of Maine; and from Arthur Gorges, author of *The Olympian Tragedy,* the first epic poem written in the English language; and from Lucy Gorges, Dean Jonathan Swift's "blue-eyed nymph"; and from Dickie Gorges, one of the three rogues who stole the Irish crown jewels at the turn of the century. Desmond's maternal grandfather was P. J. O'Farrell, an Irish robber baron during the industrial revolution. His Uncle Willie was William Cosgrave, the first president of the Irish Republic. Desmond has pictures in his scrapbook of his time with London's premier gossip columnist, Nigel Dempster, at the bullfights near Cadiz; with Sean Connery in Sotto Grande; with Patrick, earl of

Lichfield, the aristocratic photographer, on the steps of Shugborough Hall, the earl's 365-room house.

No, Desmond was not born to butle. In fact, during the first ten centuries of Gorges history, not one Gorges ever worked. It finally happened in his grandfather's time, when one of the Gorges became a solicitor. The whole affair was so frightfully scandalous that it kept Desmond's father engaged, his entire life, in nothing more strenuous than shooting, hunting, and bad-minton.

Ten years ago, when Desmond went into personal service and moved to New York "to make my fortune in the New World, as it were," his brother discovered his circumstance and phoned him all the way from Sydney.

"Is it a penthouse you're working in?" inquired Kevin John Beres-ford Gorges.

"Yes," said Desmond.

"Well, why don't you throw yourself off?"

At the moment, however appealing, such action is not under considera-tion. The dining room is on the third floor of the town house, and besides, the beans have arrived. Truly, on the scale of potential disasters, late dinner isn't so bad.

At his first position, with the Saudi ambassador in London, Desmond felt himself briefly suspected in the theft of grandmother's jewels. At movie mogul Sam Spiegel's in New York, he once brought in pretzels instead of bagels, which doesn't seem like much, unless you knew Sam Spiegel. At another employer's, he had the misfortune to inform madam that sir was off in the Hamptons in a house that madam didn't know they were renting. And once, he served the chairman a caviar other than beluga. Compared to that, late dinner is nothing.

Truth be told, something's always threatening to blow; in the complex minds of the rich, the famous, and the petty, disaster—real or perceived— usually looms, and it is just these times that bring out the best in a butler, or bring out the worst. Desmond, much to his own surprise, is known as one of the best.

Daily the calls come from other butlers, from other employers. Staff is needed for a party. Can Desmond set it up? What about so-and-so, Desmond, can I trust him? Old madam's getting tired of vegetable puree, any suggestions?

"To me, Desmond is the greatest," says Philippe Abela, a Maltese butler who was formerly in the employ of Lady Elizabeth Anson, cousin to the queen. "There is nothing Desmond cannot handle. There is no disaster too big."

The wife of a once-prominent New York political figure is equally glowing: "Desmond is the best person to work for you. He isn't really like a servant. Most of them have tantrums or heart attacks at the least little thing, like if you tell them an hour before dinner that the party is downsizing from ten to six, or the other way around. He's like a great friend who helps you out."

A gentleman's gentleman, a butler's butler, a rogue's rogue, Desmond Patrick Hamilton Gorges may have written his own first references, and he may have risen to his present stature "by faking it as I went along," and he may see butling as "the most ridiculous situation I've undertaken in my entire life," but the fact remains that he's come to America with a product to sell, and it's selling. In addition to Spiegel, he has worked for Marvin Davis; Xenon owner Howard Stein; the former Mrs. George Barrie, presently Mrs. Buzz Mossbacher; many others. And each time he has changed situations, usually on friendly terms, his price has gone higher.

At current market value, you can have Desmond—his Irish twinkle, his arrogant air, his touch of class, his family tree, his whiplash tongue—for $90,000 a year, including bonuses, but not including food, clothing, shelter, and medical, all of which must be provided. Or rather, you can have Desmond for slightly more than that. You'll have to lure him away.

Call it "Jeeves Meets Horatio Alger" or "Desmond Does New York," call it anything you want, but remember, too, that once upon a time, not too long ago, Desmond was down and out and living at day rates in a cubicle at the New York YMCA. Desmond knows very well that the money comes from performance and that the money is easily cut off.

At this very moment, the most important thing on Desmond's mind is that the chairman is here and dinner is late, and worse, now that the dumbwaiter has arrived, Desmond has learned something else: the string beans are cold.

With no other choice of action, Desmond takes the beans onto his silver serving tray, backs through the door from the serving kitchen, glides serenely into the dining room to his place at the elbow of the chairman of the board.

"—dynasty," the chairman is saying. "If we looked at it more as the kind of person we want and then go out and see if that kind of person is available—"

"I mean, you don't really expect that kind of person to find a deal, only to bring one—"

"*Haricots verts,* sir?" interrupts Desmond.

"Oh yes, thank you," says the chairman.

He lifts the spoon and fork, scoops, stops. "That's garlic on the beans!"

"I don't think so, sir," Desmond says.

"You know very well it's garlic. Christ, Desmond! Take them away!"

Another day at the town house.

The chairman is gone, and so is madam, the chauffeur, the chef, the French maid, the regular houseboy. This is condition normal for Desmond. The chairman jets in for a few days here and there, as does madam. Sometimes the house is occupied by directors or clients of the company. Most of the time, however, Desmond and the regular houseboy are here alone. It may appear that Desmond has it easy, but after four years with the chairman, Desmond still goes to pieces every time he calls. In some ways, Desmond's job is like a fighter pilot's. Most of the time, he hangs around on standby. But when the phone rings, it's war.

There are an estimated three hundred to four hundred butlers currently in service in the New York area, and, according to Glenn Scott of the Pavillion Agency, the demand is getting greater all the time. Scott, whose agency placed Desmond in his job with the chairman, says Desmond is the highest-paid butler in New York. Currently, he says, rates for full- or part-time butlers start as low as $400 a week. One-night rates range from about $75 to $200. Depending upon circumstance, employers also furnish cars, apartments, clothing, or partial allowances for these items. And some butlers find their loyalty rewarded in the form of cash bonuses, airline tickets, expensive gifts. One prominent New Yorker, upon the recent death of her longtime butler, had his ashes inserted into a tree and planted near his favorite spot in Central Park.

Ivor Spencer, proprietor of the world-renowned, London-based Ivor Spencer School for Butlers, says he has placed more than three dozen butlers in America in recent years. With the Reagans, the return to glamour, the fattening of the yuppie, butlers, says Scott, "are becoming the new status symbol. We have way more requests than qualified people to fill them. It used to be people bought a Rolls when they made it, but now, you got to get a butler. It's impressive. And once you get one, you kind of get addicted to him."

Indeed, in some ways, Desmond is much more like a drug than a servant. The chairman keeps a ledger on a table in the front hall. In it he puts his comments and commands:

Book of matches in each ashtray
Always twelve lite beers in icebox
Leave dressing gown in bathroom
Silver water jug!
Lay out dressing gown and slippers in my office
Chinese manservant for Mrs. Carlisle
Always lay out dressing gown on bed, on an angle
Return videos
Only eight lite beers in icebox!
Slow down and do things properly
Smell in halls
Always beluga!
Where is my dressing gown!

Despite the appearance, Desmond is more than just a servant. Given his responsibilities, he's more like the president of a small company. He oversees a food budget of more than $60,000 a year, a laundry budget of $500 a month, a flower budget of $250 a week, a staff of six that costs the chairman well over $200,000 a year. There are gardeners in residence nine hours a week at $30 an hour; a maintenance man on call ($100 an hour), a window washer on retainer ($550 a month). Workmen come regularly to service the elevator, spray for bugs, fix the security alarm, fix the air conditioner. With or without the chairman, the house has a life of its own.

At the moment, late in the afternoon with the chairman gone, that life is considerably sweeter, and three butlers pass the time in Desmond's room.

Ricardo (a pseudonym) is sitting on the convertible sofa bed, beneath one of the Gorges family heirlooms, a 1725 George I looking glass worth at least $25,000. Ricardo is currently in service to a prominent name, excused for a few hours while madam is at the health club.

Next to him, William (also a pseudonym) sits akimbo in a Georgian chair. William is on his way from his day job with a prominent name to his night job with a prominent name we'll change to Mrs. Smith.

Desmond sits across from his guests on an ergonomic desk chair, the kind with a rest for your knees. The back door is opened to the garden. Birds sing, cement cherubs spit water into a pool. Inside, Ricardo is spitting bile.

". . . and then, when I finally got the cats there, the airlines wouldn't take them because it's cruel."

"Well, you had the tickets for them didn't you?"

"Of course!"

"What are you talking about?" asks William, always a little behind.

"The cats, you ninny," says Desmond. "You know madam over there has to have her pussies wherever she goes."

"Yes," says Ricardo, continuing. "I said to the airlines, 'These cats have been traveling for ten or twelve years in the aeroplanes,' and the airlines said, 'Yes, but not with us. This airline is very much concerned about animals.' "

"What's to be concerned about?" asks Desmond.

"I don't know," says Ricardo. "These cats have been everywhere. They even had root canals the other week."

"Where are the cats going?" asks William.

"To Palm Springs."

"Oh, yes," says Desmond. "Madam *looooves* to go there, doesn't she?"

"I think that she has many lovers who are tennis instructors," says Ricardo.

"Beautiful men!" says William.

"Yes," agrees Desmond. "And madam looks like the back end of a cab, as we say in Ireland."

"And when she's in bad humor, which is most of the time," adds Ricardo, "she is really a bitch."

"Desmond, what do you think I should do about Mrs. Smith?" interrupts William, obviously troubled.

"What do you mean, what should you do about Mrs. Smith?"

"She never likes the food," says William. "You see, the problem is she stuffs herself with cheese and biscuits. At five o'clock the so-called maid gives her a big plate, and she eats all that, and she eats chocolate Sneekers, as well."

"Your problem, William baby, is that you haven't got old madam where you need her. You haven't got her here," says Desmond, twinkling and pointing to his palm.

"They have to complain! You have to understand, the old madam doesn't have anything else to do but complain. She's been that way her whole life. What is she going to do, cook her own dinner?"

"You think I should shave my mustache?" asks William, all at once changing the subject.

Desmond looks at William, looks away, looks back—a finely constructed double take. Then he laughs. "No wonder I make so much money!"

Friday evening, late dinner, upper 50s near Second Avenue. Desmond is free-lance butling. There are eight attending the party—neo-Yuppies fresh out of college, all on their first jobs, dressed up in evening clothes, sitting around a trendy glass and brass table. The host wears blue contact lenses on his brown eyes, braces on his bottom teeth. His accent places him somewhere in Long Island. This is his first experience with a butler. When Desmond arrived, and the boy shook his hand and addressed him as "sir," Desmond was so startled he almost reacted.

Now, each of the guests holds a little book entitled "How to Host a Murder." This is a "Murder Party"—the nineties answer to dinner conversation.

"You know," reads one of the guests, "I once heard him say, 'The only way you'll bring the railroad into the valley is over my dead body.' "

"He strongly opposes anything of the sort."

"He's in financial trouble, you know . . ."

Desmond and the temporary houseboy are corralled behind a plastic three-fold door in the kitchen, standard size for a one-bedroom apartment like this, three feet by three feet with a dishwasher. Between the fillet in the oven and the bisque on the stove, the temperature is well over ninety in the airless space, but Desmond is making close to $200 for six hours work, a set-up from the agency. No matter how much he makes with the chairman, he's a man, remember, who once found himself in residence at the YMCA. It is something he's learned late in life—the necessity of a work ethic. He'll take the extra when he can.

While the actual work required tonight is easy, the pain is registered in Desmond's face: Nothing moves an aristocrat in quite the same way as a par venue. For starters, the kid has no bread knife, no serving tray, no napkins. The silverware is stainless steel, the wine is all wrong, the bisque is terrible.

One of the guests has served himself salad onto his dinner plate. Another has held up her champagne glass for a helping of red wine. Come time for coffee, the host has instructed, Desmond is to call the deli on the corner and order up cappuccino in paper cups.

Desmond, of course, says nothing about all these "abhorrations," this lack of preparation, this lack—we might as well say it—of any semblance of class. Once, Desmond Patrick Hamilton Gorges would have walked at the sight of sweet white wine. Now he's pouring it for twenty-year-old Americans. Standing in his place near the elbow of the party's host, he is the picture of the perfect butler, composed and invisible, a Victorian android in a black coat, black tie, striped pants, silent and serene, totally without attitude, existing only to serve the whims of one Mr. Parker and his guests for this Murder Party, addressing all as "madam" and "sir."

"You know," says Desmond to the temporary houseboy, his brow beaded with sweat, "I do try to do my best. And I've never done that before in my life, anywhere, even when I was doing proper things. I'm sure the reason is the money. The *money!* And also, I guess, it's really the easiest way to do it. I mean, one spends one's whole life trying not to do anything, but it's really harder that way. It takes a long time to find that out. I've never been anywhere where people weren't just trying to avoid doing work. Getting through the day without doing anything.

"Maybe sort of for the first time in my life, I've decided that I should be successful. I mean, now, I've defined the world in a sense. Before, I was just hiding. Even though the chairman treats me like a human being, he still treats me like a servant. But he treats me with a certain amount of respect. He pays me to be an executive. . . . The facts is, there's a kind of rapport between my present employer and myself. He knows when he says, 'I want so-and-so,' he gives me the honor of not having to explain anything. He expects me to complete a task, to get a job done, to do it on my own. No one has ever expected that of me. No one! I like it.

"Of course," says Desmond Patrick Hamilton Gorges, "I do wish I'd chosen banking."

Manhattan, Inc., September 1987

Fifty Grand in San Diego

Rising with effort from the overstuffed couch, the baby secured in the crook of his mahogany python of a limb like an M16 rifle at shoulder arms, Stacey LaShun Ducksworth, thirty-two years old, lets out a bone-weary sigh.

"Lordy, Lordy, Lordy," he declaims, his eyes rolling heavenward, toward the rough-textured plaster ceiling of his eight-hundred-square-foot duplex condo, secured as of now with a rock-bottom, interest-only loan, due to balloon in three years, another of the myriad swords of Damocles hanging over his head. He sniffs the air in the vicinity of his daughter, Addison Leann Ducksworth, ten months old, dressed in a pink-and-white Ralph Lauren onesie, a hand-me-down from friends. His nose wrinkles; his face contorts into a mock-hideous mask.

"Let's go, Jackson," he orders the three-year-old. His voice is a deep baritone with a hint of Mississippi Delta twang—the only giveaway his tendency to drop his *th*'s in favor of *d*'s—a commanding voice, perfectly suited to a man who rose to the rank of sergeant after only four years in the Marines. With the index finger of his right hand, in which he holds Addison's bottle, her blankie, and a plastic toy bird from McDonald's, he pokes off their thirty-two-inch Zenith television, bought on special seven years ago at Costco, as was much of what they own. Did you know that Costco even has real estate agents?

"Let's go, Jackson," he repeats. With children, unlike marines, you *always* have to issue an order more than once. "Let's go, buddy," a tad louder this time. "I need to change your sister. Are you ready for your nap? Come over here and let me blow your nose." A decade ago, he was ducking bullets in Mogadishu.

Jackson William Ducksworth is sitting on the floor with a forty-eight-piece farmyard puzzle, just completed. He was born two weeks before his mom was supposed to start her internship at a naval hospital, a requirement for her master's degree in social work. Despite the emergency C-section, she reported ten minutes early on the scheduled day. That is her trademark; she is *always* ten minutes early. (Another trademark: proving people wrong. Like the time her father told her she would surely flunk out of college if she transferred to be closer to a man he had yet to allow inside his house.) Back in those days, during her internship, Tuesdays were the worst: work from 6:30 A.M. till 3:30 P.M., home to breast-feed Jackson, night classes, studying, bed. At the time, of course, her husband was the breadwinner, making nearly $50,000 a year as a manager of a Footlocker. His closet is still full of vintage Air Jordans. She herself owns exactly six pairs of shoes. Every time she buys a new pair, she donates an old pair. That is her personal policy. The kids do the same with their toys.

Like his mom, Jackson has asthma, which seems to open him up to every bug and flu that comes down the pike. He's been sick now for several days—most of the last several months, if you add it up. They've begun seeing a homeopathic doctor, $400 for the first consultation. They put it on the credit card, even though they vowed to use it now only for emergencies, like the $600 vet bill after their cat was attacked by a coyote, or the brand-new KitchenAid mixer—in black to match the self-timing coffeemaker—that Stacey Lashun Ducksworth bought recently as a surprise for his wife, Heather Marie Peterson Ducksworth, even though they can't afford it.

Twin rivers of viscous green snot flow from Jackson's nostrils, puddle above his lip. From the moment he awoke this morning—if you can call it *awoke,* because he never really went to sleep, he was really up all night, on and off, off and on, waking up his little sister, calling for his mommy . . . *Mommy . . . MOMMY! . . .* even though Mommy was immobilized with a pulled muscle in her back and needed her rest so she could go to work the next day—from the moment he woke up, asking again for Mommy, who was already gone, Jackson has been cranky and high maintenance, couldn't walk down the stairs himself, couldn't go potty himself, knocking over the orange juice that he insisted on having in a big-guy glass instead of his sippy cup, asking every minute for a tissue, literally every minute, *Blow my nose, Daddy, blow my nose,*

Daddy, the word like an exclamation point, a direct order, a command from on high . . . Daddy . . . *Daddy* . . . *DAAAAAAAD-DYYYYYYY!!!!!* . . . the inconsolable trill of a three-year-old, which, every parent discovers, is the true age for terrible twos.

"Jackson," he implores, as calmly as he is able, "put the puzzle back in the box, please."

"I very sick, Daddy."

"I know you are, buddy." Another sigh. "*Please.* Put the puzzle in the box. You need your nap. And I need to get some studying done. Remember? My classes?"

"Your *college* classes, Daddy."

Jackson sticks out his tongue and coughs—phlegmy, pitiful, an Oscar-caliber demonstration of the truly dire state of his health. His skin is eggshell white with a squirt of brown tint, like what they do with ceiling paint at Home Depot. He has his mom's pointy noise and prominent chin, her smallish down-turned eyes, her impish stick-out ears. His head is covered with a woolen thatch of tight yellow ringlets, which his daddy—who once did a six-month stint as the ship's barber on the USS Essex—trims painstakingly, using a comb, scissors, and electric trimmer, one little ringlet at a time.

Jackson sticks out his tongue and coughs again for effect, the tiny pink tongue of a baby doll, curled at the edges, *cough, cough, cough,* and then again, *cough, cough,* and then, suddenly, he is seized by a fit of real coughing, deep rattling hacks that rack his thin and insubstantial body, touching off in turn a fountain of tears, huge crocodile tears that flow down his cheeks, mingling with the snot and the drool, splashing upon the Pergo floor that his enterprising parents installed as part of their do-it-yourself home renovation, financed by Visa, a rare and impulsive bit of live-for-today thinking that nearly ruined them.

"I . . . don't . . . like . . . Mommy . . . *working!*"Jackson shrieks, a sob set between each word, his fists balled, tears and green snot flying everywhere.

Now Addison spits out her pacifier and sputters a few times, like a chain saw trying to start up, and then she catches, and she is off, too, a full-blown cry, causing Jackson, the ever-indignant former only child, to cry even harder, the two wailing now in stereo, an ear-shattering duet of inarticulate woe. . . .

And then Jackson throws up on the rug.

Another day in the condo, part of an oldish, modest development on the out-skirts of San Diego called Carefree San Carlos. Along with its eight hundred square feet, the Ducksworth family holds title to half of a carport. Unfortu-nately, due to the placement of the communal washer and dryer in their par-ticular allotted space, they can't pull either of their vehicles ('99 Nissan Altima, '03 Honda Odyssey) inside. One load of laundry costs eight quarters. Shun does approximately twenty loads a week. Everywhere he goes, he is always scrounging for quarters. You'd be surprised how many people say no.

Postnap, the kids are on the couch, watching Disney's *Pocahontas*—a fine example of feminine pulchritude by any standard, cartoon or otherwise, espe-cially to a guy whose last night out with his wife, sans children, was roughly twenty-one months previous, a Saturday. They saw *Man on Fire*.

Jackson appears to be feeling a little better today, thanks possibly to the homeopathic pellets he's been taking every two hours, eighteen dollars for the tube, though if you tell him he seems better, he will look up at you with doleful brown eyes and declare: "I not better. I 'till very tick"—a little problem with consonants he will no doubt outgrow, provided he quits sucking his finger, which could lead to many complications, among them a need for orthodontia, speech therapy, even corrective surgery, another of the many worst-case scenarios rattling around inside his parents' skulls. He is sit-ting on the far north end of the overstuffed couch in his customary pose: his finger—the right index, which he says is chocolate flavored—in his mouth, his sippy cup of apple juice by his side, and under each arm his faithful Momos, two identical furry monkeys that go everywhere.

Baby Addison is propped at the south end of the couch, which was pur-chased at Macy's during the Ducksworths' more frivolous days before chil-dren, along with the matching overstuffed chair that they both hate (only the cat uses it) and an armoire to hold the television, as was the style before entertainment centers came in. Addison's lids are heavy, her pink rosebud of a mouth is working her pacifier—a continuous, juicy *suck suck suck* reminiscent of Maggie on *The Simpsons*. Her face and onesie are splotched with orange-yam and green-pea baby food, the healthy, natural kind from Trader Joe's. As often seems the case in two-child families, the male Ducksworth child resem-bles his mom, the female her dad, both in looks and temperament—two little copies, the sexes playfully reversed. Round-faced and big-eyed with a small, flat nose and twin topknots of fine chestnut hair, Addison puts you in mind of a darling baby bear cub—clearly her papa bear's child, though much lighter in complexion, the same eggshell white with brown tint as her brother. (Family joke: Heather's white genes are very dominant.)

At the moment, Stacey LaShun Ducksworth is sitting cross-legged on the floor, trying his best to gift-wrap a largish cardboard box, his thick fingers struggling with the intricacies. For long stretches of time, he stops what he's doing and stares upward, lost in *Pocahontas*. Back in Soso, Mississippi, population 382—where he went to church three times a week with people who spoke in tongues, where he ran the hundred-yard dash in ten-something, and where he was the first black guy ever to be elected Mr. West Jones High School, quite the Romeo despite the fact that his parents wouldn't let him go to dances or movies—everyone called him Stacey. It was only after he got to boot camp at Parris Island (where no one bothered to advise him of the long-term benefits of surrendering $1,200 of his pay in order to qualify for college-tuition benefits under the GI Bill) that he started going by the name Shun. It's supposed to be pronounced the same way as the word meaning "to avoid someone deliberately." Most people, however, pronounce it *Shawn*. He never corrects them. It's as if he's not quite committed to that name, either.

Years ago, when he was still in high school, he asked his mom, Ora Lee Ulmer Ducksworth, how come she named him Stacey. The prettiest of three girls (and seven boys) born to a sharecropper and his wife, Ora Lee was a stern disciplinarian, taken sometimes to using a tree switch, a hairbrush, or a piece of model-racing-car track to emphasize a point with her two sons, Stacey and Jermaine. Shun's father, Norman Ducksworth, no middle name, is the son of S. L. Ducksworth, who was also a sharecropper. No one ever knew what the S. L. stood for. S. L. himself said it didn't stand for nothin'. Shun sometimes wonders: Maybe it stood for Stacey. Shun's dad was a short-distance truck driver; for many years, he delivered chicken feed. He brought home a good enough living to move his family, after the second was born, from their double-wide trailer to a proper brick house on a street inhabited mostly by white people. They still live there today, hard by Big Creek, across the main highway from a little community called Cracker's Neck.

So why did his mom name him Stacey?

"Saw it in a book and liked it," explained Ora Lee in her husky, molasses-slow monotone, the prettiest girl in Soso in her day, perhaps, and still a looker at fifty-three, but never a woman of many words. The name LaShun came from his girl cousin LaShunda. Their family is close: two sisters and a brother who married two brothers and a sister. Twenty-two aunts and uncles in all; uncounted cousins.

Within the cardboard box that Shun is wrapping is a Kitchen-Aid Artisan Series five-quart mixer. His wife, Heather, is one of those women who bakes. A lot. *A lot.* And *goo-ood*, as they like to say in Soso: two syllables, musical, emphatic, like in church. Sugar cookies. Peanut-butter cookies. Chocolate-chip cookies that Shun swears put Famous Amos to shame. Maybe too *goo-ood*, Heather jokes: Over the course of the last four years, she has been as large as a size 16, though she's presently down to a 12. Ironically, in the months leading up to her first pregnancy, she was down to her smallest ever, size 8. She knows a lot of women like that. They lose all their weight, they're looking the best of their lives, the rose in full bloom. And then, bingo, they're pregnant. They never see their waistlines again. Compared with some of the women she knows, Heather looks pretty small.

Anyway, Heather's a great baker. It's something she and Jackson do together; Shun and Addison do their part by eating whatever is baked. While Jackson is a problem eater (and a problem pooper, truth be told), Addison, like her daddy, never turns down a morsel of food. Previously, Heather always used this eight-year-old Proctor Silex hand mixer she'd taken from her mom, MaryAnne Burroughs Peterson, who is sixteen years sober and smokes her fair share of cigarettes but doesn't do much baking. Two months ago, in mid-batch, the old mixer blew. There haven't been any homemade cookies since.

In a way, buying this mixer for Heather—the gesture itself, the thought behind it—is a perfect metaphor for Shun. As the saying goes, it's what you *do* that counts. Heather and Shun met eleven years ago on a fix up. He was stationed at Camp Pendleton. His marine buddy, a white guy, knew of a busload of high school chicks from Rio Vista, California—a farm town in the central valley north of Oakland—who were coming south to San Diego for spring break.

The first time they met, first impression, Heather had no interest in Shun, who at that point was going by the nickname Duck. Part of the reason was his race, though she was by far the most liberal of her friends, the only one who ever hung out with Mexicans, which she did a little too much for her mother's taste, tooling around at all hours in her VW Beetle, primer gray with mismatched front fenders, chugging Zima and smoking Newports.

Let loose upon Pacific Beach in San Diego, the spring-break revelers, with their detachment of marines, slogged from bar to bar, re-enacting their own version of an MTV reality show. Because she was eighteen and away from home, Heather got a tattoo, a small crescent moon at the bikini line. As the night wore on, this guy Duck—with his sweet smile and courtly manner, his chiseled shoulders and rock-hard biceps—began to look more and more attractive.

When they got back to the motel room, Heather recalls, "People were passed out all over the place, and I'm trying to sleep with Shun, and he's, you know, rejecting everything I'm trying. He's saying, like, 'No, you're too drunk. We'll do it another time.' And I'm like . . . in shock. That never happened with guys at home. So we go to sleep and we wake up and he's still there, which was, like, another shock, and I was like, 'I didn't think you'd stay.' And then we all went to Disneyland and he came, too. We took the bus and he drove in a car. The whole way, my friends, they all kept saying, like, 'Oh, he's just a one-night fling.' But I was like, 'No, I think I really like him.' "

Upon returning home, Heather told her parents, "I'm in love with a black guy," adding, "I know he'll make a great father." Her own father, Bob Peterson, a descendant of Okies, sells poisons and pesticides to farmers for a living. Sitting in the smoke-filled living room of his ranch house, Bob Peterson looked like he didn't know whether to shit or vomit or do both at the same time, as Heather recalls it. The following Christmas, Shun made his first trip to Rio Vista. He stayed at Heather's friend's place; Heather brought him back a plate of food. Nowadays, everyone gets along just fine. Shun has never begrudged Heather's dad his initial feelings. "Some people just need time," he says.

What Heather needs, Shun has decided, is a mixer. More specifically, a KitchenAid Artisan Series five-quart mixer. She's spoken of it many times. Price: $300.

There is just one little problem.

Ducksworth regular monthly expenses, including mortgage, utilities, homeowners' fees, gas, insurance and other auto expenses, health insurance for the kids, credit-card minimum payments, preschool tuition, cell phones, Costco, Trader Joe's, regular groceries: $3,298.

Special expenses (projected, upcoming), like extra food for Shun's parents' visit, road trip to Rio Vista, gifts, clothes, personal items: $700.

Amount of money Heather has taken home in four weeks as a part-time, substitute social worker at two different area hospitals: $3,800.

Amount of money in the Ducksworths' savings account: $0.

Seven months ago, the impossible happened: Stacey LaShun Ducksworth, Mr. West Jones High, was fired from his job. He'd worked for Footlocker for seven and a half years—almost ten if you include the years during high school. Though his store was the fifth-highest producer in the San Diego area, his superiors took issue with Shun's work on several counts, some of which he could have controlled (recruiting more people into the Footlocker management system, keeping more up-to-date with paperwork, cracking the whip harder on employees) and some of which he could not have controlled (the lack of square footage at his store, leaving no room for inventory, which continued nevertheless to arrive in daily shipments from two different sources, piling up everywhere, causing Shun to feel very much like Mickey in *Fantasia*, fighting a flood tide of bewitched and overpriced athletic shoes).

With the job, of course, went the health care. Also into the latrine went the deal for the new house. They'd been days from closing: three bedrooms, two baths, a washer and dryer, a yard . . . they'd searched for more than a year. Luckily, they were able to persuade the buyer of *their* condo to shut down the deal, which was also about to close. At first, the guy threatened to sue.

Selling price of an eight-hundred-square-foot duplex condo, two bed-rooms, one bath, some renovation, twenty-five minutes from the Pacific Ocean: $323,000.

Within days of Shun's dismissal, Heather had him on unemployment. Though he'd sobbed via cell phone on the day of his firing, by the time he got to the condo he was dry-eyed, and he has remained so ever since. For the next six months, he received a check for $781 every two weeks. Meanwhile, Heather increased her part-time hours at a clinic run by a pair of married chiropractors; she did the books and also baby-sat their son. The Ducksworths also refinanced their condo, folding in all their debts (car and motorcycle payments and $20,000 on three credit cards), lowering their monthly nut considerably.

After looking for work with disappointing results, Shun realized that he was never going to find the kind of high-paying job he needed if he didn't have a college diploma. In Shun and Heather's estimation, you need at least $100,000 a year to live comfortably in California. To command that much, you need a sheepskin—or preferably, in today's America, two people with sheepskins. Their course was clear: Heather would go to work full-time; Shun would take care of the kids and go to college at night.

Now, for the first time since sixth grade—when he started his first job, at one of the chicken houses his dad delivered to—Shun is unemployed. More to the point, he is a kept man, dependent upon a woman for his very subsistence. "I feel like I'm the female," Shun says in his deep baritone. "It's like, Can I go buy this? Can I go do that and stuff? I asked her, 'Am I gonna get an allowance or anything like that?' "

Heather looked at him like he was crazy. Wives know how it works. Back when he was making the money, working fifty-five or sixty-five hours a week, Heather never thought twice about buying a new duvet cover at Bed, Bath & Beyond—provided, of course, that it was on sale. "Both our names are on the checking account," she told him. "It's your money, too."

And so it was that Shun decided that he was going to buy Heather a KitchenAid Artisan Series five-quart mixer, the kind she'd always talked about, the kind she really wanted, the kind she would never have bought for herself. Though he didn't say it out loud, and though he didn't even think about it this way until he was asked—like his mother, whom he resembles, Shun is not a man of many words—the reason he really wanted to buy the mixer for Heather wasn't just that he was hungry for some of her chocolate-chip cookies. It was just, well . . . he wanted to let her know how much he loved her and the kids, how much he appreciated her and stuff, how sorry he was that the Footlocker thing worked out the way it did, sorry that he let everybody down. The truth of the matter is that he and Heather had known it was coming. The district manager had warned him to shape up. He had offered to let Shun step down to assistant manager. But Shun was determined to make it. He wasn't going to take a pay cut, no way. He went to Home Depot and spent his own money on shelving for the stockroom. Heather helped with the backlog of paperwork. In the end, of course, it was useless. When Shun first called Heather to tell her the horrible news, the words he chose were these: *It finally happened.*

To find the mixer, Shun turned to his computer, an old Dell wedged between the wall and his side of the bed. Over the next few days, Shun spent a considerable amount of time searching on-line, most of it during the children's afternoon naps, the only free time in his day, time he might have better used studying for one of the four finals he has coming up this week—sociology, psychology, criminal justice, and history—or writing one of the two term papers that are due, one of which he's actually finding pretty interesting, about the history of segregation in his home state.

At last he found it. A black one just like she wanted. "Refurbished, like new, with only a couple of small scratches." Cost: $174. "They had some older ones that were less money, but I knew she'd love it," Shun says. "I was like, *Wrap that bad boy up.*"

And then Addison woke up screaming, which in turn woke Jackson. In his haste, Shun forgot to click the option for gift wrapping.

Another day, same scene: the condo, the couch, the clock on the wall with Roman numerals, battery powered, *tick tick tick*, the gurgling of the eighteen-gallon aquarium, the water algae-green, the fish sluggish (two danios and a large tiger barb named Jake). Looking down from above the couch is a poster-sized watercolor portrait of a woman holding a rose, titled *Imperfection*. Shun painted it during his tenure as president of the Art Honor Society at West Jones High.

Shun and the kids have just returned from a brief outing. Jackson is on the floor, playing with his toy cars. When he's feeling well, as he is this afternoon, he is bright, engaging, cuddly, amusing. No hint of the demon seed of the days and nights before. Shun worries sometimes that Jackson has a split personality, that he's manic, hyper . . . *something.* He doesn't like to eat. He wakes up at night shrieking for his mom. Whenever he doesn't want to do something, he complains that part of him hurts—his foot, his tummy, his head. It's as if he enjoys being sick, weirdly craves it. Shun listens to the mothers on the playground, albeit from a distance. Every kid seems to have something these days, a *diagnosis.* Heather tells him his fears are unnecessary; she got her bachelor's in childhood development. She has further advised Shun that Jackson is perfectly fine, a normal little boy who gets clingy and moody when he's sick, who doesn't listen, who loses control. *Hello? He's only three! Of course he doesn't make any sense.* Heather would like Shun to go a little easy on the Sergeant Daddy routine. Choose your battles, she suggests. Does Jackson really have to eat that one last bite of hamburger before he's allowed to watch *The Doodlebops* on television?

And then there is Addison: good-natured, low maintenance, her chin slick with drool, *suck suck suck.* At the moment, she is suspended upright in the sling of one of those round plastic activity-center thingies, an ExerSaucer by Evenflo. Each of the brightly colored protuberances that Addison can push, turn, slide, or toggle makes a different musical noise. She pushes and pokes the buttons, delighted. Again and again and again.

Shun is sprawled on the couch, watching *The Tyra Banks Show.* Three finals down, sociology paper completed (a comparison of the number of doctors' offices versus liquor stores in rich versus poor areas of town). His history paper, due tonight, is awaiting a final proofing by Heather. Also up tonight: a five-minute in-class presentation on his paper topic, followed by a final essay. The professor is an older black man who lived through the days of segregation in central Florida. Shun likes and respects him. Though he enrolled in college to get a diploma, he is beginning to understand what is meant by *getting an education;* he can feel his horizons widening. The professor was vague about tonight's essay prompt. All he would say was that they couldn't study. That is fine with Shun, because he doesn't have any time to study. And no inclination, either. He is pooped. Whipped. Beat. *Assed out,* as they say in the Marines. After tonight, no classes again for six weeks. *Ooo-rah.*

Since Heather is supposed to take cookies to Jackson's school tomorrow, Shun has planned to give her the mixer tonight, when she comes home from work. He has removed it from its hiding place in the carport. Gift wrapped, complete with red ribbon, it sits next to him on the sofa as he watches Tyra Banks.

The camera zooms close, framing Tyra's sparkling eyes and milk-chocolate décolletage. Tyra looks good. *Goo-ood.* Maybe it's just boredom, whatever, lack of anything better to focus on, but, Heather complains, Shun is always horny. "He would like it every single day," Heather says. "Three or four times a day would be okay with him. Every time he touches me, or looks at me, or just brushes past, it's always like, 'I wanna have sex.' But I'm like, 'Could you please just get that out of your mind for a minute? Because I'm tired and I have a headache,' or whatever it is at that minute. Just leave me alone. And then when we finally *do* do it, it takes me much longer than him. And then he's always like, 'Well, if you give it to me more often . . .' and I just laugh. Sometimes, you know, I tell him, 'Go downstairs and take care of yourself.'"

Just then, the sound of a key in the door. The knob turns. Shun checks the clock: 3:35.

"Mommy!" trills Jackson.

"Mmmmmmmmm!" gurgles Addison.

Heather steps into the condo, hangs her keys on the hook, puts her purse down on the table. Hands on hips, she takes stock: Shun sprawled, Tyra on TV, a load of dirty laundry sitting on the overstuffed chair that they both hate, the cat sleeping on top. She gives him a look.

"Surprise inspection, huh?" There is a guilty sound to his voice, even though he has nothing to feel guilty about, unless fantasizing is a crime, in which case all married men are guilty.

Heather kneels to hug Jackson, who is wrapped around her knees. She is wearing the new pants she bought the other night at Old Navy, marked down to $6.97.

This morning, as she was driving to work—the commute, she is finding, isn't so bad if you leave yourself enough time—Heather was doing a lot of thinking. After a month at the two hospitals, she is still a part-time substitute. The good news is that she's jumped right back into her field as if she'd never left; her superiors agree that she is doing an excellent job—always ten minutes early, *i*'s dotted and *t*'s crossed, comfortable with the patients in a hospital setting, familiar with available resources. She is working just under forty hours a week now, making roughly what Shun was making before he was fired. It still isn't really enough, but at least it's steady. The bad news is that she's already been turned down for a full-time job because she doesn't speak Spanish. People are telling her to stay positive: Something will come up.

Driving through the traffic, sipping from her Starbucks mug, Heather contemplated going back to school to study *español*. She used to speak it with her friends' parents; how long could it take to relearn? But then she thought, *You know what? If I'm gonna be the one providing for the family, maybe I want to be making a little more money than I am now. Maybe I want to be in a different position than I am now. I've always wanted to go to medical school. That's really, like, my dream. Why should I be standing around taking orders from doctors all day when I'd rather be one? Originally, I thought I'd wait until the kids were older, but maybe I could make it work now instead of waiting. I'm only twenty-eight. After eight years of training, I'll still be young enough to practice for a pretty long time. . . .*

Before Shun was fired, everything had been perfect. That's really how Heather felt. Upon completing that first internship, the one that started two weeks after her C-section, and then another one the next semester, she was awarded her master's degree. And then she made a big decision: She would stay home and raise Jackson, who would be her only child.

As the months went by, however, Heather's heart began to change. She'd always wanted a girl. Having one kid was *so* great. How much harder could it be with two? As she always did with one of their home-improvement projects, the first thing Heather did was go out and buy a book, *How to Have a Girl*, by J. M. Young. Per usual, Heather worked diligently toward her goal, keeping charts of her temperature, checking regularly the viscosity of her mucus, eating healthy foods, the works. Shun helped, too.

And they know exactly when it happened: Heather called Shun to tell him to come home from work immediately. It was the only other time in his life that Jackson has been left with a baby-sitter.

The next thing she knew, Heather was waking up each blue California morning with two kids in the condo, and it was good. She'd make plans for their day, go to the park, to museums, do the errands and the laundry, clean the house, no problem. She loved it. She loved her kids; she was part of their lives every minute of every day. And best of all, she was the absolute queen of her domain. She set the rules, the schedules, the agenda. Everything was totally under her control. It was awesome.

But then again, she had also gotten to the point where she was kind of wanting a little more time of her own. Time away. Time to be herself, to further her goals, of which there have always been many. She hated being this helpless woman who needed a man to support her. Because Shun was on commission—as manager, along with his salary, he drew a percentage of sales—his check varied from month to month. She never felt really secure. As the family bill payer, she was always juggling. "Our credit cards were our best friends," she says ruefully.

Even when Shun was in his heyday with Footlocker, Heather never really felt as if they had a cushion. She is not one to complain; she doesn't have a lot, she doesn't need a lot, she's never been one of those women. But truthfully, she never felt as if she could buy herself anything, either. Granted, with Jackson, she bought every little baby and toddler thing you could possibly buy. That didn't last long. Fifty grand just didn't go very far. Luckily, they'd bought the condo at the right time, in 2000, for $132,500. (Though when they bought it, it felt like a huge rip-off.) It has more than doubled in value in six years. But that is money on paper, not money you can spend. They lived okay, didn't deprive the kids of anything. But they never spent anything on themselves. She bought nothing, really, no makeup, no new clothes, maybe just a pair of sweatpants from the Gap on clearance. Shun cut his own hair. She had her hair cut only every six or eight months, never had it highlighted like her friends. And pedicures: Oh. My. God. *Pedicures.* How she loves them—the foot massage, the vibrating chair, the lush feeling of total self-indulgence. If she had money, she would get one every week. *Every* week. *That* would be success to Heather. That's how it would feel to her, a thirty-dollar pedicure every week. That and a new place to live, of course, their own house, not too large, say eighteen hundred square feet—a place where more than one person could go potty at one time. And a little bit of travel maybe, as long as she's on the subject. She grew up thirty-five minutes north of San Francisco. The first time she saw the city, she was sixteen. Total list of places she's been in her life: Oregon, Mississippi, Texas, Arizona. She'd love to go to the East Coast. To New York. To Maine. To New Hampshire. She'd love to see the leaves change.

Maybe when I'm a doctor I'll make enough money so we can do some of that stuff, she thought to herself, commuting to work, applying lip gloss as she inched along the exit ramp. And then she thought, *One thing's for sure: I'm never gonna not have an income again. Not after what happened this time. I'm too anal for that. I need more control.* And then she started thinking about medical school, about where she might go, how she might pay for it, how it would play out . . . and that's when it hit her: her student loans! College and grad school: $45,000. She's supposed to start paying them off this year. Oh. My. God. *Note to self: apply for extension of forbearance, due to economic hardship.* At 2 percent interest, why hurry?

Now, in the condo, home early from work, meaning fewer hours this week, less money, Heather spies the gift-wrapped box on the sofa. "What's that?"

Shun raises an eyebrow. "Something for you."

She takes a seat in the glider rocker. He sets the heavy, cube-shaped package on top of the ottoman. She looks at him archly: "It's not a KitchenAid, is it?"

Totally busted: "You're smarter than the average bear."

"You keep asking me to make you cookies," a slightly condescending tone, *you big galoot.* She pulls off the wrapping paper, confirms her suspicion. Her lips tighten with disapproval.

"But not just any KitchenAid," Shun sings brightly, *ta da*, playing the pitchman, trying to keep the applecart upright. "It's . . . a *refurbished* KitchenAid."

"Refurbished?"

"Like new."

"From Overstock.com?"

"Amazon."

She turns the box over, reading each side. Some of the writing is in *español.*

"Why are you trying to read the box?" Shun asks, annoyed. "I just told you where it came from."

"I wanna know what *color* it is," she snaps back.

"It's green. What do you think? It's harvest gold."

She opens the top. "It's black," she says, obviously tickled.

"To match the coffeemaker." He aims his face toward hers, seeking eye contact: "Just like you always wanted, right?"

Now Jackson comes over to inspect the box. Heather removes the mixer. It is a huge thing, sleek and black, as if made from the same material as a stealth bomber. Heather pats her son on the butt with a cupped palm, lets it linger there. "With this machine, Jackson, you could make cookies all by yourself."

Jackson's face crumbles. "I don't *wanna* make cookies by myself!"

She pulls the five-quart bowl out of the box, places it on the cradle. An upbeat, mommy voice: "All you do is put everything in there and then press the button. It's simple."

"I don't wanna make cookies by myself!"

At last she meets her husband's eyes. "Thanks, Shun."

"Sure, babycakes." He gives her one of his big, big smiles.

But then he notices. Something's not right. She doesn't look happy *or* thankful. Not one bit. "What's wrong?" he asks.

"I thought we weren't gonna get each other any presents."

"It was cheap."

"How cheap?"

He straightens himself, voice deep and confident. "The *original* price was $300. I got it for $174."

She eyeballs him. "That's not cheap."

"How much you wanna bet?"

"One hundred and seventy-four dollars." She pronounces each word clearly. "On a *mixer*."

"Yeah . . ." he says, his tone uncertain. "On a mixer for *you*."

"My hand can do $174 worth of mixing."

"No, you can't."

"Yeah. I *can*."

"Mommy?"

"Yes, Jackson?"

"Can we make cookies now, Mommy?"

"Not right now, Jackson." She puts the KitchenAid back in the box. "Mommy's gonna go take a shower."

Bedtime now, one month later, 9:00 on a Sunday night. There are two bedrooms upstairs in the condo and one full bath, small enough that you can spit in the sink while sitting on the toilet. All of the Ducksworths are wearing their jammies.

Jackson is in the master bedroom, eleven by thirteen feet, playing on the computer. Everyone else is in the smaller room that the kids share, Jackson's big-guy bed along one wall, Addison's crib along the other. For the past three weeks, while Shun's parents were visiting from Soso, Heather and Shun were sleeping here in the kids' room, on a queen-size AeroBed. On the penultimate night of their exile, the AeroBed sprang a leak. They all four awoke on the floor.

Addison is playing with toys, which means putting first one thing in her mouth and then another. In a couple of minutes, she will pull herself up by the crib's leg and start making her way via handholds around the room—a sign she is almost ready to walk. Next household project: childproofing. It will be the last time. Shun had the snip a few months ago.

As part of their childproofing efforts, Heather has ordered something for Addison's crib called a bumper. It serves the same purpose as the padding around a goalpost. One side effect of the cruising stage is a lot of falling down. Addison has two big welts on her forehead; Heather keeps making nervous jokes about somebody calling Child Protective Services, which is what she sometimes has to do in her capacity at the hospital. Included with the bumper, which was ordered online, is a matching dust ruffle, another of the many and varied household necessities that Shun doesn't understand the need for—as if that mattered. To install the ruffle, the crib had to be virtually disassembled. That job was his.

Now Heather is bent over the reassembled crib, tying the little ribbons from the bumper around the slats. Shun is on his knees, folding laundry, putting it away in drawers. As she works, Heather is talking about the future, a subject she very much enjoys. Heather is a planner. She wants to know who, what, where, and what time—as far in advance as possible. She wants to put it on her calendar, in ink, so she can be certain of what to expect next; in this way, she can be sure to arrive her usual ten minutes early. Shun is just the opposite. Invariably, when they're driving somewhere in their Odyssey minivan, on a longish trip, there will come a moment when the kids will finally be asleep and Heather will ask, "Where do you see yourself in five years?" Shun always has the same answer: "Don't bother me while I'm drivin'."

So, tying the bumper to the crib, Heather is talking about *her* vision of the future, this one involving possible renovations to their condo. A washer and dryer would make life easier; it's disgusting to wash your clothes in a machine where strangers' underwear has been. Another idea is to finish the attic; some people in their complex have built lofts up there, adding to their square footage by nearly 50 percent. The only problem: You'd need a ladder to get to it.

"I'm thinking that might not work," opines Shun, folding one of Addison's little shirts with his big hands, laying it carefully in the drawer.

Heather shrugs dismissively. "In two years, I wanna move out of here anyway. Three tops."

Shun looks up at her from his place on the floor. There is a hurt expression on his brown, papa-bear face.

"What?" Heather asks, clueless.

"There you go again," he says.

"What do you mean?"

Shun looks at her, not sure how far to push. For the most part, these last few weeks have been pretty okay. School was out; his parents were here to help take care of the kids. It was good to see them, especially his dad, who'd had a heart bypass two months before Shun got fired. When Norman got sick, it hit Shun hard. For the first time, it dawned on him: He was less than eight years from forty. *Man, the time really goes quick.*

Meanwhile, Heather's job prospects continue to look good. She has been subbing mostly at one hospital now, getting five full days a week. Combined with the money she makes doing the books at the chiropractor's office—the people keep begging her to stay—they are doing all right financially. And more good news: After eight months without health insurance, Heather and Shun have finally been accepted by Blue Cross, $350 a month, with no restrictions on treatment for Heather's allergies and asthma. Overall, with their restructured debt, they probably have a few more dollars in their pockets now than they had when Shun was working.

The only real negative thing that has surfaced is Shun's grades: one B, one C, two D's. The D in psychology was his second in the same course; he'd taken it previously, hoping to get a jump start on his freshman workload. The other D was in criminal justice, which is what he was thinking of majoring in, though he doesn't need to declare a major until the beginning of his junior year. The problem is, you don't get credit for D's. He'll have to take both courses again. All that time and money, completely wasted.

When Heather first went online to check Shun's grades—he hadn't shown any inclination to check them himself—she was very surprised, to say the least. There had to be a mistake. She was like, "You went every day, you attended classes, you participated in class discussions—isn't any of that taken into account?" Maybe there was some wiggle room, she thought, a point or two somewhere to be found, enough to get him up to a C, so he could get the credits and move on. E-mail your teachers, she urged him. Tell them about your situation. It's called grade grubbing, she explained—a very important part of college academics. "The worst they can do is say no," she said.

"I asked him, 'Do you wanna go back to work? Do you want to find a job?' " Heather says. "But he's like, 'No, I don't.' And I said, 'Well then, you better figure out how you're gonna continue in school, because you can't take a semester off, because then it'll take you even longer. And you can't really go to work because I'm working and we don't want the kids in daycare.' I told him, 'We all have something to hold up in order to make everything work. I'm holding up my end of the deal here. You're not holding up yours.' "

Shun's reply: "I know Heather has a point, but I think that's my problem and stuff. I know it's just a simple e-mail she wants me to write and stuff, but I still haven't done it. I don't know why. It's not that I'm putting it off. I'm not even . . . well, it's just not a priority for me. Maybe I should, you know, but I just don't. I don't feel like I should piss and moan about my grades. I feel like I should have done better, and that's it.

"I'm still committed to the college route. It's not like Heather's forcing me. It's something I've always wanted to do. If you ask me about my biggest regret in life, it's that I didn't go to college. It was just that after high school, nobody was encouraging me to go. Nobody said, 'You should really go to college.' Then I had the whole break from school, the Marines. Trying to get back into college mode was hard for me. There's a little pressure. It's tough with the kids.

"By getting a degree, I'll be able to support my family better. That is my first priority. I still want to go the criminal-justice route, but I don't want to do anything that'll be too hazardous. Like, part of me wants to be a cop. I could see myself—I mean, I wouldn't mind falling back into that whole military-type role. I would probably still be in the Marines if it wasn't for Heather; she didn't want to live that life, and I can't blame her. I could go into forensics. That's pretty cool: CSI, you know. Or corrections: I could work in a prison—though you have to literally stay in the prison for several days at a time. I can't see doing that, not right now, anyway. That's the thing—the kids. I used to work all the time, so I missed them and stuff, but I didn't really know them. Now I'm used to seeing them every minute. I'm attached. I don't like to miss out on stuff. So it's kind of like a big catch-22."

Now, back in the kids' room, Heather is staring down at her husband, upon whose dark and handsome face is probably the most deflated, defeated, wrenchingly vulnerable expression she has ever seen grace his countenance. She feels her throat catch: "What?" she beseeches. "What is it?"

He looks at her reproachfully. "You said *I*."

"What do you mean?"

"You said: 'In two years, *I* wanna move out of here.'"

"And?"

"And . . ."

"Do *you* want to be living here in two years?"

"You said *I* instead of *we*."

Dumbstruck, Heather stares at her husband of almost six years. Stacey LaShun Ducksworth: the guy who refused to do it with her because she'd had too much to drink. Her only lover since she was eighteen—though she did kiss a guy once in Tijuana, another marine, a black guy, no less, when she and Shun were temporarily broken up. It was the only other time she had known Shun to cry. *Such a good man,* she thinks. *A great husband, a great dad.* He does so many things right. He just doesn't have the—she doesn't know what to call it, the thing he's lacking. The drive to compete, maybe, the drive to be better than others, to run in front of the pack instead of in the middle. For him, it's always like, *Status quo: Great, this is working for us.* For her, it's always like, *No, it's not. How do we make it better?* Says Heather: "His purpose in this world isn't just to be a husband and a dad. You can't do everything for everyone else. You can't be okay with that. Every person needs something of their own, a goal to accomplish that doesn't have anything to do with anyone else. You have to do stuff for yourself. That's my thing: What's your goal?"

Heather smiles at him. "I'm sorry. I didn't mean to say *I*."

"Well, you did. You do it all the time."

They look at each other for a moment, considering, and then Heather laughs. "I do *not* do it *all* the time," she says dismissively, like maybe she knows she does but is not about to let on. She bends back down over the crib, proceeds to tie the remaining bumper ribbons.

Shun returns to folding clothes, putting them in the drawer, grumbling silently to himself—*Yeah, right*—as husbands do, knowing full well you can't get into trouble for things you don't say aloud.

"Who asked who first?" Shun challenges. The kids are asleep. There is a large, goofy, cat-ate-the-canary smile on his face.

"You did," Heather says, somewhat dubiously.

He looks at her with hooded eyes. "Okay, so now I'm lyin'?"

"No . . . it's just like . . . you make it seem like I came to you with a ring and stuff."

"Who asked who first?" Shun repeats.

"You said, 'If you ask me to marry you, then I'll ask you.' "

"Who asked who first?"

"So I said, 'Fine, will you marry me?' "

"Who asked who first then?"

"I asked you."

"Exactly. You asked me to marry you."

"But I didn't ask you in a *formal manner*," Heather clarifies.

"It don't matter, formal or informal. *Who asked who first?*"

"Jeez, Louise!"

"Don't bring *her* into this now."

"Fiiiine."

Long pause.

Then Shun speaks: "So tell me: Who asked who?"

"I didn't deny it."

"Exactly."

Esquire, July 2006

Volleyball Gods

"You're gonna grovel!"

"Well, ah——"

"You're finished!"

"I, ah——"

"You might as well stick a fork in yourself, 'cause you're done, bud, you are *dooooone!*"

Indiana Hov is on a rampage. Stomping his size 13s, spilling Coors on the pile carpet, rocking the whole wheelbase of a Ford Chieftain motor home. Poodle the promoter is twitching. A tiny nervous pulse at the corner of his eye. He's sitting at the dinette, behind a mound of empty cans. Hov's looming over him, shooting at Poodle with his index finger and thumb, like a kid playing guns. Only Hov's not playing guns. He's playing life. What he's shooting is L for loser, L for anyone who isn't as tall and tan and talented as he, anyone who doesn't get laid as much as he, anyone at all who can't sky high over a net and whip arm snap wrist smack palm, *wail* a 12-ounce ball so it blurs and then bounces in the sand.

This is Indiana Hov, Tim Hovland, Mr. Southern California. Six feet, five, 200 pounds. Blond, blue-eyed, perfectly jawed. Overwhelming choice for best buns on the beach. Twenty-five years old, $100,000 a year. Playing volleyball.

But he's not playing today.

"No waaaaaay!"

Indiana Hov is on strike.

"No money, no Hov" is what he told Poodle, the promoter of two-man beach volleyball. Then he told him, "Eat shit and die." Put Frick and Frack against Larry and Moe in the finals of the world championship. Put your mother out there. Hov's not touching sand. Not without double the purse and player sanction of all events. Not until you open the books on this pop stand. Say no? Righ-ti-o. You don't need Hov, he don't need you.

My beach, my girl, my way, fuck off.

"Now get the hell out of my motor home!"

Poodle isn't budging. He's just as stubborn as Hov. Last time they tangled, Poodle earned his nickname. Hov threw him into a swimming pool at a motel in Fort Lauderdale. Poodle tried to retaliate and ended up splat on his back on concrete. Someone said it reminded him of a poodle attacking a great Dane. Then, as now, on this Friday morning in September, the first day of the 1984 Jose Cuervo World Championship of Beach Volleyball, Poodle is trying to make Hov remember who's in charge. It was *his* idea to turn two-man into a professional sport. *He* created Hov. *He* created the volleyball gods. Without *him*, they'd still be playing for fun.

And besides, even without Hov, even without the other top gods, Poodle has seventeen teams signed to play in his tournament. Seven thousand fans are already in the bleachers at the Seaside Lagoon in King Harbor, Redondo Beach. And the bikini contest hasn't even started yet.

Poodle doesn't have to listen to Hov. Right now, the sponsors are behind him. They have a one-year contract with Poodle, so they have no choice. They've refused to negotiate with the players. They're backing Poodle all the way, so Poodle is staying put. It's not really Hov's motor home, anyway. It belongs to A.M.C./Renault, one of the sponsors of the tour. Hov is Renault's spokesplayer. In Hov's mind, though, he's here in the motor home, so it's his. He commandeered it because walking around in the hot sun, carrying a picket sign, doesn't suit the defending world champion.

Problem is, it doesn't suit the sponsor, either. Two hours ago, Wally the Renault rep got so pissed over the players' strike that he threatened to take the keys to Hov's Turbo Fuego. The car—like the personal appearances, per diems, flight allowances—is part of Hov's contract. But so is playing volleyball. The big boys from Renault were supposed to be flying in for this one. The motor home, the cases of Coors, the $20-an-hour bimbo in the custom bikini with Renault's logo, the ones to watch, printed across the ass—all of this was for the bosses.

But the players had to go and strike. And Wally had to phone the pale, flabby bosses in Detroit—on the very weekend that the United Auto Workers had closed thirteen General Motors plants—and tell them that the players here had walked out, too, that the barefoot guys who go to the beach for a living were marching around with semiliterate signs, shooing away fans, playing *Solidarity Forever* on a boom box.

Wally didn't dare tell them what Hov had done to Andy Fishburn. Wally had guaranteed Hov personally when he sold the sponsorship. Hov's responsible, he told them. Hov's got a degree in public relations from USC, he told them. How could he tell them now that when Fishburn, a former world champion himself, decided to cross the picket line and play, Hov had threatened to piss in his Gatorade and to fuck his wife, then hocked the biggest, greenest lugie that anyone had ever seen onto the windshield of Fishburn's car? The fact that Hov had a Renault towel wrapped around him when he did this didn't help, either.

So Wally threatened to take the car.

And Hov ran to the Fuego, kicked in the turbo and roared off, not to return until he'd hidden the car in a garage in an alley six miles away.

By the time Hov returned to make peace with Wally, to let Wally make peace with him, Wally had downed two double Dewar's and had started on the Coors. Hov took a seat in the motor home, started helping with the beers. Things were calming down.

Until Poodle came in, sat down at the dinette and said, "Look, Hov, can't we talk about this thing like adults?"

"No waaaaaay!"

Poodle's real name is David Wilk. A former PR major and student-body president at Cal State Northridge, Wilk, 34, started professional two-man volleyball in 1976 as a promotion for *Beach Volleyball* magazine. He and his partner, the magazine's circulation director, advertised a two-day event, put up $5000 in prize money, drew 30,000 fans. Following their success, they left the magazine, formed Event Concepts, went into volleyball full time. By 1984, they had built pro beach volleyball into 13 tournaments and 500,000 fans in six states, from Florida to Hawaii, with a total purse of $200,000. Such sponsors as Cuervo, Renault, Miller High Life, Coppertone, Honda and Hobie were climbing all over one another to give money, to take part.

By 1985, Event Concepts and Poodle Wilk were gone. Poodle the promoter was hanging up on long-distance calls from a national magazine. But the tour is still on, handled now by Group Dynamics, Inc., of Santa Monica and Tokyo, a proven international PR concern. The tour has been expanded to 15 dates with the addition of Hyannis Port, Massachusetts, and Wildwood, New Jersey. The total purse has been raised to close to $300,000. Depending upon whom you ask, the reason for Poodle's ouster was the players' strike, the work of an ambitious lawyer or a sudden change of allegiance by the sponsors, after the 1984 season, from Poodle to the players.

In any case, the strike was the beginning of the end for Poodle, the beginning of a new beginning for the tour. Although Renault is now out, Bollé eyewear and G.M.C. will come aboard, and the other top sponsors are hanging in, looking forward to bigger exposure from a more experienced firm. Group Dynamics has handled Virginia Slims Tennis and Paul Masson Marathons and Volvo All-American Tennis. The owner of the firm, Jack Butefish, was a founding owner of the Quebec Nordiques and of the International Track Association. His firm has handled accounts for Union Oil, Philip Morris and Seagram's.

It was only a matter of time before Poodle had to fall. Like a smalltime agent who found himself a superstar in a honky-tonk, he had created a monster. At first, the gods were happy: Someone was providing a crowd and a little money. Beat a pitcher of beer all to hell. But as the young years of the tour passed, the gods started realizing that they could demand as well as accept. They started realizing that two-man pro beach volleyball was more than just a game. It was the symbol of a lifestyle, the California lifestyle, the American Dream of the Eighties.

Hold a tournament and here they come, straight from the Pepsi commercial, disposable income on parade. Two together on roller skates and two more riding skate boards, joggers in Norma Kamali and heavyhanders in Speedos, BMX bicycle tricksters and Fuji 12-speeders with sheepskin saddles, each more beautiful, more tan, more blond or bunned or legged than the next. This is Southern California, Oneida of our times, capital of the kingdom of I. A place where headphones don't disturb conversations and cars never get dirty. A place where people don't care "How ya doin'?" but always notice, "Ya lookin' great!"

String up six volleyball nets and offer some money, and you can have it all packaged to go. Zoom the horizon—a powerboat race. Pan the middle distance—a regatta of sloops. Cut close to the crowd—a guy from *Playgirl* interviewing potential centerfolds. A crew from Honda making commercials about scooters. A radio jock playing Trivial Pursuit, giving away Coke visors and Frisbees as prizes. A Coppertone-sample girl rubbing some Number 2 on a pectoral. The bimbo from Renault doing her crotch-to-camera-lens back bend, telling everyone within earshot that she also writes prose, poetry and songs. A guy with a ring in his left nipple guzzling beer. A giant balloon bottle of Cuervo Gold swaying in the breeze atop the refreshment stand. Cut, cut, cut to the California lifestyle, all of it under a sky as blue as tinted contacts, on a beach as rocky-fine as cocaine, next to an ocean as stirring as a Jacuzzi.

All of it because Poodle Wilk and his partner knew a product when they saw one. "It couldn't lose," Wilk had said back in September in Redondo, at the Cuervo world championship, a time when he was happy to talk to reporters. "It's free admission. It's at your favorite beach. You've got great-looking athletes, great-looking girls who come out to see the athletes and guys who come out to see the girls. It's a day in the sun; you go for a swim, you drink a beer. It's the same thing these people would be doing anyway, but they've got a giant party going on all around them. And besides, you have some great volleyball, some amazing athletes."

The athletes, of course, never have ordered things this way. To them, the marketability hinges on the game. To them, beach volleyball is a test of strength and skill. A contest like tennis or golf, played by talented athletes. In high school, Hov was named first-team all–Los Angeles in football, basketball and volleyball. He was Southern California's Athlete of the Year as a senior, beating out football 49er Ronnie Lott. Hov could have been quarterback at Nebraska, strong forward at Houston. He could have been on the 1984 gold-medal U.S. Olympic volleyball team. In fact, he *was* on the team for a while. But the coach wouldn't let the guys play on the beach. He imposed a curfew. Then he took some of the team to Utah in the dead of winter for Eastern-bloc training techniques. Hov was training in Ohio at that time, but for three weeks, the boys from California climbed rock faces, slept in igloos, went without food. They got cold. This period was the end of Olympic hopes for Hov and several others. The newspapers called it a "personality conflict."

During the winter, Hov and some of the others play indoor volleyball in Italy. Last year, Hov was M.V.P. of that league. Playing as an amateur, on a team sponsored by a sportswear manufacturer, he made 40 grand, plus free car, meals, room, athletic-club membership. Hov's partner, Mike Dodd, also played in the Italian league for a year. Although Dodd, like the rest, grew up playing volleyball on the beaches, his first choice of sport was basketball. He played college ball at San Diego State, was drafted in the eighth round by the N.B.A. Clippers. Also on the tour are Karch Kiraly, M.V.P. of the gold-medal U.S. Olympic volleyball team, and Steve Timmons, another Olympic standout. Steve Obradovich, known as O.B., the Beast, played wide receiver on USC's 1977 Rose Bowl team. He tried out for the Dolphins.

These are athletes of some standing. Volleyball is a great sport. No one's arguing that. But the hook of the sport is the lifestyle. That's what the sponsors are banking on. That's what Group Dynamics is banking on. And that's where the gods' talents really lie. Hov and Dodd and O.B. and the rest *are* Southern California, high priests of the way Madison Avenue tells us we should live—cars and women, beach and beer, board surfers and orange pop. Hov has no books in his condo in Manhattan Beach. He has two magazines. Both have his picture on the cover. He reads the sports pages and the financial pages and throws the rest of the paper away. He doesn't own a watch. He doesn't wear shoes. Some days he gets out of bed and rides his bike. Some days he sees his broker. Some days he plays tennis. Some days he goes to lunch. Some days he practices volleyball. Some days he does two of those things. All of Tim Hovland's time is Miller Time. He'd be a great commercial.

The lifestyle, of course, is not new. The Beach Boys and Annette Funicello were telling America about it years ago. But it's only lately that it's scuffed its thongs across the continent and become an aspiration. Just the thing America needs for the eighties—a remake of *Happy Days*, set at the beach.

The root of the lifestyle is a four-by-four, ten feet high and stuck in the sand. Volleyball posts began appearing on the beaches of Southern California in the thirties, a California interpretation of a Depression-era pool hall. But the lifestyle as we know it really blossomed in the happy vacuum of the late fifties, early sixties. They had volleyball gods back then, too, amateur ancestors of the modern, professional kind. They lived in vans or under piers or at home with the folks if allowed. They made a little money picking up returnables on the beaches or slinging hash in the diners. They were the classic beach bums, later the classic beach hippies. They drove their cars onto the beach. They roasted wienies, played cards, necked. The surf pounded, the girls squealed, bongos were heard on the breeze.

But mostly what they did, along the Coast from Sorrento to Long Beach, was play two-man volleyball. They played it from dawn until dark, honing the art of the dig, the pass, the spike, eating sand for nothing more than the thrill. There was an occasional trophy, a first-prize pitcher of beer from the Sorrento Grill, a dinner from the Wharf.

Guys such as Ronnie Von Hagen, 62 open-tournament wins, never won a nickel for greatness. Von Hagen didn't drink, smoke or chase women. His parents gave him vitamins for Christmas. He lived to do nothing but play volleyball. Yet, a half mile from the beach, nobody knew his name. He couldn't have cared less. Von Hagen and the rest played to keep center court for the next game, to feel the hard throb of being best.

These days, the volleyball gods sweat only for money, for the hard throb of being paid, being recognized, being loved. Top players are watching the stock market and investing in real estate. They're negotiating personal-appearance fees with sponsors who want to beefcake up their images. Like the old-timers, they don't have jobs. But they aren't living on returnable RCs. They're living on purses and interest and per diems. Hov is no Moondoggie. His condo isn't made of palm fronds.

His world view may be. He bets his dick, "no small wager," that "70 percent of the people out on the beach know me. Maybe even 70 percent of the whole South Bay know me. When I started wearing striped trunks, everybody on the beach bought striped trunks. I switched to plaid and now everybody's got plaid. I own the beach, me and Mike and Karch and those guys. We own the beach. We're like gods, fuckin' gods, *fuckin' goooooods!*"

But hear Hov's declaration and you detect a little grit in the ego. This is why he and the rest of the major gods struck the Cuervo world championship, why they tried, and eventually succeeded in, ousting Poodle. As Hov and the rest know well, they may be recognized in their little world; they may be making money and setting trends in swimwear. But their lives aren't like Jimmy Connors's. They have their flights to tournaments paid for, but they always go coach. They get some free meals now and then, but usually from a local diner, The Kettle. A few of the local bouncers know them, but they still have to stand in line in L.A. Hov and Dodd rate free cars, but none of the rest do. Of the 70 to 100 top professionals, only a dozen do nothing but play volleyball. The other ones have jobs. Not that the gods care that the other ones work. More to the point, it makes them look bad. How much credibility is there in beating a waiter and a house painter in the world finals?

What they want is to see volleyball become a real professional sport. They want management that can get them *Life* magazine, ABC Sports, millions of dollars, instead of *Volleyball* magazine, a German documentary, thousands of dollars.

There is a chance, as years pass, that the gods will get what they're after. One day soon, perhaps with the help of Group Dynamics, ABC will find the beach and America will discover that many of the best players in the country weren't even on the Olympic team, that they were down the Coast an hour or so from L.A., playing two-man for money. And when that happens, when more than just the cultists know their names, gods like Indiana Hov will know that they sat out a world championship for good reason.

For now, though, Hov and the rest will have to wait and see. They'll have to be content with excelling at the lifestyle. For now, says O.B., the Beast, they'll have to be content with "getting to know an astronomical amount of people and everybody knowing who you are . . . keeping your name in the papers . . . having all these people watching me with my shirt off, jumping high and hitting hard, entertaining them, showing them how this game should be played. . . .

"We might not have the illustrious careers of tennis players," says O.B., the oldest god at 30. "We don't get to travel around in Rolls-Royces; we don't get rental cars or penthouse suites. We're still kind of rough and vagabonds. . . .

"But still, basically, without volleyball, I'm just another good-looking guy."

"I'll bet your neck is pretty sensitive. Like, if I did this, you'd get goose bumps."

Indiana Hov feathers a finger down the girl's neck. She arches her shoulder and purrs, then pulls away.

"I know who you are," she says.

Hov smiles ultrabright. Scrapes a toe. "Yeah. I'm Tim Hovland."

"You're the one on those commercials for———"

"I'm a volleyball player. A professional."

"Oh, yeah, that's right. My little sister has your picture in her room. She's in love with you. . . . Those other guys—they're players, too, right?"

The girl is pointing to 12 large humans who line a wall in the bar, loom there like the skyline of Century City. They are here on Wednesday night, two days before the Cuervo championship, following an important meeting to affirm their commitment to the strike. The meeting started an hour late, lasted 30 minutes and concluded with a resolution to go to the bar.

Outside Orville & Wilbur's, valets park the cars, and inside, it is crowded, as always, with ferns and brass and repro-antique signs and people with tans. A live band plays oldies. Three guys in the bathroom are offering free toots if you'll buy. They'll take a personal check or offer a ride to a moneymatic. Two men in ties discuss Johnny Carson. Two girls in dresses discuss at-home bikini wax.

The players have been here 15 minutes. Already they're landscaped with girls. The girls pose just so: chin raised, one foot balancing on the heel of an open-toed pump, one hand resting on a hip. They smile, widen their eyes, giggle. They throw their hair back a lot. The players stand with their arms crossed. The talk is about MTV, automobiles, cable TV, tennis, movies, going to the beach, getting wasted and, of course, volleyball. Whenever one of the girls looks away from the player she's talking to, checks to see how her friends are doing with the other players, the player she's talking to looks down, checks to see how the girl's tits are doing.

An important concept: Here in Manhattan Beach, you call them girls. Fifteen miles down the Coast from L.A., in the heart of the heart of the lifestyle, there are no women, and there are none in this bar, except, perhaps, for the older lady in a pants suit who looks like someone's mother visiting from back East. Here, a place that residents gleefully call the herpes capital of the world, "I'm active!" is a greeting and Alan Alda might as well be the Ayatollah. Men are men. Girls are volley dollies, fringe bennies or, more universally, trim.

Girls are measured in numbers. Guys don't fuck, they notch. They build numbers. A few years ago, Hov tried to count. Lost track at 300. Numbers like that require a strange sort of selectivity: This one has a good face, so she's notchable. This one isn't so pretty but has great tits, so she's notchable. This one does laundry; this one likes to cook. This one looks bad in a bathing suit but good in clothes, so she's a wintertime notch.

Notch and tell. That's the name of this game, and the girls play it as well as the guys. Singles bar at the mailbox, in the parking lot, on the sit-up board.

Any time, day or night. Sniff. You hear so many stories, you start to believe that some percentage must be true. While the gentlemen on the East Coast are whining and dining, these guys with the blow-dried hair are notching. They're notching in the toilet. Notching with a few friends watching from the closet. They're bringing home a notch, notching, passing the notch to a roommate. The roommate notches and then passes her to a third. The third guy takes her away for the weekend. This may happen more than once with the same girl. That's what they say, anyway.

Spend a few weeks out here and you begin to realize that people aren't going to restaurants or record stores to eat or buy records. They're going in search of notch. They're not running and biking and lifting for health. They're doing those things so their calves will look good when they angle their feet on the heels of their pumps. So their biceps will strain at the sleeves of their T-shirts. So the numbers on the Manhattan Beach notch exchange will be forever bullish.

Hov hunts notch on the theory of space invasion. Say anything just to enter the bubble of a girl's awareness—just to get her to focus on the product. The product has been on the cover of *U.S. News & World Report.* It's been July on a calendar. If she doesn't buy, one of the next ten or fifteen will.

Tell her her neck is probably sensitive. Ask her if she really needs to eat that whole plate of nachos herself. Offer to help her lose some calories. Guess her bra size. Ask if she'd like a drink: "May I buy you a cocktail?" And if she counters with a smirk and a line of her own, something like, "I have a daughter your age," riposte quickly with, "I'll buy her a cocktail, too."

They have some kind of style, these volleyball gods. Standing there against the wall of the bar, on this Wednesday night before the most important tournament of the season, they are an awesome group.

There is Sinjin Smith, world champion in 1979, 1980 and 1982. Great name. Lives at his mom's house, in a separate addition in the back. Trophy shelves run the circumference of the little room, the centerpieces of which are the 1979 N.C.A.A. volleyball-championship trophy—he was M.V.P.—and a king-size bed. On the back of his door is a Levi's-jeans advertisement, poster size, featuring Sinjin Smith.

Sinjin is managed by the high-powered Nina Blanchard and Ford agencies. He has modeled in *GQ, Vogue* and *Playboy,* has done television commercials for Woolite, Alberto VO-5, Coppertone and Arrow Shirts. He appeared in an episode of *Magnum, P.I.* as Tom Selleck's two-man-volleyball partner. Sinjin's body washed ashore shortly after the first station break. Two years ago, Sinjin was the billboard boy for the Milk Advisory Board. There he was, two stories tall, all over California, bare-chested in tennis shorts, with a woman draped over his shoulder. The message: MILK—IT DOES A BODY GOOD.

Jon Stevenson wears his hair like Prince Valiant. Has the most devoted groupies of anyone on the tour—an entire family in Clearwater, Florida. When Stevenson comes to town, the family puts him up at their home, feeds him, gives him a van to drive. The family has a son who wants to be just like him. The father is always saying to Stevenson, in that Florida drawl that all the players mock, "Why don't you take Jeffrey here down to the schoolyard and do some one-sets with him, give him a few pointers? Just as a favor now, hear?"

Stevenson and the other players can't stand the family. They invite young Jeffrey to parties that don't take place. They feed the mother's home-cooked dinners to the dog under the table. But they always go back.

Missing from the group tonight is Andy Fishburn, the one whom Hov will later assault with lugies. Fishburn thinks the strike is stupid, that they've come pretty far in eight years, that the rest of the players don't understand business.

Fishburn understands business. He is a project manager for Barclay Hollander Corporation, the real-estate-development firm that drained Marina del Rey and introduced condominiums to Southern California.

Fish played his college volleyball at Stanford and Yale. He looks like Robert Redford. Once, he went to Magic Mountain with his wife. Six women asked if he was the actor. He does resemble him, only Fish is prettier—upturned nose, no moles. Fish has some Hollywood in him, though. His grandfather directed the original version of *Ben Hur.* His grandmother played Maid Marian in the original *Robin Hood.*

Also absent are Gary Hooper, who works in his father's insurance and brokerage firm, and Dane Selznick. Selznick owns two surfboards, drives a chocolate-brown Eldorado, models and acts in movies and commercials. He played the medic for a team of girl football players in *Oklahoma City Dolls.*

As always, O.B. is here. He is a former world champion, and the players respect him. He is the personality on the tour, the John McEnroe of two-man pro volleyball. Wherever they go, the local press writes a story about him, even though he hasn't won a tournament since 1981. When O.B. makes a bad play, he bites the net. When he doesn't like a ref's call, he pulls down his trunks. In the finals of the 1983 world championship, he and his partner had game point on Hov and Dodd, but for some reason, O.B. felt the need to hit an easy set with his head instead of his palm. The crowd cheered. They won the point but lost the game. But people remember that head. Just as they remember the time he stopped a match, called over a waitress and ordered one of those tropical drinks with an umbrella garnish.

Dodd is talking to Karch. Both of them have new flattop hair styles. Karch is probably the best player on the tour, but in general, the Olympic players are not as good on the beach. The two-man game requires more all-round skills than the six-man indoor version. In six-man, players are specialized. There are spikers, setters, blockers. They play on a fast floor. On the beach, two players have to have all the skills, have to cover the same size court on a slower surface.

Also present are a few of the lesser gods. Under any other circumstance, they'd be rated L for loser. Earlier this season, at a tourney at Santa Cruz, two of the losers had made reservations a year in advance for an ocean-front room at the Dream Inn. Hov and Dodd had made no reservations. They landed in a motel two miles away. So they drove to the Dream Inn and liberated the room from the losers—just told them to leave. They vanished.

Tonight, this Wednesday before the Cuervo world championship, and for the course of the planning of the upcoming strike and the eventual switch to Group Dynamics, the losers are included. The cool guys are clapping them on their backs. Someone has to make the picket signs and write the press releases and find a Xerox machine. In exchange, the gods have allowed an invasion of the nerds.

The losers are loving it. As Hov and the rest of the gods engage in their various space invasions, one of the losers, 5'8", brown hair, adenoid problem, gets up his new courage of association and approaches two beautiful girls.

"How you doing, girls?"

No answer.

"May I buy you girls a cocktail?"

"No."

"I've already got a drink."

"Well, then how about some dinner?"

"No."

"Thank you, no."

"I'm a professional volleyball player. What do you girls do?"

"We work."

"Downtown."

"Oh. . . . Well. . . . Would either of you girls care to fuck?"

Mornings at Manhattan Beach belong to mothers, tan but not so beautiful anymore. They wear shorts over their scant bikinis. Their towheaded children play naked on blankets by the volleyball net. It is Thursday, the day before the Cuervo world championship. There's a group of six women rotating games on one court, four more on another, two alone on another, waiting for their game to begin. The group of six plays twice a week. The same six, more or less, have been coming here for five years for two-woman volleyball, house-wives getting together for the South Bay version of mah-jongg, bowling or tennis.

Above the courts, people play body mania on a concrete boardwalk called the Strand. They jog, bike, skate. They have deltoids. It's not like back East. There's no such thing as "You have to know me to love me." On the beach, you can't wear a bulky sweater to hide your flab. The ten extra pounds are harder to ignore. Here, there are no fat people. Here, in a town two miles square, there are, by informal count, ten places to pump iron and only one bookstore. The marquee at the Manhattan Beach Health Club advises, THERE'S A PROBLEM WHEN PEOPLE THINK YOU'RE OVER 40 AND YOU REALLY ARE. The weekly tabloid is called *Easy Reader*.

Off the Strand, a cramped line of mansions and then a sharp rise in the land. The slopes are stippled with cracker-box houses, peopled with stew-ardesses who live in efficiencies for $600 or $700 a month, salesmen who live in illegal converted garages. Lots of stucco, balconies, windows, weathered wood. Take a look inside. Just the necessities—tubes, tunes, beds. A heap of running gear in the corner. Beer and Gatorade and lunch meat in the refrig-erator. Cars are parked everywhere on the narrow streets, on the sidewalks, on the postage-stamp lawns. Except for a handful of vintage Americans and quite a few jeeps with surfboard racks, most are lifestylemobiles: Hondas, Porsches, Zs, BMers. The cars head north in the mornings and south in the evenings, back and forth from livelihood to life.

There is some industry around Manhattan Beach. TRW and Hughes are nearby, as are several refineries and a pottery factory. But mostly, during the day, the feel is deserted village. Echo of waves, hum of neon, tinkle of bicycle bell. Nice.

Soon, at lunchtime, the beach will fill with car pools of men breaking for two-man volleyball. The students will come after that, planting their surfboards in the sand, playing a few games before the waves come up, and then the men will return again about five. Most of the day, the eight courts here off Marine Avenue will be busy, as will thousands of courts up and down the Coast.

But at the moment, on this Thursday morning, the beach belongs to the mothers. They've stopped playing volleyball to sing *Happy Birthday,* give out cookies to the kids.

Nearby, Hov and O.B. are sitting in the sand. Hov is bouncing a volley-ball on his knee. O.B. is running sand through his hand. They've already decided to strike, but they're here to practice, because they figure the minute Poodle hears that they've decided not to play, he'll cave to their demands. Turn the books, the money, the whole pro circuit over to them.

The gods are used to getting their way. They surround themselves with people who will give it to them. Hov's father, who lives 15 minutes north, cooks him breakfast. His mother does his laundry. O.B.'s wife does those things for him. His family lets him work a flexible schedule in their restaurant so it won't interfere with his volleyball. Both Hov and O.B. get stock tips from fans. Two days ago, Hov bought Phillips Petroleum on a tip. This morning, it is up five points. Another fan has taken Mike Dodd under wing. Dodd's got a condo among his numerous investments in Manhattan Beach, a fortune in a town where an old house is usually demolished before a new one can be built.

Right now, though, the problem is getting up some games, and no one can help them with that. There are two college guys—amateur players, losers—sitting five feet away. Hov and O.B. would rather sit than play with them. Another god is bound to show soon.

"Jesus," says Hov, looking over at the birthday party. "These women really breed."

"Mother cows," says O.B.

"They play every Wednesday."

"Today's Thursday."

"Oh."

"Where is everybody? Nobody comes to the beach anymore."

"Yeah, everybody's working, I guess."

"I shoulda worked today," says O.B.

"Stop bitching. Taking a day off is the best thing in life for you. Only thing better is not working at all."

"I just can't believe there's nobody here. In the old days, I'd go up to Sorrento at 9:30 in the morning. Von Hagen and all those guys would be there. They'd play all day long. Play every game. Ten, 12 games. Play until dark. . . ."

"So they were stupid."

"They'd play with anybody. Hacks, girls, anybody. Just kept touching the ball. That's why Von Hagen and those guys were so good."

"Fuck. None of those guys would be any good today. They wouldn't make shit for dollars. We'd eat 'em and swallow. . . ."

As Hov and O.B. talk, a third loser joins the two others. Fifteen minutes later, there comes a fourth. They start a game.

Hov and O.B. sit.

Then Hov says, "You hungry?"

"I could eat."

"We can always come by later and see if there's some games."

"Fuck, there's nobody to play with anymore, anyway."

"Would you pose in the nude?"

"Nope."

"Not even for money?"

"Nope."

"For a quarter of a million?"

"Nope."

"Do you have a lot of money or something?"

"Yep."

By Sunday, the last day of the 1984 Cuervo world championship, the guy from *Playgirl* has enlisted the aid of the bimbo from Renault. She's had quite a lot to drink, is deviating from the written questions for potential *Playgirl* centerfolds. Her license plate, by the way, says FLASHHH. It's framed by a plate guard that says CHAINS REQUIRED. WHIPS OPTIONAL. She has a two-year-old daughter at home with a sitter. Her husband sells cars. You can look, but you can't touch. That seems fine to the correspondent from *Playgirl*. He's apparently taken her up because he doesn't want potential centerfolds to think he's a fag. The two are bounding from hunk to hunk on the outskirts of center court. Somehow, amazingly, the bimbo keeps her balance, even on spike-heeled sandals in sand. At the moment, though, she's kneeling on the edge of a blanket at Andy Fishburn's feet. Fish, the god who crossed the picket line, is not interested in being a centerfold. Last night, his wife had their first baby. Right now, he's waiting to play and win the finals of the world championship.

All around them, there's an event going on. The bikinis, the beer, the nipple rings and the regatta of sloops in the distance, the balloon bottle of Cuervo Gold sagging a bit after three days of boogie max. No one seems to care that the gods didn't play. No one seems to care that none of the semi-finalists were seeded. They gave a tournament without the gods and people still came.

In droves. Thirty thousand people over three days. All the gods could do was stand outside the fence at Seaside Lagoon with picket signs that said, WHERE'S THE MONEY? AND FUCK EVENT CONCEPTS. Occasionally, one of the gods would observe how small the crowd was this year. Occasionally, Hov would come out of the motor home to pick a fight, shoot a few Ls at the losers who had crossed the line to play. He kept saying the same thing: "Every time I see you at the beach from now on, I'm going to be all over you. You're going down, bro. *Doowwwnnn!* Every time I see you, you're dead. *Deaaaaaaaad!* You're a fucking scab for life."

Hov's father, C.O., came by to sit with Hov in the motor home. C.O., a semiretired school-supply salesman, was getting disgusted with Indiana Hov, with the strike, with Hov's rampage. "If you're going to drink, drink, and if you're going to talk, talk, but you can't do both at the same time," C.O. advised him several times. Hov's brother, a personal-injury attorney, also advised him to cool it. He figured Renault had grounds for breach of contract.

To this, Hov said, "In one ear and out the other. Doesn't register a twinkle." Then he opened another beer.

Meanwhile, the other gods milled around the entrance to Seaside Lagoon, telling some fans that "the best players in the world are not participating in the tournament today," flipping the bird to other fans who said, "What are you striking for, smaller bikinis and free beer?" A representative of the Abused, Battered Children's Foundation of Marina del Rey stopped by to pitch the players. He was offering five grand a player—minimum—for participation in his own event, the Abused, Battered Children's Pro Celebrity Volleyball Tour.

Some fans did leave when they saw that the gods were on strike. First, though, they asked the players questions and stood real close, patting their backs, basking in solidarity with the movement, in familiarity with the gods. Other fans hung around outside the fence with the players. These were mostly adolescent girls. The players said things to them like, "Hey, honey, want to suck some cock?" and "Come take a look at my Trousersaurus rex." To this the girls giggled and rubbed more Coppertone on their backs.

At one point, a fan with a bunch of cameras came by. He wanted to take their picture. The players told him to fuck off. He said, "But this is a gathering of the best players in the world in one place."

"You're damn right, bro," said one of the players. "Let him take the picture."

Conservatively, 14,000 of the spectators were on hand for the naming of Miss Jose Cuervo. The 1984 *Penthouse* Pet of the Year was the chief judge. More than a few of the fans commented that she was fat. She had a pimple on her thigh that could be seen three rows back. But the contestants weren't bad. Even the players laid down their signs and sneaked inside to watch Sylvia Adams (who said, in response to her question, that she would take a good-looking man and two cases of Cuervo Gold if she were stranded on a desert island), Beverly Bunn, Marissa Mendoza and Strawberry Frehoff compete for the $1000 in prize money. Strawberry wore a leopard bathing suit. Her aspiration, she said, was to get into real estate. She had the second-largest tits in the group, but the one with the largest had a bit too much stomach. Strawberry won the prize.

By today, Sunday, the number of gods has dwindled. The teeny-bopper trim is absent—something about two of them and a god in a shower at a party last night. The boom box and *Solidarity Forever* are gone, too. The picket signs have been stuck, unattended, into the Cyclone fence. Wally the Renault rep is home with his wife. Hov and Dodd are here, as are Karch and Sinjin and O.B. Hov still hasn't picked up a picket sign, but he has hoisted quite a few Coors. Between Hov and the bimbo, four or five cases have probably been drunk. That doesn't include last night. Hov went to Orville & Wilbur's, then left and went to a massage parlor to visit a Japanese friend, then came back to Manhattan Beach and hit two other bars, then returned to Orville & Wilbur's. Just about closing time, he hooked a notch. Her face wasn't too great; her tits weren't too great. She probably didn't look too great in a bathing suit and she certainly didn't look great in her sun dress. But she bought the product. She was notchable.

Hov really started going at the Coors yesterday afternoon, after Poodle the promoter, feeling that he had broken the strike and assured his continued position as king of the gods, had set the record straight on who was an L for loser.

It began after some of the players had realized that Poodle wasn't going to cave to their demands, that the 1984 Jose Cuervo World Championship of Beach Volleyball was going to be played without them, that someone else was going to win the $22,000 purse. When this had sunk in, a group of the volleyball gods went to Poodle and begged him to start the tournament over again, to let them play. Hov even came out of the motor home to hear the verdict.

"No waaaaaay!" is what Poodle said.

After he said that, Poodle had leaned back, fluffed his curly hair, screwed his small, dark eyes into the big blue ones belonging to Indiana Hov, Mr. Southern California. He let Hov twitch a moment, then said, "Be happy for yourselves. You stood up for your principles. Don't regret it. I stood up for what I believed in, too. I'm going to do what I gotta do, too. This strike will serve a useful purpose. Maybe after this we'll see we need each other, that we have to work together, that we can't screw each other."

To this, Hov had said, "Money talks, bullshit walks." Then he walked away. Poodle had won. Or at least it appeared that way. Hov wouldn't be world champion twice in a row, at least not this time. His sponsor was mad at him, might even file suit. And worse, Hov had heard through the grapevine that Dodd, his partner, had called the Olympic coach to discuss getting back onto the national team. Hov knew now that the strike was dead, that the players would be back out on the sand next week for the last tourney of the season, the Miller Tournament of Champions in San Diego. He knew now also that ABC and *Life* and the rest were still a dream away. It appeared, as he walked away from Poodle, head lowered, thongs scuffing, that tears were welling in his eyes, though that could have been just a reaction to the bright sun after all that time spent in the motor home.

Then, all of a sudden, Hov stopped and bellowed:

"I got it. I got it. I *goooooot* it!"

The players gathered.

"We can put on our own tournament!"

"Yeah. Like an exhibition," said Dodd, warming. "Like 'Come on out and see the best players in the world practicing!' "

"Yeah."

"All right!"

"We'll show them some real volleyball!"

"I don't know about this, bro," said O.B. "This could really piss off the sponsors."

"Fuck them!"

"Yeah," said O.B. "But what if nobody comes?"

"You don't think the fans would come see us?"

"Who the fuck will know to come?" said Jon Stevenson. "Poodle and those guys advertise for weeks before the tournaments. They spend all this money on radio and newspaper ads and stuff."

"So what?" said Hov.

"What, you think the fans are gonna get our vibes and know to come?" said Stevenson.

And so there convened another council of the gods, and so Indiana Hov's last-ditch solution was put to a vote and defeated unanimously. Even Hov voted against it. Then he went back to the motor home.

And now it is Sunday, and the finals of the world championship are about to be played without him. Hov is once again in the motor home. Only this time, he's alone.

"I don't know," Hov is saying between drags on another Coors. "At this point, I'd say Event Concepts has pulled it off. The people are going to show up because of the beach party. It's nothing compared to normal, the caliber isn't near the same, but the people are here. . . ."

"I worked very hard to get where I am. I find when I work hard, then I usually win. There has been an occasion when something has gone wrong, when somebody has played better. But that's rare. And once I lose to someone, I guarantee I won't lose again.

"Never again.

"No waaaaaay!"

Outside the motor home, on the beach, a tall man wearing a gold chain is kicking around in the sand, scoping the beer, the buns, the games. He has a folder under one arm that says GROUP DYNAMICS, INC. His name is Jack Butefish. He's making notes on a little pad. One thing he's written is discontent. Another is RECOGNITION/CASH. A third is HOV. The last he's circled three times.

He knows a god when he sees one.

Deviates in Love

Finally there's a knock at the door, and Walter drains his glass, sets it on the night table. A candle flickers in the dark; lurid shadows dance across two double beds in room 416 of the Sunset Lodge. Walter breathes into his hand and sniffs. *Well,* he thinks, *here goes anything.*

He drops his palms to his thighs and stands, grunting a bit, that noise a man makes when the files of personal history have begun to pile up around him, action resigned but not quite resolved. He looks down at Debbie. "You're sure now, right?"

Debbie watches the candle, a vaguely musky number from the knick-knack store in the mall. Tiny creases score her lips, the corners of her mouth, yet she has about her a gleam of trust and wonderment. She likes her drinks, usually fruit juice and vodka, with a straw. When she's done, she'll root around in the ice, search out the last little sip, make a loud sucking noise until someone gets irritated. Then she'll giggle, take one last sip.

"We can always say no," Walter says. "I mean—"

"Just open the door already, Walter. You're thinking too much again, remember?"

Thinking. Walter has realized lately that there's too much thinking in his life. He's found that once he starts thinking, a program of pros and cons starts to run. He compares, contrasts, weighs, frets. He replays his failures, sets up his odds. His mind begins to build traps, reasons not to do things. The night before they flew to Pensacola, Walter was in bed, covers up to his chin, trying to imagine what lay in store. A cold drop of sweat rolled across his rib cage. He reached for the phone, asked Deb, "Do you think we're being crazy?"

Walter was more than a little apprehensive about being with people who really had a lot of experience, who really had an open lifestyle. If he wanted, he could count on *three* fingers the number of lovers he'd had since 1977. Even he and Deb had never done it. They'd gotten naked one night and talked about AIDS. Then they fell asleep.

Now Walter takes a deep breath, thumbs his shin into his waistband, walks briskly to the door.

"Right on time!" he sings.

"Howdy!" chorus Ann and Michael.

Ann is wearing something like a wedding dress, white and lacy, see-through: garter belt, G-string, bustier, veil. Michael is wearing a policeman's uniform. Instead of a nightstick, he carries a two-foot marital aide. Flesh-colored, veined, and rubbery, it has heads at either end.

Walter looks at Debbie. Debbie looks at Walter. Nobody told them anything about costumes.

Down the hall is room 425, the hospitality suite for the Elite International Couples' Fantasy weekend. As soon as the deejay had put on the last record and announced, "Ladies and gentlemen, let's go party," a good many of the fifty couples registered had come straight here. At the moment, a number of them are arranged into a daisy chain. Its origin is way over there, two women on the king-size bed. It flows across the patterned spread, head to pelvis, pelvis to head, down over the carpet, a long train coupled orally, tresses and pates, arms and legs, mouths and breasts, writhing and flexing, diddling and bobbing, past the table of mixers and munchies, around a corner and through the sitting room, past a flickering video orgy, past the sofa, a red-haired man masturbating, his eyes wide and unfocused, past a woman in a gold lamé dress sleeping in a fetal position against the wall, on through the open door and into the hallway.

They are a wide assortment, people you wouldn't second-glance, ages thirty to sixty, from towns and cities from Florida to Michigan, Virginia to Arkansas. Mothers, fathers, grandparents. A horse trainer, a housewife, a state trooper, a minister, an owner of a travel agency, an executive secretary, a psychologist, a man high up in the music industry, a real estate agent, a salesman for a satellite dish company, a computer operator, a truck driver, a mail-order clerk, an employee of Oscar Mayer. Of course, what they do, where they live, none of that matters here. People in swinging like to say that when you enter the door of the orgy room, you leave your clothes and your labels behind you. You step out of your bikini briefs or your cutout bra and into a world of anonymity, a moist, dark place where your fantasies can be real.

Here, as one woman says in her personal ad in *Heartland Swingers* magazine, you can be a Horny Housewife from western Michigan, 5'4", 140 lbs, 38D, brown hair and eyes and shaved, very bi. Or a Voluptuous Nympho (39-22-34) into tight spread-wide-open bondage, spanking, nothing too outrageous or kinky. Or an Attractive, Rubenesque White Female; a Well-hung (9") Tom Selleck Look-alike; an Open-minded Couple looking for romance, variety, and good times.

In room 425, men and women traipse around nakedly in their alter egos, regular folks from real closet mirrors, toupees and wrinkles and bellies and stretch marks, cellulite and black socks, tiptoeing over limbs and bodies, dipping chips, taking pictures with Instamatics. A couple stands outside on the balmy, watching the go-cart races at the grand-prix track across the parking lot. Inside, a platinum blonde rides something that looks like a Naugahyde saddle. Attached to the seat, facing skyward, is a plastic phallus. The device can be set for rotation, vibration, or both. The record ride is five minutes. The blonde, dismounting after three, stays down on one knee, clasps her hands. "Will you marry me?" she asks the machine.

Cruising around the room, a fully dressed man shoulders a video camera. In a month or so, hundreds or even thousands of Americans will own a copy of the action this evening, courtesy of A'Mature Video Productions. For fifteen dollars they will be able to pop the video into their living-room VCRs and—after a brief warning about the content, a guarantee of the amateur status of the consenting players, and a short, poignant message about the need for political involvement on behalf of the First Amendment—the action will unfold on a room full of people in various states of undress, some wearing feathered bird masks, or capes, or leopard-skin bras, the floor littered with boas and toy cat-o'-nine tails and ripped-open foil condom packets, the accompanying soundtrack a symphony of moans and slurps and sucking sounds, the intimate, primal music of nighttime, heartfelt and abandoned, stirringly grotesque, Oh, God! Fuck me! Come on, baby!

Up and down the hall, meanwhile, twosomes and threesomes and four-somes and more pursue every conceivable conjunction, employ every lotion and toy. And, at this very moment, all across America, millions of others are doing the same. Here in the 1990s, the age of AIDS, the era of guilt and caution and remorse, a directory of swing clubs across the nation lists almost one hundred. These are the big fancy places, with theme rooms and exhibition rooms and even rooms for the night. Uncounted hundreds, maybe even thousands, are less formal, convening weekly in private homes for a door fee. Al and April,* the hosts this weekend in Pensacola, have more than one hundred couples that meet twice monthly in Nashville as the Tennessee Social Club. One of their employees heads up Personal Touch, a group of sixty couples meeting on alternate weekends. Add these to one other swing club in Nashville, home of both the Baptists' and the Methodists' national Sunday-school boards. Recently, a negative article in a local paper brought twenty-six new members to Al's club alone.

Al also sells annually more than half a million copies of swingers' magazines in all fifty states. There are dozens of other magazines like his, each one containing hundreds of personal appeals from singles and couples. Some couples only trade photos or videos. Others exchange first names and then body fluids. Variety, fantasy fulfillment, a hobby shared by man and wife, that is the notion. Shaving, Greek, Roman, gang bangs, girls' nights, light S and M, or maybe even romance—dinner, dancing, and sex. Husbands who want to see their wives with other women. Wives who want to see their husbands with other women. Husbands who want to see their wives with other men while they take pictures. Wives who want to be with several men while their husbands take pictures. Cross-dressing, sexy lingerie, Mistress Missy looking for a sex slave, no male bisexuality, please.

Until tonight, Walter's life had basically gone all wrong. He'd given up music to get married and raise a family. The day after his daughter was born, his wife was diagnosed with schizophrenia. Imagine the worst and that's the rest. Business reverses, legal problems, heartbreaks, hassles, years. Now Walter is forty-four, an optometrist with a renovated condo in a Victorian building in Cleveland. He works part-time, makes his money trading commodities. Through the years he's been into Nautilus, biking, liquid diets, rowing, jogging. A series of memberships at video stores has left him an expert in the

*Their real names and identifying details have been changed.

history of film; a series of lackluster weekends has left him a master of Trivial Pursuit. One day about two months ago, he daydreamed about hanging himself from the chin-up bar in the ten-foot doorway to his den. He could see the last spastic jerk of his feet. He was wearing his Nikes.

Now, with all the hope and spirit he can muster—with enough presence of mind to know that his life isn't yet over, that you can find more but only if you seek—he is sitting on a bed across from an erotic bride and her Village People police escort in a cut-rate motel room in Pensacola, Florida. Next to him on the bed is his good friend Debbie. She was married for twelve years, has two kids. Recently, her husband married her best friend.

"Well," says Michael, "you all aren't soft swingers, are you?"

"What's a soft swinger?" asks Walter, crunching a piece of ice.

"Soft swingers go along with everything right up until sex, and then they don't have sex," says Michael. The words seem to leave a bad taste in his mouth. Ann raises an eyebrow.

"That doesn't sound like me at all," says Walter. "I kinda want to get right into it."

"Enthusiastic, ain't he!" laughs Michael. Ann and Walter and Debbie laugh, too. Michael puts his hand on Ann's knee, just below a colorful tattoo of a bird of paradise. Ann smiles, catches her husband's gaze. It is a fond and loving exchange, twenty-three years of marriage, but also somehow carnal and new, sparks of lust and devilment dancing in the humid, salty air of the Gulf night. They hold it there a moment, and then Ann breaks off and turns her head slowly, seeking Walter.

Fairly attractive, Walter is thinking. *Not bad at all. Blond hair, always nice, and a very nice shape.* He wonders what he could see if she uncrossed her legs. Her breasts seem nice, not real large but swelling ever so slightly above her bustier. And very soft skin, so white. He wonders, *Should I do something? What should I say? I guess I could—*

Ann reaches out across the space between the beds, long black fingernails . . .

When I married him," Ann is saying, "I didn't know nothing."

"The first time I went down on her, she like to had a heart attack!" says Michael.

"I'd never had it done," protests Ann, giggling. "I was really, really dumb on it."

"I created a monster now," says Michael.

"I was basically a very shy person," says Ann.

Michael double-takes, smiles. "We'd heard of swinging on TV."

"He just asked me to try it," says Ann. "He said, 'If you try it and you don't like it, I'll never ask you again.'"

" 'Cause I never forced her into nothing."

"I'm a person, if I don't want to do something, I won't."

"Yeah," says Michael.

"You start talking around, and you find out there's a lot of people out there in the lifestyle. We met some of them, then we put an ad in a swinger magazine."

"They'd call and then we'd meet at the Waffle House or something. You never knew what you'd be getting into. One couple, the guy had just had two open-heart surgeries within three or four months," says Ann.

"And he didn't have a dick on him," says Michael. "He had an artificial dick. A good piece of pussy and a glass of ice water woulda killed him."

"Oh, Michael," says Ann, "be kind."

Michael smiles. "I like to see her with a guy that's a lot bigger than me. It just turns me on. There's just something there that gets to me. I think I'd also like her to be with another woman. She's never been with another woman. She's curious, though."

"I am curious," says Ann. "You could say I just like a lot of sex."

"That's what it boils down to," says Michael. "Excitement."

An hour or so past dawn, the sun edges between the curtains, rays of a new day filtering across rumpled clothes and scattered bed sheets, a smell of ashtrays, old beer, perspiration. Walter feels himself swimming slowly upward from deep, pleasant dreams. Michael and Ann had left several hours earlier, happy and holding hands, walking naked together down the hall to their own room. Now Walter dozes in the grainy silken waters just beneath awake. He stretches, rolls over onto his back, luxuriates beneath the sheets. He notices something, a certain morning tightness down there that he hasn't felt in quite a while. He clasps his hands behind his head, breathes deeply. He thinks of Ann, last night. He smiles.

It was he who got things started. Not very long after Ann had taken to edging her black fingernails along his knee, Walter stood up, pulled off his shirt, went for her. Michael, following, had gone for Deb. Walter took Ann's face lightly between his hands, gave her a deep kiss. They flopped on the bed.

More kissing, undressing, some hugging, and then Ann took the lead and dropped her head. They stayed like this until Walter started feeling guilty, so he found a way to kind of flip her over. They spent maybe fifteen or twenty minutes there, and then came a time when he and Ann reached a silent decision, well, okay, now let's go for regular. From above Ann, he could see Michael and Debbie, and as he labored, every once in a while he would reach over and touch Deb and give her a little massage, just to let her know he was there.

After a while, Walter noticed that Ann was starting her orgasm. He was glad she was first. All the pressure to please and perform was off his back. Her body tightened beneath him, her breathing became quicker and then shallower and shallower and then caught, and then there was nothing for a moment, a pause, a strained, constricted calm, a trembling, a teetering on the edge, and then a sudden eruption of breath and voice and movement, and that gave Walter the clue to go ahead and get his. He looked over toward Michael and Debbie, and he could see that Michael's movements were almost identical to his own, a counter beat, a split second behind. Walter could feel a rising synchronicity or something in the room, a multiplication of emotions, a rush of sounds and energy like a choral round. First silence, then the first voice, and then the second, and a resonance begins to build, a fullness, new harmonics and vibrations born neither of the first nor the second, but rather of the mixing of both, all of it welling up, filling the room. Walter flashed for an instant on his days with transcendental meditation. *Om mani padme hum,* the jewel is in the lotus. Walter was 100 percent into it. No mind games, no cares, totally immersed.

Now Debbie stirs in the morning light, and Walter opens his eyes, looks across the white sheets at her tangle of brown curls. Debbie purrs, scoots up close, her lips near his ear. "Walter," she whispers, singing like a little girl, "*Waaalter?*"

"Yes, Deb?"

"I still feel sexy."

"You do, do you?"

"Yes," she says, and then she giggles and ducks her head beneath the sheet.

"Smile, honey!" calls Al, trundling barefoot through deep sand, the camcorder riding his shoulder, appended to one eye. He moves in, fingers a button on the handle. A thick black lens telescopes, a tight electric whine. Close-up on April.

"Say *orgasm!*" directs Al. April lifts her head, squints into the brilliant day. She smiles wanly, raises the middle finger of her right hand.

"Fuck you very much, sweetheart," sings Al. He is forty-six, a bit of the handsome goofball, a bit of the Artful Dodger, a homespun cottonseed from Arkansas. He has a full head of gray hair combed back into a postmodern pompadour, squared-off aviator bifocals, cleft chin, eight-inch penis. And he has trouble. April. Here on the weekend that they've gathered fifty couples in Pensacola, there's a crisis. Yesterday, they had sex only twice. They seem to be breaking up.

It's a Pygmalion-and-Galatea-type story, Henry Higgins and Eliza Doolittle. Al's scared, a little desperate. She, on the other hand, is firm but ambivalent, in control of her facts and her future but not of her emotions. She knows she needs to take what she's learned and fly. Yet she feels like she owes him so much. Sitting on the beach with Al, she'll dangle her foot near him on the sand, tickle his thigh with her toes. He'll be so hopeful at the sign that he'll rare up and go for a hug, then push it, try to get sexy. She'll push it away. That's not what she meant.

"Have a *niiiiiice* day, dear," calls Al, and he turns and heads down the beach, preceded by his lens. His belly bobbles but not too bad, minimal damage considering he gave up jogging five years ago.

Now he comes to a stop, pans the scenery around him. The cloudless sky, the greens and blues of the warm, salty Gulf of Mexico, the fine white sand, an assortment of string bikinis, seashell-cup bras, mottled thighs, hairy bellies, motel towels, and rented chaise longues, the swingers from Elite. One group is huddled around the travel agent and his wife. They have a binder of photos and brochures from swing clubs and nudist hotels they've visited across the world. Out in the water, a man and a woman play catch with a second man's bathing suit. The naked guy bobs whitely in the chest-high waves, hands raised in resignation.

"Sharks!" yells Al. "Watch out for your dick!"

April checks the water. "That shark's gonna go hungry."

Al stays focused on the water, hoping the naked guy will make a break for it. He's lovable, Al is, a little irritating but willing to play the fall guy, an off-color comedian who's a tad too loud. He grew up in an orphanage, studied psychology in college, served in Vietnam. His life's work has been sales: insurance, solar power, real estate, and, for the last ten years, the swinging lifestyle. He's been swinging for twenty years, been married twice, says he's had more than three thousand women. In the chiropractor's office, under Frequency of Intercourse, he recently wrote "four to five daily."

Al twists around, shooting down the beach toward the fishing pier, and then around a little more, moving in a tight circle, panning the dunes, the highway, the hotel. . . . There! Coming down the boardwalk from the pool. He fingers the zoom. He whistles. "The Star-Spangled Banner!" he yells. "Hot damn!"

Butch and Rosemary step in tandem off the last wooden plank. Simultaneously, each kicks off one rubber thong, then the other, then bends, grabs, straightens up. Butch and Rosemary have been going to the beach together for twenty-one years. He carries the cooler, she totes the bag of stuff. He's tall, very thin, slightly bow-legged (a souvenir of his rodeo days), wearing a gimme cap over his toupee. A ponytail, one inch long, secured with a red rubber band, pokes out beneath the plastic adjuster. Rosemary is forty but has a gym in her house. When she appeared last night at the costume party in that tiny black thing, you could see men all over the room poking their wives in the rib cage. Quite a few wives poked back. This afternoon she's wearing a very small bathing suit. The top is blue with two white stars. The bottom is a patch of stripes.

"I don't know whether to salute you or stand at attention!" exclaims Al.

"Looks like you're already standing at attention," says Butch.

"You know it's you I want, Butchie," says Al, reaching with his free hand toward Butch's bathing suit. Butch jumps back. Everybody laughs.

"Al! Enough!" pleads April.

April met Al at a swingers' party four years ago. She was forty-five pounds heavier then, recently separated, two young kids, still the same ugly duckling at twenty-six that she had been ten years earlier when she'd played Monopoly with her parents on the night of her senior prom. Since teaming up with Al, she said recently in a speech to their swing club, she has grown into a swan.

Indeed, the combination of April's business ideas and Al's salesmanship has built for the couple a modest empire based on swinging. From the looks of his station wagon, a rusted woody with two hundred thousand miles on the odometer, and the number of alimony and child-support checks he writes each month, they haven't amassed a fortune. But they have taken over a warehouse in Nashville, and the payroll has grown to fourteen people. Somehow, Al and April have managed to tap a well of latent desire in America. If the exponential growth of their own mailing list is any indication, the well is deep.

In addition to the adult-contact magazines—fifty state and regional, five national—Al and April also run a set of 900-numbers with twenty-four-hour operators who can connect interested swingers; another set of 900-numbers with revolving date lines and recordings; the Preferred Lovers toy collection; the Tennessee Social Club, meeting twice monthly in the Free Spirit Lounge, a bar in the rear of their warehouse; the Elite International Paradise weekends in Hot Springs, Las Vegas, on a Mississippi riverboat. As Am-World Distributors, they produce A'Mature, Fantasy Focus, and Real Swingers Videos, offering a catalogue of ninety-two home-porn videos. All of the videos star everyday people, and many of them were made with this very same Sears camcorder. Many of them feature April, in her guise as Mary Lou.

"Mary Lou" is one of the brightest new lights in the fast-emerging field of amateur porn. Recently, her picture was on the cover of Hustler's Amateur Video guide. She is famous for her high cheekbones, her inch-long nipples, her wanton enthusiasm, and her hard, jockey-style rides on prone partners. In *Mary Lou, the Stud Finder*, a woman hires a carpenter "with all the right equipment." *Missy, Mary Lou, and 9"* has April teaming up with a housewife from Arkansas.

The video line was April's idea, though it started out before they met as one of Al's grand schemes. At first, he wanted to make professional-quality movies with amateur actors, people that the folks at home could identify with. He himself had always enjoyed watching and taking pictures. And though the women he'd swung with weren't goddesses or even of professional porn quality, they were willing, enthusiastic, and accessible. The same was true of the men. Swinging had held a considerable amount of his attention for twenty years, why not the buying public?

When April came on board, she took the idea and ran. She nixed the professional sound and video men Al had hired, bought the video camera, and threw it in the back of the wagon. Three years later, Al and April are selling about ten thousand videos annually, many of them starring their friends, some of them sent unsolicited from the heartland, all of them featuring real people having real sex, the good, the bad, the ugly.

According to the video industry, porn films account for 12 percent of all national rentals, about $325 million a year. Currently, amateur videos are the hottest new trend, written up in the *New York Times*, debated on *Donahue*, available at your corner store. About a dozen companies offer amateur videos of one sort or another, from homemade to professional.

It is impossible to say how big the market is, but the reasons for its popularity are apparent to Al and April and everyone else here in Pensacola. Like swinging, the videos aren't as much about fantasy as they are about fulfillment. You can dream about Traci Lords or John Holmes, but you can drive to Pensacola and fuck a half-dozen real men or women in one day even if you have stretch marks or a little dick. Amateur videos make everything seem possible. The stars resemble you and your neighbors, and they're not embarrassed. It looks like they're having a pretty great time, all the grunting and the straining, the unrelenting pleasure, all of it real and unrehearsed. Swingers think of it like this: Sex is the one recreation that God gave us. It costs nothing. It requires no accessories. You can even do it alone. It is a natural drug available in an almost inexhaustible supply. The Chinese, the Greeks, the Romans, the Hindus, the Buddhists, all of them believed in variety. It was only with the rise of Western civilization that sex lost all its glamour. Done among consenting adults with proper respect for health, it feels good, it is good, can even have lasting benefits. Why not make it a hobby?

All of which sounded ridiculous to April the first time she heard it. She'd grown up in a traditional upper-middle-class family in the Baptist South. Mother, father, sister, dog, cat, tropical fish. When she was twelve years old, she fell head over heels in love. He was two years older. In truth, the boy kind of dated April when he didn't have anybody else. But April had read enough Harlequin romances to believe that if you stick around long enough, eventually they fall in love with you. In his last year of high school, the boy got another girl pregnant. They were married. April went away to college.

Two years later April herself was married, to a man she'd met while working part-time at a hospital. After a few minutes of conversation, he told her, "I'm gonna marry you," and April said, "Oh, sure, right." A week later he said it again, and April thought, *Well, it would certainly be one way to get out of moving back home.* He was twenty years older, built nursing homes. They lived in a seven-foot travel trailer.

Seven years and two kids later, April got a phone call one day from her original love. The next weekend she and the two kids moved to Nashville.

And so it was, deep into her fourth week in Nashville, that the boyfriend suggested swinging, and April went along. She'd never heard of swinging. He didn't explain. The party was at a private house.

At first, April didn't see anything out of order. She had a drink, talked a while. After about fifteen minutes, she went downstairs.

It was the most disgusting thing she had ever seen. She didn't even tell him she was leaving. She took the car.

For some reason, she doesn't know why, April agreed to a second party in Memphis two weeks later, and there she met Al. For the next six weeks, Al and April saw a lot of each other. They'd go to lunch, to dinner, to the park, on walks. April started thinking, *What have I done wrong? This guy's got a reputation for fucking everything, and he isn't even making passes.*

Finally, Al explained. He wanted more from April than a swinging relationship. Soon they moved in together, though they didn't begin swinging for nine months. He just said when you're ready, you're ready. She knows now that if you try to talk a woman into swinging, she's not going to last very long.

April can't remember her first time swinging as a couple with Al, but she remembers clearly something she calls "my first real assertion of who I was sexually."

It was in Nashville, maybe a year into swinging. She and Al were giving a party at a hotel. Usually, they didn't do a lot at their own parties, too many details and responsibilities. But this time, there was a man from Kentucky she'd been trying to get with for six months. She took his hand, led him out of the dance. On the way to the elevator, she bumped into another man she knew. "Where you guys going?" he asked. "Come on," said April. In the elevator were others. They followed, too.

Later, Al came upstairs and peeked into the room. April was with six men. He stood in the doorway for a long, long time, smiling, shaking his head. His swan.

April lost weight, discovered the mall, started wearing makeup and going to the beauty shop each week, changing her hair color several times a year. She moved into the business, engineered the deal for the warehouse, took the big office for herself, decorated it in dusky rose. Currently, she has ads under twenty-five different names running in personals magazines all over the country. She also has a mini-industry in Mary Lou—900-numbers, videos, photo sales, fans.

"If you've had a traditional upbringing, and you listen to society, it's difficult to think of giving somebody you care about to somebody else. But Al says that our swinging relationships are part of our lovemaking. He says that swinging is like using a living dildo, and to a certain extent it is—it's our toys, our foreplay. We always go home and do it together, and that's always the best, though I have to say being with others helps a lot.

"I don't know if you get technically better at sex 'cause you're in the lifestyle, but I think you're a little more experimental. You're a little less embarrassed because in a lot of cases you really don't know the person that well. To me, the most embarrassing moment is taking off your clothes. After that, it's all spontaneous. You just turn off your mind and hook up your nerve endings.

"It's like the movies. I've had a few offers to do it professionally, and it's like, no, 'cause you guys would screw it all up. You'd say be here at 8:00, you're gonna do tit shots at 9:00, and this at 10:00. No way! That takes all the fun out of it.

"I have to say, getting letters from people who want pictures of my feet, who send me forty dollars for them, well, how can that not be good for you? You don't want to meet the guys, but listen: There's men out there jerking off to me. That gives you a certain amount of confidence.

"Lately, I've been noticing that my insecurities are going away. I'm really starting to feel good about myself. It's the wallflower stuff. I mean, it used to be that everything was unobtainable. Now I decide. Hell, now I turn it down in droves!"

By late Saturday afternoon, the sun has dipped, fat and orange, below the water slide at Tiki Island. Birds fly, crickets chirp, waves tongue the shoreline. The water is calm and evanescent, the color of jewels, animated in the autumn light, a Disney sea.

It is time now for the cookout, and everyone is here by the pool—even the state trooper, who has been known in the past to take a cooler full of sandwiches into the orgy room and stay there the entire weekend. Rosemary undulates on high heels across the grass, a heaping plate in one hand, an iced tea sloshing in the other. Her corn-silk hair floats on the breeze, her white spandex mini rides high on her thighs. Butch, her husband, trails a few steps behind.

Rosemary pulls up beside one of the picnic tables. "Mind if we sit down?" she sings, and then she nods backward, indicating Butch. "I already heard everything this one's got to say at least three times."

Michael and Ann, Walter and Deb, Sarah, Teresa, and Rod erupt in a chorus of laughter and commiseration. Swinging, especially a weekend gathering like this, is about social foreplay—the banter, the romance, the chase, the newness of a stranger's old stories. It's like having a quick affair, only your spouse is doing the same, often in the same room. Everyone shifts around on the benches to make room. A spot opens opposite Walter.

Holy shit! he thinks, and some saliva actually puddles in his mouth. He swallows, feels a slight blush. God! Walter had somehow missed Rosemary at the party last night. Today, he and Debbie and Michael and Ann had gone to a nude beach near the Naval Air Station. They had a nice day, walking, talking, having sex two different times. Deb and Michael really had a connection going. They couldn't keep their hands off each other. This was fine with Walter. He hadn't gotten laid this much since . . . he'd never gotten laid this much. Michael and Ann had kind of indicated that they really wanted to be with only one other couple for the weekend. That's the way they usually go, and that was fine with Walter. Until now.

"What y'all talking about?" asks Rosemary.

"That Professor Hill woman," says Sarah.

"It's on every channel," exclaims Deb.

It is the weekend of the Clarence Thomas hearings, and all day long Anita Hill has been describing her charges of sexual harassment.

"It's getting to the point where a man can't tell a woman she has a nice ass," says Michael.

"Or nice tits," adds Rod.

The women around the table chew quietly. Men, whattaya gonna do? Butch is quiet, too. *This is gonna be interesting,* he thinks.

"I still think she made the whole thing up," says Michael.

"What about you, Rosemary? What do you think?" It is Walter. He smiles, sweetly.

"What do I think?" asks Rosemary, licking some sauce off a finger. She looks across at Butch. He finds something very interesting in his plate. "Well," says Rosemary. "Men aren't fast enough on their feet to figure out when they're fuckin' up. Or maybe they don't give a shit. One or the other."

Then she stands, tugs at her mini. She says, bright and perky, "I'm gettin' me another piece of chicken! You want anything, Butch, honey? Any, y'all?"

She turns on her toes, moves away toward the barbecue pit.

Walter watches keenly. He wants her. Now.

"I was raised very religious, a Jehovah's Witness," says Rosemary. "I was dressed from here to here my whole life. My first husband was even against oral sex. Then I met this one and about three years into our relationship he said, 'Let's go to a swingers' party.' "

"I suggested it because ever since I was, I don't know, fourteen years old, one woman's never satisfied me," says Butch.

"No," interrupts Rosemary. "You just like to see two women together."

"You damn straight I do!"

"Well, darlin', I've lived with you eight years and we've had three single women and four couples, so obviously those eight years and those seven experiences don't tell me that you haven't been satisfied with just me."

"Yeah, could be."

"Thank you," says Rosemary. "When he first suggested swinging, I was curious as to what the hell went on. The thing people say about Jehovah's Witnesses is that they go to church and roll under the chairs and try to find God. I guess that brought a lot of people out to see exactly what they did do on Sundays. And I was the same way about the swingers club, wanting to know what happened.

"First we went through a phase of single women only. I have to tell you, I had my doubts. But with the right female it's very enjoyable. I've had some women who could eat pussy a lot better then men ever thought they could. I've gotten to the point where I've had to push them away 'cause I didn't want anybody in that room to see what I was going through.

"Then we went through a phase of women with their husbands, but we didn't swap, there was no total swapping. Then we tried the actual swap situation. It got to the point where a lot of the women were as attractive to me as they were to Butch, but their husbands were big, fat, and ugly, with pimples on their ass. I ended up quote unquote mercy-fucking some men 'cause Butch would say, 'I just can't live without this woman.'

"But then it got to the point that I said, 'Wait a minute, this ain't gonna work for me no more. For once I want it the way I want it even if you gotta fuck a dog.' And he said, 'Well, I can't get my dick up, but you can use lubricant.' But now, finally, it's taken us four years, but now he'll say, 'What do you think of the blonde's husband over there?' You've got to work through the games. If you don't, divorce will ensue. What's good for the goose is good for the gander.

"And I'll tell you another thing," says Rosemary. "If cleanliness isn't next to you, neither are we. One thing that turns us off is couples that will not use condoms. I realize that the guys don't get the same damn sensation, but tough luck. Hell, no dick's worth dying for."

"There's a shitload of men, and women too, that will tell you they never look at anybody else," says Butch. "Well, that's bullshit. If she tells me she'll never go to bed with another man, and then she does it behind my back and I find out, then she has lied to me. If she lies to me about that, then she'll lie to me about anything. I'll begin to get where I don't trust her with the money we make or with my truck or with anything.

"Then you get into deceit and lies and mistrust and all this other bullshit. What it comes down to is that if you can trust your wife to go to bed with somebody else and be honest about it, you can trust her about anything."

"Good evening! How is everybody feeling? Good-looking crowd here tonight! A bunch of dancin' fools!" announces Steve the deejay, breaking the music, turning up the patter. He drags on his cigarette, blows the smoke into the microphone: *whooosh.* Once upon a time, he was a stand-up comic.

Steve squints down from his platform, into the candle-lit hall. "Apparently, some of our guests didn't figure out that the costume party was last night. I see Butch came dressed as a bald guy. Where's your toupee, Butch? Oh, yeah, didn't I run over something hairy on the go-cart track? I thought it was road kill!"

"I wiped your ass on the go-cart track!" hollers Butch.

"Shoot," says Steve. "Well, anyway . . . Butch, you doin' okay this weekend?"

"Had five offers so far!"

"If you keep on, maybe a *woman* will offer before the night's over! Ha-ha! *Whooosh* . . . We're gonna keep it pumped up right now. This guy can sing his ass off when it comes to love songs. . . ."

The music starts and the dance floor fills. Some do a western two-step, working in a circle around the floor; others attempt white disco. A few couples slow dance, unconcerned with the beat. Hands move inside shirts, under skirts. At the tables, people talk and flirt. Deb, it seems, has discovered Gary. Michael and Ann have found Keith and BJ.

Al is at the back of the room, behind a partition, sulking, losing himself in the task of taking pictures of each couple, a Polaroid for them, real film for the article in the swingers' magazines. April has taken to champagne. She stopped drinking four years ago, but tonight she's bought the good stuff with the flowers painted on the bottle. She's been hovering around Rosemary, spilling bubbles on the rug, and also around Steve's girl, Shannon. Shannon is a looker, too. She partied for the first time last night, choosing Butch and Rosemary for her inaugural. To Rosemary it was a mercy fuck, but she liked Shannon, wanted to do it for her and Butch. Afterward, Shannon and Steve went back to their own room and did it until dawn. Shannon came to breakfast droopy-eyed and flushed. "Eleven times," she kept repeating. By lunch they were engaged.

Walter, meanwhile, is sitting at a table by himself. He's in a certain odd frame of mind. Since dinner he's been looking around. He's kind of decided that there are certain people he wants to be with. Really wants to be with. There is Rosemary, of course. A girl of his dreams. If she'd only ask, he'd go at it right now on the floor next to his chair. Shannon is another. He'd do her in a minute. Why won't she come over?

Walter's mind is beginning to play its old tricks on him. His mind is saying, *You really want to have sex with all of these women.* His mind is building a trap for him. Expectations. It's saying, *You have a huge appetite and you're not going to satisfy it.*

Walter is depressed. Actually depressed. His palms hold the sides of his head. There is more on my plate in front of me than I can possibly have, he is thinking. Things aren't turning out as I'd imagined. For some reason, I thought women might be more aggressive during this thing. But they aren't. I thought they'd just come up and say, "Hey, let's do something." That's basically how it had been with Michael and Ann. But that was eons ago, twenty-four hours. Why isn't Rosemary asking me to dance? he wonders. Why not Shannon? Why aren't they dragging me to their rooms?

Suddenly Walter feels a tap on his back. He twists around, hopeful, smiling his best smile.

Her eyebrows are drawn in with pencil. Through her filmy top he can see sad little pancake breasts. She has to be sixty. "Would you like to dance?" she asks.

A lone silhouette against the night horizon, Walter stands on the beach, arms crossed over his fishnet shirt, feet planted up to his ankles in the sand, head thrown back, the view of infinity. *A million stars,* he thinks. This is what they mean by a million stars. Funny about nature, about beauty, pleasure, love: Things so strong and deep and lovely and mysterious become clichés when you try to form the words, try to tell yourself what you see or feel. A million stars. A gentle wind. The smell of salt, the sound of waves, the cool, gritty tickle of sand between your toes. *Stop telling yourself where you are,* Walter chides himself. *Just be here.*

Walter is none too happy. The party had ended and Debbie had gone off in search of Gary, and Walter found himself sitting at the table, lights out, alone. He went to his room a while, watched TV, sulked. He kept thinking about Rosemary. He wondered who she was with. He imagined being with her. He masturbated. He felt jealous, cheated, confirmed in his opinion that his life had been one big waste of time, a period he was damned to endure.

Now, standing on the beach, his burden slowly begins to lift; he begins to see things in a slightly different way. There is something about a view like this, the infinity. Your disappointments have a distance to travel before falling back down to pierce your hopes. They lift off, rocket out and away. Back on the ground the smoke clears, and you can see new things. Walter realizes that he was so paralyzed by the weight of choice, the chance of rejection, that he never made any move at all. So much in his life had been that way. He fucked himself up once and he never trusted himself again, never even gave himself a break. Now here he is. He'd tried something new, sort of. For a day at least, he tried something new and it had made him happy. Then he got too happy. Then he got scared. Then he got sad.

My expectations were way up there, he tells himself, kind of up where the stars are. What was I thinking? What did I want? What more? Come on. I really did have a good time. I had a fabulous time. This isn't an athletic event. I really had a lot of wonderful things happen. Let's face it—if nothing else happens during the whole trip, it was still miraculous. If I die in an accident right now, I can go out with a smile on my face.

Walter closes his eyes, feeling the cool air on his nipples through the mesh of his shirt, the growing lightness in his heart. He stands awhile, stock-still, breathing in and out, trying not to think, trying just to feel.

"Howdy, stranger. What are you doin' out here all by your lonesome?"

Walter turns, slowly, not wanting to believe. It is Rosemary. Her white miniskirt glows in the starlight.

"Hi," he says.

"Hi."

"Ah, where's Butch?"

"Oh, you know Butch. Gettin' into one thing or another."

"If I had you, I wouldn't need anyone else," says Walter.

"That's sweet," says Rosemary, avoiding his eyes. She looks up, sighs. Walter does the same. "How beautiful," she says.

"A million stars," says Walter.

"A million stars."

They are silent awhile, facing each other, heads back, gazing up. Then Walter's head comes down, and his eyes fix Rosemary. Her corn-silk hair, the graceful curve of her neck. He clears his throat. She meets his gaze.

"Well . . ." she says, her voice trailing away. "I guess I'm gonna go on up and—"

"Rosemary?" interrupts Walter.

"Yes?"

"Ever since the first second I saw you, you've been on my mind. It was like, you were there and I just, I wanted, I . . . Rosemary, I was wondering: Would you, ah, would you like to take a little walk? Just a walk. Just to talk. That's all. I need that. Just to talk to you a while."

Rosemary meets his eyes, watery, blue, hopeful. *Not a bad guy*, she thinks. *A little neurotic, a little confused. He seems to have a little crush on me. That's sweet.* She feels a rush of emotion. Not sexual, not exactly motherly, but something tender. She reaches up, palms his cheek. "How far you think it is to that pier?"

"I've basically been really several notches above where I usually am," says Walter, home now a few weeks later. "I'm pretty happy. I feel good. And I've noticed, when I'm out and about, when I look at people, I have—I almost want to believe that all these people are also swingers. Like at the grocery store, the post office. I know that they're not, but I really want to believe that they are. I don't know why. I find myself smiling at people. I hope it lasts.

"I tried to get something going with Rosemary, but nothing was gonna happen. It didn't happen. But that's okay. I still had a great time. I'm happy that I took the time and energy to talk to her for a while. Just getting the chance to talk to her was enough. It worked out that you don't have to do everything your mind thinks you want to. I was so relieved and so happy just to have that half hour to walk up the beach and talk. It was kind of a real personal little encounter. A real little gift.

"In a way I think that I decided we'll just save it. Me and Rosemary. Someday at another gathering, we'll meet again, we'll get together. We'll have our chance. We'll—"

Walter gets quiet a moment. Something has occurred to him. Finally, he breaks the silence. "By the way—do you know what state she lives in?"

Esquire, October 1992

Is Ditka Nuts?

Iron Mike Ditka, a football man on his annual summer vacation, hunched forward in a hard spindle chair in a country-club locker room, playing a friendly game of gin. His legs are splayed, thighs like hams, right knee pumping like a piston. One hour in, he is $700 down. He blows a cloud of acrid blue smoke from a girthy eight-inch Dominican. Tap-tap-tap goes his heel, the tender meat of his swollen ankle oozing nakedly out of the low-cut upper of his dainty leather loafer.

He inserts the thirty-five-dollar Fuente Fuente OpusX salaciously into the center of his thin-lipped gob, beneath the salt-and-pepper whisk broom of his trademark mustache, then gathers up the hand he's been dealt. It is an anomalous summer afternoon, cool and dry in the suburbs of Chicago, a slow hour south through traffic and construction by stretch limo from downtown, from the Tremont Hotel, Ditka's home away from home, the site of his restaurant, Iron Mike's Grille, a sports bar with the air of a white-tablecloth meat house, a fitting amalgam of the parts of Iron Mike, featuring the Kick-Ass Paddle Steak and the Training Table Pot Roast, a cigar bar upstairs.

The restaurant is located just off the Magnificent Mile, on Chestnut Street, one block of which was recently renamed Mike Ditka Way, a tribute to a Windy City icon whose popularity seems to grow with each passing year, a loose cannon they've called "the Hammer" and "Sybil" and "Ready, Fire, Aim," a rehabilitated antihero as enduring as Mayor Daley and Mrs. O'Leary's cow, a hard-nosed coach who brought a proud, provincial city a Super Bowl it will never forget. Payton, the Fridge, Singletary, and McMahon. Buddy Ryan and the best defense the game has ever seen. A bunch of deep-hearted guys with chips on their shoulders—eternal, infernal, gut-it-out Grabowskis, commanded and inspired by the original Grabowski himself, Da Coach, Iron Mike Ditka, son of a steelworker from Aliquippa, Pennsylvania, stomping the sidelines and spitting his gum, throwing clipboards and grabbing face masks, nose to nose and bellowing.

The Super Bowl, of course, was thirteen years ago now. It's been six years since Ditka was dumped unceremoniously by the Bears. He arranges his cards dexterously into a neat fan in his left hand, the third finger of which sports a chunky diamond-and-onyx ring crested with a gold fleur-de-lis, symbol of his current team, his current town, another proud, provincial, politically compromised city by the water that prides itself on its food and music and homegrown soul. In the thirty-two-year history of the franchise, the New Orleans Saints have had eleven coaches and five winning seasons—the only club in the NFL that has never won a playoff game. Ditka arrived three years ago; his first two seasons went off at a disappointing 12–20. Now, in typical Iron Mike fashion—drawing from the same kind of inspiration, no doubt, that led him to transform a three-hundred-pound interior lineman into a running back—Ditka has traded away his whole 1999 draft and some of next year's for a dreadlocked, tattooed, nose- and tongue-studded Heisman Trophy winner with a rap star for an agent, causing an apoplectic stir in the conservative front offices around the league.

"A lot of people say I'm nuts," says Ditka about his choice of Texas running back Ricky Williams as his team's savior. "People ask me if by giving away our entire draft I'm ransoming the whole future of the Saints. Well, let me tell you: There *is* no future. This game is about winning. It's about trying to get as good as you can as soon as you can."

Ditka draws a card, inserts it into his hand. He is at Olympia Fields Country Club, a former site of the Senior Open, a future site of the U.S. Open, a rambling, stately old club whose first president was Amos Alonzo Stagg, himself a legendary Chicago football man who coached until the age of ninety-seven. The late-afternoon sun filters through the frosted skylights in the vaulted ceiling of the plush, cavernous locker room, casting an epic glow upon a faithful scene: the slap and tickle of the sporty upper class, a room full of men in various states of prime and undress, patting backs and telling jokes, reaching into lockers, padding across the sea-green carpeting wrapped in terry-cloth towels, an old black gentleman attending in the bathroom, calling everyone sir, the odors of Old Spice and Right Guard, mildew and musk and money, lingering in the air.

He discards curtly, flipping the reject to a spot just left of the tidy pile of newly cracked Bicycles at the center of the round table—one of two decks in service for this high-stakes game of three-man, round-robin gin, delivered with great alacrity by the locker-room boy, who went away with the heady flush of celebrity contact in evidence on his youthful countenance, a goofy, fawning, aw-shucks glaze, a crisp Ben Franklin clutched securely in his hand, the second such windfall of the day, proffered absently by Iron Mike from a fat roll of bills secured with a rubber band, kept in the front right pocket of his expensive slacks amid a treasure trove of special man-toys: a cigar cutter, a butane torch, a silver pocketknife with a plastic toothpick accessory, and a thick felt-tip marking pen used for signing a constant stream of autographs, the most recent of which—"Best Wishes, Mike Ditka"—was scribbled today upon the desiccated flank of a four-inch cigar butt reclaimed from the ground by a fan at a personal appearance three years ago and stored until this momentous occasion in a Ziploc baggie.

Tap-tap-tap goes his heel. That he is here at Olympia Fields for a golf tournament to benefit a Catholic nuns' home for disabled children and adults; that he is biding his time with a friendly game of gin, waiting to address a steak-and-potatoes crowd of well-heeled male contributors; that he is on vacation, in the first days of a golf holiday that will take him and his best buddy, Fred, to stellar courses all across the nation in his newly leased private jet, something he acquired at his wife's urging, in his newfound spirit of can't-take-it-with-you; that he is here to try to relax and have fun during this slim month of downtime between minicamp and preseason training— all of that seems lost at the moment. Ditka in repose. He blows a cloud of acrid blue smoke. Tap-tap-tap goes his heel.

He played like crap on the course today, shot a 95, well above his 7 handicap. Hook, slice, bunker, rough—the confounded ball was all over the con-founded course, defying his every attempt at compensation: left of the tee, right of the tee, club face open, club face closed. His nervous, fluttery setup and his odd little hip wiggle and his semi-elliptical swing with its short, mus-cular hook at the finale—it just wasn't working, it just wasn't his day, a series of solid, steely thwacks followed by the sickening rustle of leaves, and him bolting off in hot pursuit in that dwarfishly absurd electric cart, listing a bit to port under his weight, his left shoe—a bright white buck—extended precariously outside of the vehicle as he drove, as if there weren't a moment to spare, as if the game were somehow predicated upon speed, upon hopping out of the cart before it even stopped to right the mortal wrong of his last bungled shot.

Though Ditka has been known in the past to leave a scorching trail of four-letter words across the manicured fairways of the nation's top courses, this day on the links found him frustrated but largely contained. In October, he will turn sixty. His players and assistant coaches say he's mellowed, gone back to the Catholic Church, gone so far as to order an end to all cursing on the field. His general manager, Bill Kuharich—who was a fourteen-year-old ball boy, son of the coach, when Ditka played tight end for the Philadelphia Eagles—speaks glowingly of Iron Mike, calling him a regular guy with that certain something of a star, a class act who keeps morale high in the front office and on the field. He points to Ditka's weakness for giving to charity; last season alone he bailed out a Special Olympics weight-lifting team that had lost its sponsor, picked up the hotel bills for an entire group of handicapped kids and their chaperones at Disney World, performed countless other unsung acts for the needy.

Ditka's wife of twenty-two years, Diana, is a lighthearted Arkansas pistol with a 15 handicap who once told a reporter from *New Orleans Magazine*, "If I suck on something, it's not going to be a crawfish." Known affectionately as the Iron Lady, Diana says that her husband is lately feeling his age. "Mike's campaigning for a spot in heaven," she quips. "When men go through the change, they find some kind of inner peace. Mike has definitely changed. I tell him if he doesn't watch out, that halo is gonna slip down and choke him."

Ditka admits that the years are beginning to catch up. Physically, the wear and tear is evident. He walks a bit like a penguin, grimaces audibly when negotiating stairs. A permanently dislocated foot, loose ligaments in the knee, two artificial hips, an arthritic shoulder, a mouthful of replacement teeth. One heart attack, an angioplasty, a procedure last March to shock his heart back into rhythm. His large, square, chiseled face, crowned with its familiar plume of bristly hair, is sunburned a peculiar, florid shade of cherry-red, a side effect of his heart medication. Just yesterday, he sprained his ankle during his predawn three-mile run along the lakefront.

Ditka says he's "started seeing life a little differently. The things that seemed so important when you were young don't seem so important anymore. You start realizing that the greatest gifts you've got are life, health, family, friends, your spiritual beliefs. I feel a lot more secure with myself than I did a couple years ago. I think there were times when I didn't like who the hell I was. I would get mad at myself when I saw film of myself blowing up on the evening news. Not that I'll never blow up again; I probably will. But heck, you know, you gotta try. There's a great saying that says hell comes when the person we are comes face-to-face with the person we ought to be. That's about regrets. And I don't want to live a life of regrets. I want to be the kind of person I should be."

Which doesn't mean, he is quick to add, that Iron Mike has lost his edge. "You can mellow by your actions, but you don't have to lose your drive, you don't have to lose your competitiveness," he says. "Anyone can be the best person they can be. That's the whole key, see? To succeed in life you gotta have three main things. The first is attitude: That's basically the only thing you can control. If you have a bad attitude, you're not gonna do very well when you get a chance. The second is character: what you stand for, what you believe in, knowing right from wrong. And then there's enthusiasm: You have to like what you do. You have to make a commitment to what you're doing. If you don't like something, then heck, don't do it—*don't do it!* If you settle for defeat, you're gonna be defeated. If you settle for mediocrity, you're gonna be mediocre. If you're gonna play, you gotta play to win."

A commitment that brings us back to the Saints. Time was, New Orleans had given up hope. Fans referred to their team as the 'Aints. They showed up at the park with paper bags over their heads, called the Superdome the House of Blues. Though last year Ditka signed a contract extension that will guarantee him more than $2 million a year through 2002, he has no intention of playing it safe. Appearing at the press conference last spring to introduce Williams, his new $9-million-bonus baby, Ditka wore a funky dreadlock wig to silence the naysayers. He doesn't care if people like him. He doesn't care what anyone thinks. He got the player he wanted. "You look at Ricky and you see the way he looks, and people are put off," says Ditka. "But I think if John the Baptist came down to earth today, everybody would be put off by his looks, too. They'd say, 'Hey, I'm not following this guy anywhere—for gosh sakes, he eats locusts!' This is what bothers me about our society. When somebody reaches the top like Ricky, they try to tear him down. It doesn't make any sense. He's the most talented running back to come out of college in years. Mark my words: Time will prove that I'm a pretty sage person."

Ditka promises his new city nothing less than a Super Bowl of its own. "I hear all the experts say that the Saints are more than one player away from the playoffs or the Super Bowl," he says. "Realistically, everybody is, except the teams who get there. But let me tell you, we're one player closer with this guy. When people tried to stop the Bears in the eighties, they tried to stop our running game, and it didn't matter if they did stop it, because we kept trying to run the football, and eventually we made it work. And we made it work because of one guy—Walter Payton. He made our line better. He made our passing game better. He made our defense better because they weren't on the field that much. Maybe that's old-fashioned, and maybe the new gurus of football don't see it that way, but I don't really care. I'll let other people run their teams, and I'll run my team, and we'll see what happens in the end, that's all."

Iron Mike picks up a discard, inserts it in his hand. Tap-tap-tap goes his heel. When Ditka was out of coaching, it was great, it really was, don't get him wrong. He'd wake up in the morning and his big decision was whether to wear long pants or shorts, what shirt to choose. He played golf and gin all week long, thirty-six, fifty-four, sometimes ninety holes in a day—Iron Mike Power Golf people called it, polo golf—and when the weekend came, he got on a plane, flew to New York, did a TV show for NBC, then turned around and flew back. It wasn't a bad life, not in any way, shape, or form. But it was an aimless life. There was no winning. There was no losing. There was no gauge by which to measure himself, no mountains to climb—it's not as if he was out to win an Emmy for his broadcasting skills. There just didn't seem to be any purpose to what the hell he was doing. Iron Mike needs a purpose. When you read about Ditka as a player—as an All-American at Pitt, a five-time Pro Bowler, the first tight end ever elected to the Hall of Fame—the word you see most often is *relentless*. You need an outlet for relentless, something to pursue. Even when you're on vacation.

"Sevens and clubs, eh?" chimes Fred, sitting to Ditka's right, sitting out this hand. Fred has been the big winner so far this afternoon, up $1,900, but Ditka has been on a roll, is coming on strong. Tap-tap-tap goes his heel. During his playing days, having made a catch in the open field, given the choice between running for daylight and lowering his head, Iron Mike would always choose the hit. Now he cuts his eyes to the right, gives Fred a sharp, annoyed look. Freddie raises his hands in surrender, flashing an amused smile.

Fred L. Smith, of Las Vegas and Palm Springs, made a fortune in his family's food-and-drug business. Now he's retired to the good life, a great chunk of which is devoted to his friendship with Iron Mike. A handsome, convivial man with garish round spectacles and the gift of gab, he has a deep, golden tan and preternaturally white teeth, despite his fifteen Cubans a day, a stock of which he carries around with him everywhere in a portable brushed-aluminum humidor that resembles a small briefcase. Fred favors loud print shirts, always orange, and a heavy diamond pinkie ring. He goes nowhere that requires a sport coat. Don't even mention the word *tie*. As with Ditka, the things Fred loves most in this life are golf, gin, the guys, his wife, his kid, and football, the order of which is up for debate.

Fred has never known any man as intense as Iron Mike. The two men met more than five years ago at a golf tournament. For the last three years, they've taken this monthlong vacation together. Fred—who flies in his own Gulfstream IV to New Orleans for all the Saints' home games, who has his plane and pilot on standby for the next month because Ditka has no qualms about flying through perilous weather—doesn't mind telling you that this vacation with Mike Ditka is the absolute highlight of his year, something he starts looking forward to as soon as the last one is done. On the third finger of his left hand, he sports a diamond-and-onyx fleur-de-lis ring identical to Iron Mike's. Ditka gave it to him at dinner a year ago. So touching was the scene, all liquid eyes and strained voices, that Diana jokingly suggested they take it into the men's room. She also suggested, rather more pointedly, that something was missing, like maybe a fleur-de-lis ring for herself. So Ditka ordered up a ring for his wife, and a massive three-inch oval pendant as well, just for good measure.

Diana is best friends with Fred's wife, Elaine, so everything is very cozy. During this boys' golfing holiday, Diana and Elaine will crisscross the country playing golf, rendezvousing occasionally with their husbands at intersecting points. Their separate vacations have already begun. While Fred and Iron Mike bunk at the Tremont, Diana is ensconced a block away at the Ritz with another of her golfing girlfriends, a former ladies club champion and standout college softball pitcher from Ole Miss. The odd arrangements suit everyone just fine. Mike can play all the golf and gin, smoke all the cigars, and keep any hours he likes. He can meet his myriad personal-appearance obligations, hang around his restaurant and slap backs and sign autographs, Fred in ready attendance. Let the boys be boys, Diana figures. Let Mike enjoy himself. He's earned this, and it lightens her soul to see him with his friend. "Both of them can afford to do the things that make them happy," says Diana. "It's a great thing, because Mike has never really had a very best friend that he can pick up the phone and talk to about anything, whether it's me or family or whatever. He can tell this man he loves him. They're like brothers."

Ditka draws another card, inserts it into his hand. Across the table, another wealthy acquaintance, this one named Dick, is looking a bit uncomfortable. He is down $1,200 in this round-robin game of gin—not to mention the steep price tag on his philanthropic eighteen holes. The truth of the matter is he swore off cards several years ago. The truth of the matter is he has only $500 in his pocket. But, hey, he's here with Iron Mike, having come from Milwaukee to play with the coach in the name of his favorite charity, Misericordia, founded in the twenties by the Sisters of Mercy, home to almost six hundred children and adults with disabilities. Though Ditka has hardly spoken a sentence in the last eight hours—his ebullient public face actually belies a taciturn nature, a deep, brooding stillness that has you forgetting he's even around—he will later, before the gathering of patrons, wax poetic about Misericordia, for which he has helped raise more than $5 million over the last several years.

"I talk all the time about loving people," Ditka will say, totally at ease before the microphone, looking out over the blue haze of cigar smoke that envelops the crowd, voice catching with real emotion. "In life we seem to put conditions on our love. We'll love if we're loved back. We'll love if the situation is right. But the kids at Misericordia don't do that. They just love you. It puts everything back into perspective."

At the moment, however, the thing looming greatest in Iron Mike's perspective is not loving people but something quite different, something he's been known for throughout his life: coming from behind, grinding out the points, digging himself out of the hole in this game of gin. A contest is at hand, and if he's gonna play, he's gotta play to win. Hunched forward in a hard spindle chair, right heel tap-tap-tapping, he draws another card.

"Excuse me, Coach Ditka?"

The young man from Misericordia, coordinator of the event, has appeared at Iron Mike's side. He's got a xeroxed schedule in his hand. It is time for Ditka to give his remarks.

Iron Mike ignores the young man, sits up straight in his chair. He plunks a card on the pile, facedown. Four turns into the game, it is over. "Gin," he says, mildly triumphant.

"Jesus Christ!" says Dick. "Didn't anybody shuffle the deck?"

"That Ditka luck is kicking in!" says Fred. "Did I ever tell you the story about Mike playing gin against this guy with cancer? The guy was killing him, and finally Mike just exploded. 'You are the luckiest son of a bitch I have ever met,' he told him. The guy died eight days later."

"Skill, baby," says Iron Mike, ignoring the story, cracking a smile, lips elevating on either side of the girthy Dominican.

"Coach?" says the young man timidly. "Sir? Excuse me? Sister Rosemary says she's ready for you. She says it's time for you to come on out."

Ditka picks up a nub of a pencil and a pink score pad, adds his points at the bottom of a column that he has labeled coach. He pushes the chaotic rubble of the just-used deck out of the center of the round table, gathers up the second deck, begins dealing the next hand, a football man on vacation, playing a friendly game of gin, closing the gap. Seventy minutes in, he is now $620 down. He blows a cloud of acrid blue smoke. Tap-tap-tap goes his heel. "Tell Sister I'll be there in a minute," says Iron Mike Ditka, once and for always Da Coach, gathering up the hand he's dealt himself.

Esquire, October 1999

Old

Morning filters through the bedroom window in delicate, slanted rays, dust motes and sounds and memories drifting in the air. Doves coo, a horse-shoe clangs, quails skitter across the rain gutter. The clock radio on the night table whirs and vibrates; the number card flops: 6:33.

The old man sleeps on his left shoulder on the right side of the bed. His name is Glenn Brown Sanberg. He is ninety-two. He is peaceful in repose in plaid pajamas, a colorful floral spread pulled snugly to his neck. He has white, flyaway hair and bushy eyebrows, a flaky irritation at the point on his forehead from which his pompadour once issued. His cheeks are soft and deeply furrowed, speckled here and there with brown spots. His mouth is open, top lip buckled a bit over the gum line, chin stubbled with fine white whiskers. His left hand rests upon the pillow on the unmussed side of the bed, a queen.

Starlings chatter. Water gurgles in an ornamental pond. A draft horse pulls a wagon full of housewares down a cobblestone street. Glenn stirs, sighs, floats toward wakefulness. He thinks of the lake cabin he once built. Laying the foundation, he used a pancake turner for a trowel. He thinks of woodpeckers, of ducks, of fresh blueberries. A Studebaker with a rumble seat. A player piano in a speakeasy. Stealing apples from an orchard, buckshot whistling overhead, the double row of brass buttons on the blue serge uni-form of the town constable. Smoking corn silk under the porch. Joan leaning against the radiator in his office in the collection department at the Mayo Clinic, drying her stockings on a cold, rainy day.

The paper thuds against the front door. Glenn's eyelids flutter. An electric golf cart hums past, tires swishing through sprinkler runoff. He thinks of an address book left behind at a riverside telephone booth, a thermos left behind at a seaside hotel. Mount Rushmore. Old Faithful. Shaking hands with Lawrence Welk. Napping on his favorite divan. The odd, modest undershirt and boxers worn by his Mormon son-in-law.

He opens his eyes, blinking against the light. Through the cracks in the partially opened vertical blinds, he can see the sky, a wan blue, vectored with contrails, overhung with wispy clouds. He thinks of the cold, clear sky of a northern Minnesota winter. He thinks of Joan digging in the garden, a smudge of mud on her nose. Dad sitting in President Eisenhower's chair in the White House, a proud and grave expression on his face. Tom bagging his first buck with the Savage .303. Mickey reeling in a fat pike on a sparkling mountain lake. Little Eleanor, limp in her bed, scarlet fever. Joan falling against a door. Lucy falling against the curb. Ann Black, front row center at the Greek Week songfest, legs crossed, dark eyes beaming. Jeffy's warm, tiny hand inside of his.

A lawn mower sputters and coughs, catches, begins to drone. Glenn slides his left hand beneath the covers, places it palm down beside his hip. He reaches behind himself with his right arm, grabs a handful of bedspread. Pushing with one hand, pulling with the other, he rolls himself over onto his back with a grunt. There is little pain to speak of—a twinge of nagging soreness, perhaps, in the knuckles, the left shoulder, the right hip, the neck—but there is a certain acute stiffness in his muscles and ligaments and joints that enfeebles his every action, renders his every movement a task. Think of the first few turns on a rusty lug after it has finally come unstuck—such is the effort. Winded, Glenn lets his head settle into the pillow. He thinks of hoeing weeds in a five-acre bean patch on a hot summer day. Walking across a golf course in the early morning, meeting Lucy at the fountain for a sip of water and a little hug. Martin Luther King Jr. at the Lincoln Memorial. Eleanor in the car on the way to her freshman year of college: "Don't drive so fast, Daddy."

Stretching both arms above his head, he yawns deeply, luxuriantly, then brings his right hand forward, uses his thumb and forefinger to wipe away the cakey dryness that has accumulated at the corners of his mouth. His hand trembles. He's not sure when it began, this shaking. His son pointed it out not long ago when he came to visit. Glenn was taken aback by the revelation; he simply hadn't noticed. You live in your body every day of your life. Things change slowly, inexorably, in increments too small to measure. You gain weight, you lose weight, your hair falls out. Your skin slackens, your voice thins, your bones become brittle, your ankles swell. Your prostate and a piece of your colon are removed. Your back bends with the weight of gravity and passing time. You wake up twice during the night to pee; once in a while, you wet your pants. Crossing your legs has become a project that requires your hands; getting out of a chair has become a gymnastic routine; eating a bowl of soup has become a logistical feat. Whenever you go to the store, you can't remember if you have coffee at home. There are two blue cans of Maxwell House in your refrigerator, six more in your cupboard. You buy another can just to be sure. There is a tiny droplet of moisture suspended from the bottom of your nose. There is food crusted on the front of your shirt, the crotch of your pants, the tips of your shoes. You ask people questions several times over. Sometimes, just as you're asking, you realize that you've already asked this same question, that you've already heard the answer. You go ahead and ask again anyway. It's too embarrassing to do anything else. Your parents and your five siblings and your spouse have all died. Your late-life companion has moved on to constant care. You visit her three times a day. She lights up when you're around. Your children have entered their own retirement years in distant states. People talk to you as if you were a four-year-old; they are always trying to give you hard candies. You are old, diminished, alone. You can't even cut your own toenails. The podiatrist does it for fifty-five dollars. His nurse calls to remind you about your appointment. It was thirty minutes ago.

All of this happens; everything changes. But the odd part is, you don't really notice. You're aware of it, sure, but somehow it doesn't integrate. Deep down, to yourself, you are always just you, the same pair of eyes in the mirror, the same familiar voice inside your head still wondering, "When will I feel grown up?"

Glenn runs his pink tongue around the inside of his mouth, tries to swallow. He is thirsty, but he can wait, the thought of the effort needed to get himself a glass of water displaced for the moment by the pure, sensual pleasure of lingering beneath the covers with no place special to go. It isn't all bad, this diminishment, this narrowing of the circle of friends and activity and influence and competence. You can see it as a long, slow march toward death. Or you can see it as a distillation, a paring down—as the last leg of a journey, the jump-off point, perhaps, for a great new adventure in the next world, a chance to reunite with your loved ones. It is truly a second childhood, only this time you're the one in charge, as long as you still live on your own, as long as you can still dress yourself and feed yourself and get to the store. As long as you still have your driver's license. You can wear the same clothes two days in a row. You can stay up half the night watching *National Geographic* videos. You can nap. You can eat dessert for dinner, pour mocha crème on your cornflakes, stay in bed until you feel like getting up.

At the moment, Glenn feels like staying in bed. He places his hands behind his head, interlaces his fingers. He pans the room, eyes blue and elfin, the eyes of his grandfather, a blacksmith from Sweden, and of his father, a school superintendent from Minnesota. There is Lucy's wig hanging from a hook on the towel rack in the bathroom. Joan's desk, Mother's lamp. A copy of the *Physicians' Desk Reference.* A Snoopy doll holding a tiny box of Whitman's chocolates. Portraits of Lucy's kids and grandkids and great-grandkids. A small, silver frame on a dresser with a picture of Joan on their wedding day. Joan: She was quite a gal. She wasn't a superwoman, but he never knew anybody who was more honest. The first time he saw her, she was leaning against the radiator in his office in the collection department at the Mayo Clinic, drying her stockings on a cold, rainy day. She could read him like a book. One night in bed, in the dark, she slapped him. He doesn't remember what the argument was about. Boy oh boy oh boy. Right on the cheek: *Slap!* That was a wake-up call. Yes sirree. A female voice, digitized, robotic, calls out from the living room: "6:30 A.M."

Glenn's brow furrows. He sighs. *Where am I?* he wonders.

He closes his eyes. The lids tremble with concentration. You can be ninety-two years old and have your eyesight, as Glenn does, need glasses only for reading. You can have hearing good enough to pick out whispers in a crowded room, reflexes good enough to drive on busy streets. You can have a medicine chest with nary a prescription pill or bottle of ibuprofen in evidence. But when you get to be Glenn's age, things are different; things like this happen all the time: A situation comes up and suddenly you are stymied, baffled, lost, confused; the information needed proves elusive. *Why did I come into this room? When did they board up this bank? What's Tom's daughter's name? Wasn't the meeting supposed to be here? When did I order these pictures of myself from Olan Mills? Where am I?*

Glenn knows that he knows the answer. He knows that he knows where he lives. He just can't put his finger on it right now—this little scrap of knowledge stored, along with so many other disparate pieces of information gathered over a lifetime, somewhere in the crammed and dusty attic of random rooms that is his memory, an archive chockablock with electrobio-chemical renderings of pictures and dates and facts and ideas, words of wisdom, personal milestones, nouns and verbs and adjectives particular to his life. Like the facts that he was born in Bird Island, Minnesota, in 1905, grad-uated from the University of North Dakota in 1927, married Joan in 1929, just before the Depression. He was an air-raid warden in Minneapolis during World War II, stepped down as executive vice-president of the American Society of Association Executives in 1964, lost Joan in 1987. Twenty-nine years he's been retired. He knows that fact, too, can do the math in his head right now if he chooses. He knows that Tom lives in Chicago, that Jeffy lives in Oregon and deals in lumber, that Saturday is the most dangerous day of the week to drive your car. That in order to live happily in retirement, you must find something to be important to. That the best excuse is the one you never make. That you should back up your files on a floppy disk. That the knocking noise in the hot-water heater is probably due to sediment buildup. That you need to separate the laundry before you wash. That it is best to eat the biggest strawberry last. That the first income-tax law was enacted by the U. S. Congress in 1862. That if you are big enough, your troubles will always be smaller than you.

Lying there with his fingers interlaced behind his head, his lids trembling with concentration, Glenn searches the borders of his awareness for the infor-mation he seeks. *Come on, Sanberg, you old coot. Boy oh boy oh boy. You're in a fine state, Sanberg. You don't even know where you are!*

The voice that is speaking, the old familiar one inside his head, the one he grew up with, seems oddly amused at the turn of events. A little embar-rassed, a bit nonplussed, just the slightest bit self-pitying, the words punctu-ated with a phlegmy, nervous laugh, *Ah ha ha!* You learn to go with the flow in these matters, to let nature take its course. Patience: That is what you learn with age. You can rage against the dying of the light, or you can feel fortu-nate that it's not yet totally dark, that there's still time left and things to see, things to remember, even things to forget. Glenn thinks of the other places where he has woken up, the other places he has called home. The cabin they named Spikehorn—the best idea he ever had, enlisting the whole family to build from scratch a one-room cabin in the woods. The three-bedroom house in Minneapolis—he hated to leave the place, but the nation's capital was calling, and he was a man of some ambition. The trailer in McAllen, Texas, their third abortive attempt at finding a place of retirement—too many old farmers with creased necks, nothing to do, too much bingo, and too much square dancing, no way to spend the rest of your life. You don't think about it when you're young, even when you're middle-aged, even when you first retire, but if you're lucky, if you're blessed with hardy genes, as Glenn has been—and that is the only reason he can give for his longevity and good health, the fact that his father died at eighty-nine of the colon cancer they caught in Glenn a few years back, and that his mother died at ninety-three of natural causes—then your retirement years can last for a period of time that is longer than your youth, almost as long as your working adulthood. It's been almost thirty years since Glenn had to set an alarm clock.

Now, as he lies in bed with his eyes closed, it comes to him at last: the answer he's been seeking, materializing out of the shadows, floating toward him like an autumn leaf. Of course, of course. Of course! *Ah ha ha!* He is in Sun City, Arizona, fifteen miles northwest of downtown Phoenix. Nine thousand acres, forty thousand residents, almost all of them over fifty-five. City of Volunteers, home of the Active Retirement Lifestyle, the nation's first large-scale experiment in retirement living. Glenn's home since 1972.

He studies the sky through the cracks in the blinds, a bit amused, a bit relieved. *Sanberg, you old coot! You ain't dead yet!* Doves coo, a lawn mower drones, quails skitter across the rain gutter. Another fine day in Sun City. Another fine day of retirement. Another fine day to—

His brow furrows. He sighs. *What day is this?* he wonders.

The waitress unlocks the door, and Glenn steps lightly across the threshold. He is a handsome man, five feet ten, 190 pounds, with a prominent nose and a broad, friendly chin, another trait passed down from his father. He is wearing a crisp, pale-blue guayabera shirt that he washed and ironed himself and navy-blue flared trousers, polyester, with western stitching. He tips two fingers to his forehead in a modified salute. His eyes twinkle. "Thank ya kindly, ma'am."

"No problem, dear," says the woman, thin and sixtyish, with a cigarette rasp. "How you doin' this morning?"

"Pretty good for an old coot," he says cheerfully.

She smiles wide, lays a hand on his shoulder. "You're just the cutest thing!"

Glenn arches his bushy white eyebrows, makes his mouth an O of surprise. He attempts a step or two of soft shoe, then takes his leave, stage left, heading at his usual good clip toward the banquet room at the rear of Nancy's Country Cupboard. He has an odd, stiff, jaunty gait, torso rigid and bent slightly forward, arms pumping from the elbows, feet working from the knees, weight shifting quickly from side to side, the sole of his left shoe scuffing the floor. Seeing him walk, you detect pride and good nature in the face of adversity; you sense that here is a man who understands the value of progress made one step at a time. A man undeterred by what he cannot do, focused instead on what he can, determined to do it well. He holds his head high.

Had this been a Monday morning, Glenn would have driven his '91 Buick Park Avenue the three hundred yards from his garage to what he likes to call the Chamber of Commerce, the snack bar in the main building of Royal Oaks, his fifth residence since retirement. Had this been a Wednesday, he would have tidied up a bit in anticipation of a visit from Maria the cleaning lady, a pretty young Mexican woman who tells him stories about her little boy. On other days, he might have had a meeting of the Lakes Club board of directors, or the Sun City Community Fund grants committee, or the New Horizons club, wherein outsiders are invited to dinner to discuss topics of general interest, from health care to the state of today's teens.

Thursdays are his busiest, with a Lions Club meeting at noon and his weekly column due at four o'clock. For almost thirty years, in various venues, Glenn has been writing a newspaper column called "Retired in Style." It began in 1952, long before he retired, as an extracurricular attempt to satisfy his lifelong desire to be a writer. A self-published weekly broadsheet containing words of wisdom, encouragement, and solidarity for busy executives like himself, it was called LIFT, as in, "Have you given someone a lift today?" A sort of support group in the form of a newsletter, with subscribers all over the country, LIFT was a bit ahead of its time in sentiment and sensibility, rather touchy-feely in an era of Sputnik and Joe McCarthy. Later, when he retired, Glenn remembered how lost his father had been without something important to do in his golden years. Never much for hobbies, he decided to make the column a late-life career. For five years, "Retired in Style" was carried by *The Arizona Republic*, the major daily in Phoenix. When the long drive downtown to drop off his offerings became problematic, he switched to the *Daily News-Sun*, the chronicle of Sun City and environs, a snappy little afternoon paper conveniently located two blocks from his house. True to his late-found profession, he waits until the last possible moment to flip on his Gateway computer, which features Windows 95, WordPerfect, and America Online. He writes about what he knows, what he thinks, what he sees, what he remembers, what he reads. Increasingly, he writes about what he's already written, borrowing material from the reams of old clippings he keeps filed in the den he uses for an office. He usually finishes thirty minutes before deadline, then drives it over. The column runs Saturdays on the front page of the second section, along with his picture.

Had this been a Sunday, Glenn would have driven a hundred yards to the constant-care center and picked up Lucy for church. Though he spent most of his life with the Methodists, he now attends Faith Presbyterian, Lucy's church. He sometimes finds comfort in prayer, in the calm, meditative state it brings, in the fellowship of worship with others. He doesn't subscribe to the whole hellfire-and-brimstone story. His beliefs are centered more on the kind of living you do than on what happens when you die. He's not hung up on denomination, either. The way he figures it, God is God is God no matter what house you're in, and Lucy cared more than he did about which church they attended. Faith Presbyterian was also the sponsor of the Royal Oaks Life Care Community, where Glenn and Lucy moved three years ago when they decided to set up house together. A sort of retirement development within a retirement community, Royal Oaks offers laundry, housecleaning, repair services, a cafeteria, social workers, and shuttle vans to shopping and doctors. Within Royal Oaks are three grades of living arrangements—ranch-style duplex garden homes, assisted-living apartments, and full-care nursing facilities. For $40,000 down, $800 a month, Glenn will have food, housing, and care for the rest of his life.

As it is, today turns out to be Tuesday—a fact he finally confirmed by consulting the newspaper tossed every morning from his driveway to his front door by a friendly neighbor on his daily walk—and Glenn has come to

Nancy's. For twenty years, Tuesday mornings have been reserved for the Walk-Jog Club. Once upon a time, all the members would jog or walk for an hour and then convene in Nancy's banquet room for the $1.99 breakfast special. Nobody jogs anymore. The big joke these days is how they lose a half pound walking, then gain a pound and a half at breakfast. Glenn contents himself with driving the mile or so to the restaurant and walking one circuit around the parking lot. At his age, you need to get your circulation going, relieve some of the stiffness, but there's no sense getting all worked up. Actuarial tables say that Glenn will likely be dead in 3.4 years. He knows this. He's all right with it. As he often says: "It's been a good life."

Glenn enters the banquet room, the first to arrive. He takes a seat at one of the two large, round tables that have been set up to accommodate the group. He looks around. He sighs. He pats the tabletop like a set of bongos, pat-a-pat-pat.

A man enters, takes a seat across from Glenn. He is in his early eighties. Glenn can't remember his name. "Good to see you," says Glenn.

"How do?" says the man.

"Pretty good for an old coot."

"I'll say," says the man. It occurs to Glenn that he was once a banker. Possibly from Chicago. He is wearing his official Walk-Jog Club T-shirt.

Glenn points to his own chest with a crooked finger. "Looks like I forgot to wear my T-shirt."

"Yeah, well," says the banker, pinching his T-shirt between a crooked thumb and forefinger. "I came to find out if there's anybody still alive down here."

"Alive and kickin'!" says Glenn. He pushes a fist into the air before him, rah-rah.

Soon the others begin to arrive. The younger crowd, sixties and seventies, goes to one table; the others go to Glenn's. Big John is a retired attorney. Edith, in a wide-brimmed straw hat, was one of the founding members of the club. Harold is a retired Westclox executive from somewhere back east; Pearl is his wife. The banker, it turns out, is named Frank. The only other person at the table in his nineties is Reggie. He carries a wireless contraption that he places on the table; it helps him hear. His speech is nearly unintelligible, his glasses are thick, and he walks with a slow shuffle. Though the median age in Sun City is about seventy-four and 25 percent of the residents are over eighty, ninety-two-year-old men who are up and around and healthy like Glenn are a rare commodity. The life expectancy of an American male today is seventy-three years. According to the Census Bureau, there are about fifty-three thousand ninety-two-year-old men in the country, but that number is increasing. All told, people over ninety are the fastest-growing demographic group in America. Edith pours him a cup of decaf coffee from the carafe on the table. They wait to order. No one needs a menu.

"It was a nice breezy walk, wasn't it?" says Frank. "We were bucking the breeze going, but we got a nice rear-end push on the way back."

"Is that what it was?" asks Edith, raising her eyebrows.

"Oh!" exclaims Frank. "You mean you thought that rear-end push was me?"

Edith swats the air in his direction. Everyone laughs. Glenn is sitting with his arms crossed casually, like an executive at a meeting. "You can't beat a little good, clean fun, now can you?" says Glenn.

"No sirree, you can't," says John.

"Nope," says Edith.

"Did I tell you about my Northern Tissue stock?" asks Frank.

"Go ahead if you must," says John, rolling his eyes.

"I guess you're going to anyway," says Edith.

"I bought a hundred shares, but I got wiped out on it," says Frank. He crosses his arms, proud of himself.

"Groan!" says Glenn.

And so it goes. The food comes: oatmeal and eggs and French toast, lots of warm syrup. They chat about summering in Utah, motor homes, cruises up the Colorado, bus trips to Laughlin, Nevada, to play the one-armed bandits. About the traffic on Bell Road, the exploits of sons and daughters, the times they played golf in the 115 degree heat. They swap stories about the legendary Del Webb, the six-foot-four-inch former minor-league pitcher who built Bugsy Siegel's casino, who once owned the Yankees, who, almost forty years ago now, saw acres and acres of sun-bleached cotton fields in the Arizona desert and envisioned a new kind of lifestyle for people in the winter of their lives, the next logical post-Levittown step for the citizens who peopled the American century.

Sitting back with his arms crossed, tossing out a reminiscence here, a comment or a bon mot there, asking a question when the conversation hits a lull, Glenn has the relaxed air of a man at a cocktail party in the 1950s. You can imagine him in a dark suit and skinny tie, puffing on a pipe, passing pleasant time with pleasant associates over a manhattan, two cherries. Since he came here, in fact, Sun City has impressed Glenn as being just like that, like one big floating cocktail party without the booze, a gathering of familiar, friendly acquaintances, all of them of similar type and class and background, with shared values and customs. People from a genteel era, a time when men wore sport coats to baseball games, held doors open for ladies, paid their bills on time, gave backyard cookouts for neighbors, had a friendly word for all, whether they meant it or not.

Glenn pats the tabletop like a set of bongos, pat-a-pat-pat. It is a pleasant feeling, this comradeship, this diversion, this activity that takes him outside his ranch-style duplex garden home, outside his own head. But it is also somewhat hollow and boring. Glenn may be old, but he still knows the difference between acquaintances and true friends, between quality time and killing time. Though he's been living among these same people for many years, he doesn't really know them, and they don't know him, his little offerings in the newspaper every week notwithstanding. They have no idea that he married into the Mayo family, helped set up the world-famous clinic's first collection department. That he started his own successful business, went on to be executive secretary of the American Collectors Association. That by the time his career was at its peak, he could claim good friends among top people in the White House. Like the trophies and plaques and framed citations stored in dusty boxes in his garage, none of that matters much anymore; it happened so long ago now, he can hardly remember the details. You spend thirty or forty or fifty years bulking up your résumé, throwing your weight around, polishing your reputation, playing the game, planting your legacy. It matters what you do in life, it really does—the impressions you leave, the contributions you make, the money you earn, the people you touch, the children you send off into the world. But as the end draws near, as the scope of your life narrows, none of that seems very important anymore, none of that *is* very important anymore. What becomes important are things like your health and the state of the weather, things like putting one foot in front of the other, making sure the chair doesn't roll out from under you when you go to stand, getting a phone call now and then from your sons or daughter, tasting a warm, sweet Entenmann's bear claw. Being able to sit with yourself at the end of another day and feel that you have no regrets about the time you've spent on earth, that you've done your best to live a good life, to give others a lift.

A woman named Barbara comes over from the younger table. She is carrying a newspaper clipping, two inches square: an obituary. She is in her early sixties, the only one in the room wearing shorts.

"There she is, Miss America," sings Frank.

Barbara throws him a dismissive look, walks over to John, shows him the clipping. "Is this the Bob Thompson from Sun City West that used to walk with us?"

John tilts his head up, reads down through the bottom of his trifocals. "Sure," he says, "that was him."

"How old was he?" asks Edith.

"Says here he was eighty-four," says John.

"Bob Thompson?" asks Harold. "Which one was he?"

"Remember?" reminds Pearl, his wife. "Little Bob Thompson. He used to . . . what do you call that? Race walk."

"He used to jog with the boys, then his legs gave out and he got to walkin'," John confirms.

"So that was Bob Thompson," says Harold.

"Guess so," says Frank.

"Yep," says John.

"Hmmm," says Edith.

"Hey, Miss America," says Frank. "Did I tell you the one about my Northern Tissue stock?"

"Say yes!" exclaims Edith.

"Say yes!" exclaims John.

"No matter what, say yes!" exclaims Glenn.

Everybody laughs.

Glenn struts into Lucy's place, full of vigor and good cheer, a fresh pink rose in his hand. The room is a standard nursing-home double painted in pastels. "How you doing, old gal?"

"I never know," says Lucy. She is a small woman with large, brown glasses and short, gray hair, sitting on the edge of the narrow bed. She giggles a nervous laugh, *Ha ha ha.*

"I like that black-and-white outfit."

"Do you?" She looks down to see what she's wearing, adjusts the drape of her blouse. "I have to stop and think. Where am I? Who am I?" She giggles again, *Ha ha ha.*

"That's all right, dear," says Glenn. "I have to do that, too." He reaches out with a trembling hand and cups her cheek.

Lucy sighs, leans her face into his palm. "Oh, well," she says. She has been in the constant-care center for almost two years. Her Alzheimer's is still at an early enough stage that in her good moments, she seems to be aware of what is happening to her, this process that is slowly taking her away from the world. It seems to embarrass and frustrate her, yet at the same time she seems resigned and good-humored, willing to accept what comes. She no longer complains about the food, no longer asks about going home. Rarely is she sad or angry anymore. During her active lifetime, she was smart, pleasant, witty, a little feisty, willing to see the silver lining. Now it is as if the disease is slowly distilling her to her essence, rendering her a fond memory of herself. "It's really a very nice day," she says. She is a bit difficult to understand without her dentures.

"A little breezy out there right now."

"It's a little tricky."

"It's always a little tricky," says Glenn. He laughs nervously, *Ah ha ha!* He is embarrassed and frustrated, too. He visits three times a day. He makes it a policy to stay upbeat, though he secretly wonders sometimes why he bothers to come at all. He always hopes, whenever he walks through the door to her room, that this time things will be different, that this time Lucy will show signs of getting well. He knows she won't get well. More often than not, a few moments after he arrives, he feels ready to leave. He sticks it out anyway. It's a rough deal, this thing. Having her here is very tough. A real push/pull, if you know what he means. If he didn't show up, she probably wouldn't know. Yet something deep compels him to return time after time, day after day, with a cheery expression on his face: a deep gratitude for the years they spent together, for what they meant to each other. A deep solace in knowing that he is not alone here in Sun City. He steps to the bed, turns, slowly lowers himself down next to her.

Glenn and Lucy met many years ago in Minneapolis. She and her husband, they called him Bake, lived near the Sanbergs. He was an accountant for the railroad. The two couples were quite friendly, members of the same social club. Glenn and Bake hunted together. Lucy worked for a time as

Glenn's secretary. Years later, her daughter had a summer job with him. When Glenn and Joan came to Sun City for the first time to check it out, the Bakers and another couple were their hosts.

When Joan died in 1987, just before Thanksgiving, Glenn got a call late at night from the hospital, saying she was gone. It all happened so fast. That summer, vacationing in Logan, Utah, she had fallen and hit her head. Four months later, she was dead. Fifty-eight years of married life were over. He never thought he'd be the one who was left behind. He listened to the words, delivered by a stranger, a nurse, over the telephone. Then he replaced the receiver on its cradle. "I'm all alone," he said, speaking out loud into the darkness. He will forget a lot of things before his time is up, but he will never forget that.

It was rough for a while, real rough, boy oh boy oh boy, though he came to enjoy the parade of widows with their casseroles who started showing up at his door. He learned how to sort the laundry and make coffee, how to fend for himself after so many years as a husband. He was doing okay; it wasn't great, but he was getting along. Then one day he ran into Lucy. Bake had died a few years before; Joan and Glenn had helped her through her grief. Now, coincidentally, both Glenn and Lucy were on a walking kick. He began phoning her in the mornings to say he was leaving for his walk, and she'd leave, too, and they'd meet at the water fountain on the golf course, a point equidistant from their houses. At first, they'd just hang around and talk. Soon, they were giving each other a little hug. That's the thing you come to miss the most: a little hug, the warmth of someone next to you, her body against yours, her breath on your neck. They began eating meals together, some days at his place, some at hers. Lucy took Joan's place in a way that was very positive, Glenn believes, and he thinks he took Bake's place in the same way. After a few years, they decided to cut out the foolishness and move in together.

Before they finalized their plans, however, they went to see the pastor of Lucy's church. They told him their intention, to live together in the open, out of wedlock. He regarded them gravely. Then he cracked a smile. "Go for it!" he said. Three other words that Glenn will never forget.

Glenn and Lucy had similar likes and dislikes. They both played golf and bridge, enjoyed dancing. They both cared about who was president, who was senator, what was going on in the world. She was easy to be with, very accessible, had a sense of humor, was a very sharp gal, a college graduate, very involved throughout her life with the American Field Service. You couldn't put anything over on her. She was that kind, like Joan in many respects. They went on trips to see each other's children, drove all the way to Florida, took a cruise once through the Panama Canal. In the years they lived and traveled together, they slept in the same bed—he on the right, she on the left—but never had sexual intercourse. Thinking about it, Glenn wonders if it was kind of unusual to be so close and yet never be intimate in that way. Their spouses had been their lifelong lovers, their only lovers. And so it remained, though it wasn't like he couldn't have, physically—he still feels the call now and then. No matter. They were at an age in life when that wasn't very important anymore.

Then one day Lucy fell against the curb in the parking lot. It didn't seem like that big of a deal—a few cuts and scratches, a badly bruised hip. But tests at the hospital revealed Alzheimer's. She never returned home. He still keeps her things in their proper places in the house, the way they were the day she left with him to go out for a simple lunch at the Lakes Club—the wig hanging from a hook on the towel rack, the pictures of her family on the walls. To do otherwise would be unthinkable.

Lucy leans her head against Glenn's shoulder. Glenn looks distractedly around the room. Through the doorway, he can see the slow procession of Royal Oaks residents up and down the central corridor, aged figures caterpillar-walking in their wheelchairs, pushing with their hands and padding with their feet, eyes fixed on the distance. A woman is slumped in her wheelchair just outside Lucy's door. She is holding a teddy bear. "Help me," she calls again and again. "I have to make a BM."

Glenn notices the rose in his hand, holds it out in front of Lucy. "I brought you this rose. It's from our yard."

"No kidding?"

"Yeah, right from our yard."

"Our yard?"

"The one at the house."

"It's lovely this time of year."

"Yes it is, dear, yes it is." He puts the rose on the dresser. "I had break-fast this morning with Harold and Pearl. Frank was there, too."

"How are their families doing? Or are you only interested in whether or not the little boy can jump the fence?"

"I guess so," says Glenn. He laughs, *Ah ha ha!* Lucy looks at him questioningly. She seems to realize that she is not making sense. She laughs. *Ha ha ha.*

"My whole back is bad," says Lucy.

"Itchy?"

"It's just wonderful when they come by and scratch."

"Here, allow me, madam," Glenn says with mock formality. He shifts his weight, moves his arm slowly behind her back, begins to scratch.

A look of pure bliss crosses Lucy's face. *"Oooooooh, ahhhhhhh, ooooooo,"* she purrs. She closes her eyes, shrugs her shoulders, wriggles her back. "It's almost worth paying extra," she says. *"Ahhhhhh."*

"You can leave me a tip."

"Absolutely!"

"Boy oh boy oh boy," says Glenn. He laughs, *Ah ha ha!* He continues scratching.

Glenn slips beneath the floral spread, rolls effortfully onto his left side, one hand resting beneath his cheek. Street light filters through the bedroom window; a night bird sings, a single voice.

He breathes deeply. He thinks of the beautiful birch tree that guarded the breezeway at Spikehorn. The carpenter from across the lake thought he was crazy, but he couldn't bring himself to cut it down. He ended up building the roof with a big zigzag in it, leaving plenty of room for the stately old tree to grow. He thinks of playing run-sheep-run and kick-the-can and gyp, playing trombone in the high school band, shaking hands with John Philip Sousa, listening to Stan Kenton on a superheterodyne radio. A Model T milk truck. A flapper in a beaver coat, dancing the Charleston. A thank-you note from Wendell Willkie. A letter from Bennett Cerf. Pounding nails into a scrap of two-by-four on the back porch while his mother snaps beans. Lucy in her square-dance outfit. Joan leaning against the radiator in his office in the collection department at the Mayo Clinic, drying her stockings on a cold, rainy day.

Water gurgles in an ornamental pond. The air conditioner kicks over, cycles up, begins to blow. Glenn sighs. He pushes his head deep into the feather pillow. It feels soft and cool. The clock radio on the night table whirs and vibrates; the number card flops: 10:35.

Esquire, September 1998

Mike Sager
by Mike Sager

Somewhere east of Lost River, along a narrow ribbon of slippery asphalt that dipped and climbed and meandered like a goat trail through the George Washington National Forest, I pulled my rented Trailblazer to a stop before a line of mailboxes—a pitted, muddy road called Sager Hollow.

The rain was falling harder now, a thick mist against a white-gray sky, visible above the spindly bare trees and high ridges. The engine idled, burning low-test, $2.59-a-gallon. The front wipers went *swish-swock;* the back one countered in a lower register, *hunk-thunk,* reverberating through the long, empty vehicle, the rental of which—my wife's idea—had first seemed like overkill but now seemed pretty darn wise. It was Easter Sunday. I was in West Virginia. I'd been driving for hours though the mountains, through the fog and the rain, eyes glued to the center line for navigation, big rigs pushing up on my tail. My nerves were frayed, I needed to take a piss. I needed to finish this job and get back home.

I lowered the window, the familiar electric hum, and peered down the road into the gloomy afternoon, not quite sure what to do next. The air was heavy with the smells of earth and mold, wood smoke and wet livestock. I'd started this trip in San Diego, within sight of the Pacific Ocean. I'd seen the night lights of Las Vegas, the night stars over the Great Plains, the ghostly vapors of dawn in the Louisiana bayou, the glare of morning sun on freshly fallen snow in the Allegheny mountains of Pennsylvania, the stuffy blackness of the guest room in my parents' hermetically sealed condo in Pikesville, Maryland, my bar mitzvah photo on the nightstand—I had a cast on my right hand, broken on a kid's head during a bus fight. Seventeen days, sixty-eight hundred and forty-some-odd miles, by air and by Avis, much of it spent clutching a MapQuest printout, trying to manage the trick of using my reading glasses while driving eighty miles-per-hour, the wind buffeting my high-profile vehicle, the truck drivers playing cat-and-mouse (some of them, no doubt, sprung to the eyeballs on crystal meth), and me hoping fervently that the much ballyhooed computer intelligence at MapQuest had not forgotten some small but critical detail—say, a right turn onto a certain gravel road, as had been the case only yesterday, leaving me with my bald head craned out the window in the cold and driving rain, backing down a steep slope leading to nowhere. I shall never again decline the extra insurance.

Now I was in Hardy County, in the Appalachian Mountains. Or rather, I was back here for second time in as many days, having decided to try one more time to complete my mission—excuses are not an option to the self-employed. Sitting there in my rented Trailblazer, idling in the middle of the rain-swept road, eyeballing the line of mailboxes—the design and arrangement of which might just as well have incorporated a blinking neon sign that said Dogpatch, USA—I felt a slight pang of self doubt. Maybe this whole thing was foolhardy. Maybe I hadn't done enough prep. Maybe I should have called first. It was, after all, the holiest day on the Christian calendar. (And here I come, a reputed Christ killer.) There'd been no telephone number listed on the Web site, no e-mail contact either. Just a street address—and I use the word *street* generously—for the Salem Mennonite Church, dating to 1868, average weekly attendance twenty, which had turned out to be a picturesque whitewashed meeting house on a sweet little hill, with a volleyball net out front and a little graveyard behind but not a living soul in evidence. I searched my personal data banks for any knowledge of Mennonite customs and practices. Are Mennonites the same as Amish? Do they wear those bonnets? Do they carry firearms? Do they even *have* telephones?

And then something else occurred to me: I couldn't have called them even if I wanted to. My cell phone was not in service—confirming, once again, my experience that cell phones never work in places you really need them.

I took a deep breath and exhaled, lips pursed, a muscle memory from my smoking days—times like this, I still crave a cig. And then I thought, *Let's do this thing*, which is corny, I know, but my ten-year-old likes me to say it before his basketball games. In five years, I'd never missed one of his games . . . until yesterday, which happened to be his first game of a new season in a tough new league, his first without me coaching. Right about tip-off time, I'd had my head out the window, backing down that hill.

Beyond the mailboxes, the denuded winter forest revealed its underlying typography, a large depression on the down side of a mountain slope, known in geologic terms as a hollow, pronounced *holler* in movies like *Deliverance* or *Coal Miner's Daughter*, a sort of backwoods cul-de-sac, this one home to an eclectic collection of buildings and ruins, placed with no apparent aesthetic strategy or consideration for zoning: here a ramshackle barn; there an A-frame log cabin; a wood shack, smoke curling from its crooked chimney; a tarpaper outhouse; a suburban-grade split level with whitewashed siding . . . all of it landscaped with an assortment of junked autos and rusted farm vehicles, discarded major appliances, trailers—occupied and not—and every manner of truck from every era. Presently the dogs appeared, prancing beside the road, barking, talking shit, tracking my progress through their territory like so many homeboys dogging a stranger in the 'hood. I could feel the human eyes watching me from the windows. I wondered: Had my message preceded me? Did they even know I was coming?

Down the road a piece, I came upon the place, exactly as described: "A little house with tan siding and a white picket fence, with a green sofa settin' yonder beneath an oak tree."

I parked and gathered my things. Before I could reach the steps to the front porch, the door swung open. Out stepped a ruddy-faced man in a camouflage hunting cap. Next came a woman in an ankle-length jean skirt. Her hair was swept back primly, pinned atop her head. Atop that was pinned a small piece of black lace. It reminded me of a doily. The man and woman stood side by side: American Gothic with an edge.

"Afternoon, folks." I tipped my watch cap with my first two fingers, playing it casual, down home. In fact, this was my home, my ancestral home, or nearly so. My great-grandfather, Yaakov Labe "Louis" Sager, born in 1869 in a shetl in Lithuania, had raised his nine children not far from here, just on the other side of the mountains, in Front Royal, Virginia. I'd spent last night there, having backtracked nearly 130 miles, across the state line, to find the nearest viable motel room.

My great-grandfather Louis had begun his American sojourn at the age of twenty-two. To make his living, he'd take a train from his home in Hagerstown, Maryland, where he lived with landsman from the old country, out to rural Virginia, and disembark at a crossroads that looked promising. From there he went farm to farm with a large pack on his back, selling needles and thread, soaps, small kitchen utensils, bolts of cloth, pieces of lace, and other lightweight items targeted to farmers' wives, whose language he could barely speak. He'd be gone a week at a time, overnighting in the barns of friendly customers or under the stars, eating the kosher food he'd brought along. Soon, he purchased a horse and wagon—a rolling department store. Since cash was scarce among the hardscrabble subsistence farmers in the territory, he began taking fur pelts in trade, which he in turn sold to big city furriers. Later still he would own four stores on the main street of Front Royal, three offering clothing (men's, women's and children's), the fourth a grocery, which did a booming business in pint bottles, twenty-four to a box, used for moonshine. When the grocery was sold, in 1926, he began selling the bottles from beneath the front counter of the men's shop, the sign over which said "Sager's Bargain Store—We Sell for Less." He continued to sell the bottles during Prohibition, albeit for a slightly higher markup.

The ancestral Sager house, where Louis and Fanny Schindler Sager raised their four boys and five girls (two attorneys, a pharmacist who became a beer distributor after Prohibition was repealed, an operating room nurse, a grade-school teacher with a masters from Columbia University in New York, two housewives, and the eldest, Willie, who died at twenty-one in the flu epidemic of 1918) still stands at 126 S. Royal Avenue. It is located about a block from the town center, where sits the county court house and also the town's Confederate War memorial. My great-uncle Bill Sager—one of the attorneys; a retired marine major who saw action on Guadalcanal with a rifle platoon during WWII—was the runt of the family, the youngest by many years, named after his dead brother. He remembers watching Ku Klux Klan parades from his father's storefront. The house is now a real estate office; the little outbuilding, in which my great-grandfather dried the fur pelts for resale, serves today as the firm's property management department—its image adorns the front of their brochure. After checking into my motel, I'd found the house, introduced myself to the owner. She told me about a friendly ghost who sometimes appears in the front room. As it happens, according to Uncle Bill, my great-grandfather spent all of his time in that room after his leg was amputated, due to diabetes. He died in 1960, at the age of ninety.

Of course, the man on the porch in Sager Hollow knew nothing of all this. He went about six foot two, 240. The way the house was built, upon a little rise, the porch was elevated, six steep steps. Looming there on high, like a preacher on a pulpit, he eyeballed me in my North Face ski shell, Gap cargo pants, and muddy Dr. Martens boots, the strap of my man-purse slung across my chest like a bandolier. He worked his shoulders a little bit, uncricked his neck, an audible pop. "How can we help you today, friend?"

The way he said *friend* . . . it didn't sound very friendly. Obviously, my message had not gotten through. I rose up to my full five foot five and put on an earnest smile. "I'm looking for a guy named Mike Sager."

The couple exchanged glances. "Who wants to know?" the man asked.

"Well," I said, "you're not gonna believe this . . ."

Call me Mike Sager.

Everyone does.

It's the way I answer the phone, the way I introduce myself. It's how I think of myself—my symbol, my logo, my brand name, like Prince's glyph. Mike Sager. A random collection of nine letters from the Latin alphabet, arranged into two groups, one space in between, the first group upthrust and masculine, like the monuments of the West, the second group rounded and feminine, like those of the East. Mike Sager, the yin and the yang. Three syllables, easy to say. Short and sweet—which my wife, in one of her occasional playful moods, would say describes me perfectly. Mike Sager. A simple name. A name that leaves room in a conversation for the next sentence. Not a fancy show-off name like Brandon Miller-de la Cuesta. Not a cool exotic name like William Least-Heat Moon. Not a tragic name like Richard Kuntz, a decent kid who went to my high school. His parents called him Dick. He called himself Dick. I always wondered: What were they thinking?

Mike Sager. A name with no baggage, no connotation. Just a name, an ordinary name. Not too Jewish-sounding, thank God—my mother's line; the first anti-Semite I ever knew. A name like a blank canvas or a raw hunk of granite, a name you can work with, chisel into something. Mike Sager. A name of my own choosing.

My given name, of course, is not Mike Sager. It is Michael Andrew Sager. *Mi-kul*, as the people in Baltimore used to say, *Miiiii-kuuuuullllll*, one of eight Michaels in my first grade class, an overweight boy in husky-size corduroys who cried easily but never backed down from a fight, whose handwriting was "poor" and whose spelling was "attrocious," who spent his entire third grade year sitting in the front of the room, his desk pushed against the teacher's. By fifth grade, I was the only member of the "smart class" who was being shuttled off to the "dumb class" for math. By junior high, having delayed taking algebra and a foreign language, I was placed full-time in the "dumb class." A few years later they'd start special ed. Some of my colleagues would end up there.

Then I started going to summer camp, two months away from home. I discovered sports; I got pretty good. I ended up on the soccer team at Emory University, eight hundred miles from Pikesville. New start, clean slate. I made varsity my freshman year. They listed me on the roster as Mike Sager.

From there, things began to turn around. Mike Sager was not Michael Sager. Mike Sager was a winner. He was popular. He did well. He got into a good law school, and then he quit law school after three weeks to work at one of the world's best newspapers, albeit as a copy boy on the graveyard shift. And then, in 1978, the really big thing happened: I got my first big-league credit.

By Mike Sager.

That's me.

A body of work. A lifetime of actions large and small.

What's in a name?

To me, everything.

So you can imagine my surprise, on that day some years ago—being newly connected to the Internet, a bit of a late adopter—when I decided to type the nine Latin letters of my name into this wondrous new tool they called a search engine.

Remember your first Google?

In a matter of milliseconds, the results appeared.

I was gut shot: There were *other* Mike Sagers.

Tons of them.

At first, I was outraged. I mean, Mike Sager is not exactly John Smith. How could there be others? What right did they have to use my name? A name I'd built from the ground up.

Time passed—the demands of everyday life interceded. I tried to forget them. But as is often the case, the things you hate become a prickly fascination. I found myself wondering: *Who are these guys?*

I started clicking around. There were 3,650 Google entries for "Mike

Sager," fifty-three pages. Going through them over a period of several days, I identified thirty-nine other Mike Sagers. This did not include the hundreds of still *more* Mike and Michael Sagers listed in the various telephone data bases on the web.

There was Lutheran pastor Mike Sager in Spokane; motorcycle racer/sound technologist Mike Sager in Wenatchee, Washington; car salesman Mike Sager in Perrysburg, Ohio; rock 'n' roll roadie/blogger/political campaign worker Mike Sager in Reston, Virginia; and high-tech-company owner Mike Sager in Southern California, who declined a meeting though his personal assistant, saying he preferred not to divulge any personal details—making me wonder immediately what he has to hide. Third generation stucco and plasterer Mike Sager lives on a small island near Vancouver with 500 other humans and a large number of bald eagles. There were three Captain Mike Sagers: a Louisiana state police officer; a jail warden in exurban Virginia (he also played semi-pro baseball); and an avid poet, ex-Navy, sailboat enthusiast, and all around renaissance man (just ask!) living in early retirement in a river town called Daphne, Alabama. And then there was help desk coordinator Mike Sager, who works for a tire and auto business in Tampa Florida. He calls himself mIKEY™, a name he is attempting to trademark.

All of them Mike Sager

None of them me.

What's in a name?

I needed to find out.

Mike Sager twisted my arm behind my back, slapped on a pair of handcuffs. "This guy claims his name is Mike Sager," he drawled.

Louisiana state police captain Mike Sager was wearing an enormous straw campaign-style hat, royal blue, the type seen on lonely highways in bygone days, usually in the company of mirrored sunglasses.

His lieutenant stepped forward, seeking a more strategic position. "Smile," he ordered. He snapped our picture with my wife's digital camera.

We'd just returned from Drusilla Seafood, a Baton Rouge landmark, where Mike and I had fallen quickly into a comfortable state of familiarity, like long-lost kin. Forty-eight years old, Mike is an imposing six foot two and a half, 230, with silver hair. His uniform shirt was festooned with ribbons and medals collected over his twenty-three years of service, during which time he has seen action as a road trooper, SWAT-team member, hazmat expert, tactics instructor, and member of the headquarters brass. Beneath the shirt, he wore a bulky Kevlar vest, as is regulation, despite his current, rear-echelon position as training-academy commander. On his right hip was strapped a .45 SIG Sauer with an eight-shot clip. He prefers it over the 9mm because, he said, "The .45 has a little bit more knockdown power to it—you can be a little off target."

Mike comes from a cop family. His grandfather Bill Sager immigrated to America from Canada and eventually became a Brooklyn police-precinct captain. Mike is married to the wife of a cop who killed himself in a gun-cleaning accident. They met at a party. She came up to him and asked how tall he was. When he told her, she said: "That's good. You'll do." They have a daughter, Amanda, with whom Mike sometimes shares a ride to classes at Louisiana State University. By the time you read this, he will have received his bachelor's degree in sociology.

Having grown up in Garden City, Long Island (he moved to Louisiana his senior year of high school, when his father took a job as a sales manager at a chemical company), he remembers the delights of living near the Westbury Music Fair, seeing *Fiddler on the Roof* with Zero Mostel and *Man of La Mancha* with Howard Keel and Lainie Kazan. After he gets his degree, Mike hopes to audition for an upcoming show at the Baton Rouge Little Theater, where he had a nonspeaking part a few years back in *Inherit the Wind*.

Invariably, when Mike talks with civilians, they ask him about his most dangerous moments. This is the story he likes to tell:

Early in his career, Mike was a Baton Rouge city police officer working a one-man car. A call came in—armed robbery at a fried-chicken establishment. By the time he arrived, the suspect had already fled, a black man in a brown leather bebop hat, last seen entering the bar across the street.

Mike called for backup, waited outside the bar. While he was standing there, the door swung open. A guy in a leather bebop hat was drinking at the bar. He saw Mike. He bolted.

Mike caught up with him at the back of the joint, grabbed him by the collar of his jacket with his gun hand, his right. His gun was still in his holster. The suspect was a short guy, about five foot five. As Mike struggled to control him, the suspect started to turn to his left, toward Mike, coming around to face him. Then Mike noticed: He had a gun.

"I grabbed the gun with my left hand, still holding him by the scruff of his neck with my right. I kept telling him to drop it, 'Drop the gun! Drop the gun!' but he kept on fighting. The next thing I knew, I had him lifted off the ground by his neck with one hand, still holding on to the gun with the other, and I was hitting him against the wall, banging him again and again, until finally he dropped the weapon and I fell on top of him.

"I took out my radio and called immediately: 'Officer needs help!' Then I sort of crouched there for a few seconds, holding him down on the ground, my knee in his back, catching my breath. As my adrenaline began to subside, I started to look around. This was not a very good neighborhood. There were a lot of thugs in the bar, and here I am, I've got one of their fellow thugs held to the ground. I could feel them closing in on me.

"I drew my weapon and I yelled at the top of my voice: 'I want this bar emptied. *Now!*'"

He looked at me with a crooked grin. "You never saw a bunch of *skels* move so fast."

Mike Sager and I stood on a flatbed trailer decorated with felt and bunting, rolling slowly through the streets of Kansas City, Missouri, each of us wearing a green plastic derby with large, furry mule ears attached to the brim. Stretching before us on either side of the street, the throngs cheered the city's annual Saint Patrick's Day parade. According to politician Mike Sager, who'd invited me to ride with him on this float, 40 percent of the population hereabouts is Irish. Mike is full of numbers and useful facts, which he recites while waving to the crowd. How he was the first Democrat to hold his seat in the Missouri state legislature in sixteen years. How he won by 416 votes out of 12,903 cast in 2002. How his opponent, during his failed reelection campaign in 2004, ran eleven different ads against Mike after he voted against a bill banning gay marriage, making charges on the order of: "He's a fag lover. If you elect Mike Sager, men and women are going to be kissing each other in the street."

Politician Mike is forty years old, five foot nine, 165. He majored in business in college, then worked as an environmental consultant, then chucked it all to market a card game he'd invented, a sword-fighting simulation called Highlander, based on the movie. For seven years, his game was one of the top ten sellers on the market; Mike was a big player in the gaming world, attending conventions, winning big competitions, doing whatever it is that gamers do. He still collects a modest sum in royalties.

Currently, Mike is focused on one mission: returning to public service. He is trying this time for Kansas City alderman, representing the blue-collar district of Raytown. Lucky for Mike, his wife makes a "sufficient living" as a history professor, allowing him to campaign full-time. He describes her unabashedly as "a beautiful, large-breasted Vietnamese woman" whom he married, he likes to say, "for her mind, something that will still be there when everything else is sagging." In addition to his wife, he shares his house with five other females—three daughters, a mother-in-law, a sister-in-law. "Seven if you count the dog."

Mike is Irish on his non-Sager side; he sports a trim red beard and an elfin grin, easily evoked. On the Sager side he is German—the beakish nose, the almond eyes, the glasses . . . he looks very much like a photo I'd eventually come across in Illinois, of one Georg Michael Sager, known in America as Mike, born in Pfaltz, in Bavaria, Germany, in 1816, more about whom later.

Mike's dad was a carpenter. He walked out on Mike and his mom and little sister. His mom put herself through college, worked up the corporate ladder. She retired from her corner office in 1999, at the age of fifty-five. She died of cancer one year later. It hit Mike very hard.

"Not a day goes by that I don't hear her, the things she taught me. I never leave home without an extra jacket or something. I look both ways before I cross the street. I never pick a fight, but I never back down from a bully, especially if he's going to pick a fight with someone else. That is my mother in me, speaking to me every day. Probably the most dangerous thing I ever did in my political career was vote against the ban on gay marriage. But gay and lesbian people had worked for me. They'd voted for me. You don't prove that you're somebody's friend by standing with them when things are going well. You prove it by standing with them when nobody else will. That's how my mom raised me. I know she was up there cheering."

On April 5, Mike lost his race, finishing a distant second in a three-candidate field.

"I was on the sidelines, like usual, just watching the game," said Mike Sager. "Then somebody yelled down the line: 'Hey, Sager! Get in there!'

And I'm like, 'What?' This was my second year on the team; I'd never once left the bench. I ran over and found my helmet and then ran out onto the field."

Tulane University backup placekicker Mike Sager is a twenty-year-old walk-on from Bird City, Kansas, population 482, where his family owns the second-tallest grain elevator in town, McDougal-Sager Grains. He was sitting in a little restaurant off campus, the kind of place college girls like to be taken, with tofu and brown rice on the menu. Mike is five foot ten, 194. His eyes are "bluish greenish grayish"; a handsome kid with a strong jaw, a slight underbite. In high school he always got red in the face at the Scholars' Bowl matches, probably caused, he says, by "the scrutiny, you know, of having all eyes upon you."

A former member of Future Farmers of America, Mike still works every summer at a Methodist-church camp and also at Bird City's famous tractor show. He's thinking of becoming a lawyer. He is known to his Tulane football buddies as Woody for his resemblance to the actor Woody Harrelson. He earned their respect about midseason of his freshman year, in 2003, when he started dating the senior captain of the women's varsity soccer team. That Halloween, Mike and his soccer girl went to several big parties, then went back to her place. He woke up the next morning in her housemate's bed. The housemate was lying next to him naked. He still had all his clothes on. "It was one of those moments, you know, when you're like, Whoa, what happened here?"

Kind of like his big football moment.

Tulane was leading Navy 42 to 10 last November, on its way to one of its five victories (in eleven games) last season. "I got out there on the field and I was just lost," Mike recalled. "The holder's like, 'Sager! Get over *here.*'

"He showed me the spot. It wasn't very far, twenty-eight yards. I did it all the time in practice. I was really nervous. The roar of the crowd. It made me feel kind of dizzy."

The center hiked the ball. The holder placed it down. "I guess I was too excited," Mike said. "I attacked too quickly. My leg swung right to left instead of just swinging through." Wide left.

"Everybody came up to me and groaned. They all said, 'Sager, that's the only chance you're ever gonna get.' But I didn't care. I was like, 'At least now I'm in the record books.' "

Mike Sager strode long-legged through the clatter and din of the new Maloof brothers casino, the theme of which seemed to have something vaguely to do with large-breasted women. At six foot four, Las Vegas Mike Sager was the tallest of the Mikes. Twenty-three years old, he is, like me, descended from Lithuanian Jews, with black hair and green eyes. He was wearing a white shirt and a purple patterned tie beneath a windbreaker. He had just punched out from his job as a food-and-beverage shift supervisor at Sam's Town, an off-strip gambling hall that caters to locals. The parent corporation has casino properties all over the U.S.—meaning lots of future career options if he plays his cards right, so to speak.

Having grown up in Canarsie, in Brooklyn, New York, Mike speaks with an accent that is distinct and musical, the vowels turned inward, the consonants swallowed—Manhattan comes out sounding like *Mah-hattan.* In college, at Widener University in Pennsylvania, people always remarked on Mike's accent. Because there were so many other Mikes at his school, he became known as Brooklyn Mike, and later as just Brooklyn. "And then they started calling me Brooklyn Zoo, and then Zoo, and then all kinds of crazy names," he said. "And I'm like: I'm not strange, youse guys are strange. Where I come from I'm normal."

Mike makes about fifteen dollars an hour at Sam's Town. He drives a '98 Infinity I30 because he wanted a car that was businesslike. His one-bedroom condo cost $135,000—why throw away money on rent? In his spare time, he does charity stuff, like delivering food to the poor. He'd like to take some university classes. He'd like to learn to make sushi. He'd like to have a steady girlfriend but doesn't think it's in his budget, not at the moment. But give him a little time. All things come in time.

"You say to yourself, When I'm thirty years old, this is my goal. When I'm forty, this is my goal," Mike said, yelling over the disco music at the in-house Asian restaurant between sips of his Komodo Dragon, a mix of Baileys Irish Cream and Jagermeister that tasted like an oatmeal cookie.

"When I was first here, one of my bosses told me, 'Mike, you're a great worker, I can see you as a food-and-beverage director someday'—which is a top position. So that gave me a lot of anticipation to work."

He wants to be a VP one day. Maybe a general manager. "I'm willing to work hard for it. That's my deal."

Mike Sager lives a couple of miles outside the town of Kell, in southern Illinois, population 231. It is quiet country, rolling and wooded, closer to Kentucky than it is to Chicago in both mileage and state of mind.

Pistol-packin' Mike Sager—so dubbed by his uncle Mike Sager for his habit of walking in the woods with a stout stick and a .22-caliber handgun— is forty-nine, five foot seven, 180. His left eye is hazel, the right one is brown. While most of the other Mike Sagers, including me, pronounce our names with a long a, pistol-packin' Mike pronounces his name as if it were spelled with an *o*, as in *blogger.*

Mike's father, Pete Sager, who is Uncle Mike's brother, lives two miles away, across Sager-owned woods and fields. Pete spent most of his life as a farmer, logger, and sawmill worker, as have most of the Sagers here for generations. The name Sager, according to genealogy experts, is derived from several sources, one of them being the Dutch and North German occupational name *sager,* meaning "sawyer," a person who works with wood. Other roots include: French/Germanic, from sag meaning "quarrel" or "lawsuit," and *hari,* meaning "army"; Jewish/German, from *sagen,* "to say"; Yiddish, from *zeiger,* meaning "clock" or "timepiece"; Russian, a person from the village of Zhagory, in Lithuania; German, a person from the village of Zager, near Wollin.

Like his father—who in his later life became an expert leather craftsman—Mike started as a farmer. It was tough. He ended up having to borrow money just to pay his taxes. Now he works as a farm advisor for the USDA, focusing mostly on ag-waste systems. You can imagine what a big problem ag waste can be on a dairy farm.

Mike and his wife, Deann, grew up together and share a lot of history. They also have a nine-year-old son, Jacob. And they have something else in common: They're cousins.

Deann's maiden name is Sager. Her people own Sager Farms, known for its sweet peaches. They pronounce the name with the long *a.* Deann *Sayger-Sogger.* Mike and Deann's common ancestor is another Pete Sager, after whom pistol-packin' Mike's father was named. Old Pete Sager outlived three different wives, had three different families. Mike is a descendant of one wife; Deann is a descendant of another. Old Pete, it turns out, was the son of Georg Mike Sager, the beak-nosed German fellow who, I mentioned earlier, resembled politician Mike (and who, pistol-packin' Mike and Uncle Mike agree, looks very Jewish in pictures).

According to family lore, Georg Mike Sager immigrated from Germany in the 1840s on a boat called the *Wester*. He settled for a period in New York, but then killed a man and fled west to the banks of the Missouri, where he worked in a logging camp. There, the story goes, Georg Mike killed *another* man and then fled to Kell. Around the time of the Civil War, Kell and its environs had a reputation as a "butcher-knife town," a hole-up for renegades and people on the run. Nearby Horse Creek was known for a big old sycamore tree used by vigilantes for hangings. The tree was still standing when pistol-packin' Mike was a kid.

According to Deann—who had come home from work, nearly twenty miles one way, curious to meet a man with her husband's name—pistol-packin' Mike is happiest when he's in the woods. Sitting at the kitchen table, the aroma of Deann's frying pork chops filling the air, we watched the purple finches and titmice at the bird feeders just outside the window. "I can spend all day in them woods," he said. "Sometimes I come in and eat and go back out."

"Just like your son," Deann said.

Mike smiled. "One time, I was coming through the woods, creeping through the underbrush. I bent down to go under a limb, you know, and here's this little bitty bird sittin' up literally right under my nose. Only this far away. And he just set there and looked at me, you know how birds do? And I looked at him. I studied him, 'cause I had never seen that particular bird in these parts, and you know I been walkin' these woods my entire life. I come back to the house and get out my bird book. And wouldn't you know . . . it was a Golden-crowned Kinglet. That really tickled me."

For most of my career, I've followed the same basic routine when doing an interview. Having schmoozed my way through the door, having explained my intentions, I turn on the tape. And then I say, charmingly, open-endedly, "So: You were born in a log cabin. . . ."

A little bit of levity to break the ice.

And so it went when I sat down with seventy-eight-year-old Mike Sager and his wife in their seldom-used living room in Eureka, Illinois, the town where Ronald Reagan attended college, five hours upstate from the home of his nephew, pistol-packin' Mike. Hearing my cute little opener, Uncle

Mike Sager replied matter-of-factly: "That's right. Did my nephew show you the place?"

Mike Sager (also sounds like *blogger*) was born on September 29, 1926, making him the oldest Mike Sager I've met. He has been married to Genevia—whose mother spelled her name wrong, Mike likes to point out—for fifty-four years. They have four children, two grandkids. He calls her Granny. "She's wearing my first paycheck," he said, indicating her engagement ring.

Over the last decade or so, Mike has survived prostate cancer, heart surgery, glaucoma, and cataract surgery. He lost parts of the three center digits on his left hand to a workshop accident in 2002, after which he put the fingers in a bag and drove himself to the hospital. He still does beautiful work with wood, all of the standard stuff, and also more wondrous things, like a large, flexible link chain whittled entirely from a solid tree branch, and custom walking sticks, also made from branches, one of which he gave me as a gift, a beautiful piece of work with his name, *Mike Sager*, carved in script beneath the handle. Mike also insisted on giving me lunch, a savory local steak he grilled behind his house, meanwhile pointing out the suspension bridge over the creek and the freestanding workshop—both of which he'd built himself—the latter constructed in odd harmony with a huge old tree, as precious and irregular as a workshop for elves.

Mike grew up during the Depression, endured the proverbial hardships, leaving before sunup each morning from the family farm to attend a high school twenty miles away (where, incidentally, his classmate was former UN ambassador Jeane Kirkpatrick). He served in the Army toward the end of World War II, where his "ability to print real tiny" won him a job as a clerk in the general headquarters at Camp Robinson, Arkansas.

He is well known in some circles for his important contributions to agriculture. After attending the University of Illinois and becoming a farm-extension agent, Uncle Mike helped pioneer something called conservation tillage. Previously, farmers used a moldboard plow to turn over the soil before planting, thus exposing the rich soil underneath. In the fifties, as America began applying its scientific might to farming, it was discovered that much of the rich soil turned over by moldboard plowing was being eroded away by wind and rain. Hence, conservation tillage: no more plowing; the seeds are planted right on top of the stubble and residue from the last crop. Due to Mike Sager's efforts, most Illinois farmers now practice conservation tillage.

A few years back, when Mike Sager received the Illinois Farm Bureau's most prestigious award to commemorate his achievements, he was handed a trophy.

At the top of the marble base sat . . . a large chrome replica of a moldboard plow.

Mike Sager wore a buzz cut and semi-baggy jeans, not baggy-baggy, like hip-hop, more just like casual, like preppy or whatever, which was how he characterized his style of dress, like American Eagle and stuff, like button-down shirts.

Seventeen years old, six foot two and still growing, he is a junior at Central York High School in York, Pennsylvania, where he plays varsity basketball and soccer. Though he is right-handed and shoots righty in hoops, his stronger foot in soccer is his left. The same is true of his sister, who is two years younger. "Having strong left feet, they've always been hot commodities in soccer—it's helped them to be starters," his mom explained.

High school Mike is sitting in the living room at the end of a half day of school. His mom makes him turn off the TV. He is willing to talk, a little shy, thinking maybe that this whole interview thing is a bit, like, freakish or whatever, this grown-up Mike Sager guy calling his high school vice-principal (who at first thought I was some kind of pervert), and then tracking him down, coming all the way across the country from San Diego, showing up at his door a few minutes before his mom got home.

Mike has lived in York all his life, as has his mom, who is divorced from his dad, meaning that Mike doesn't know a whole lot about his Sager history. He thinks they came from Lancaster, Pennsylvania. That's where his dad is from.

Mike hangs out with the soccer guys and some of the basketball guys. He likes poker, eating out, hanging out. Nobody goes to the mall anymore. It's all about texting, being online, IM. He met his girlfriend, Kasey, in a chat room. She goes to Eastern, where his mom teaches. His favorite dish is seafood au gratin. He likes watching sports on television; he likes his PlayStation 2. All-time favorite game: NBA Live 2005, followed by Madden Football. He is hoping to play college soccer; he wants to go into sports management and work for a pro team.

His mother calls him Michael. Like me, he prefers to be called Mike.

"He will deliberately tell people to call him Mike because he knows it bugs me," she said.

High school Mike shrugged. Then his cell phone started vibrating.

His mom shot him a look. "I thought I asked you to shut that off."

"Lemme just get this," Mike said.

Mike Sager spent much of his childhood looking out the window, watching the sky. "It drove my mother nuts," he recalled, stroking his trim goatee, sitting in the narrow living room of his starter house with his coat on.

The town was Bellefonte, Pennsylvania, in the mountainous center of the state. The time was 7:30 P.M. The temperature was 34 degrees, the wind was from the north at six miles per hour, the humidity was 96 percent. Snow was falling—a three-inch accumulation since the afternoon, necessitating the use of my TrailBlazer's four-wheel option to negotiate the steep approach to Mike's driveway.

AccuWeather Mike is twenty-seven years old, five eleven, 180. He was born in Patterson, New Jersey, a half-Jewish Sager with dark hair and blue eyes like my own great-uncle Bill Sager. His great-grandfather Sager came from Lithuania or Romania, he's not sure. His grandfather lived in Brooklyn and drove a cab; he later became a calligrapher. Mike's parents split when he was two and a half. He lived with his mother most of the time. She remarried twice. Mike remembers "acting out" a lot. They moved frequently. He went to ten or eleven different schools.

"I'd remember weather events," AccuWeather Mike continued. His wife, Caitlin, was sitting with us. She has long red hair. She cradled one of their cats like a baby, listening intently—a newlywed still fascinated by her husband's childhood stories. "I'd be like, 'Remember that time when it was snowing really hard?' And my mother would be like, 'No, I don't remember that.' And I'd be like, 'Well, it was only a couple of years ago.'"

Now the unhappy boy is a Rutgers-trained meteorologist with the important title of Data Acquisition and Utilization Manager for AccuWeather, Inc., the forecasting service headquartered in nearby State College. Not only that. AccuWeather recently agreed to purchase from him something called Mike Sager's Weather Forecast Model Animator, which explains why he is always at the top of the list when you Google our name. Over the last several years, in fact, Mike Sager's Web-based forecasting tool—a software program that generates moving maps of weather systems—has become a favorite of meteorologists all over the nation, even the world.

"Part of the agreement," he told me proudly, "is that it's always going to have my name on it. So from now on, if you Google Mike Sager, you'll come to AccuWeather, along with my Web site."

Mike Sager and his son, Mike Sager—from Springfield and Mundelein, Illinois, respectively—are descendants of the most famous Sagers in history. Their story is the subject of a classic juvenile book, *The Valiant Seven*, a vivid historical novel based on the lives of the seven brave Sager children whose parents died while the family was en route by wagon train from Missouri to Oregon. A movie version, made in 1974, was called *Seven Alone*.

Warren Mike Sager is a youthful fifty-five, five foot eleven, 175, with brown eyes and brown hair done up in spikes. A former high school teacher turned corporate-communications and video guy, he is now self-employed as a distributor for Coach House Garages, an Amish concern that makes prefab garages and houses.

Mike Garth Sager is twenty-three, six foot, 160, a handsome kid with dreamy blue eyes and a little goatee, a backward baseball cap, a taste for the journalism of Hunter S. Thompson. An ag-business major with a degree from Illinois State University at Normal, he is working as a landscaper for a big company. By the time this is published, he will be a married man.

Through the years, Mike and Mike have found a common interest in canoeing, often taking trips together. Once, when Mike Garth was about ten or eleven, they were members of a small group plying the Boundary Waters between Minnesota and Ontario, about thirty miles from Grand Marais, near the end of the Gunflint Trail—the absolute middle of nowhere.

They had pulled the canoes out of the water in order to carry them over a portage, a sandy strip between two lakes. Usually in the Boundary Waters, you could canoe for days and never see another human. As luck would have it, on this day there was another party already at the portage, six men.

The folks in Mike and Mike's party busied themselves carrying their canoes and equipment. Then someone in his group wanted Warren Mike's attention. He called out, "Hey, Mike Sager!"

Though Mike Garth was typically oblivious, Warren Mike heard this and turned around. As he did, he noticed two men from the other group looking his way quizzically. They walked over. The older one extended his hand to shake. "Mike Sager," he said, introducing himself. "Was someone calling me?"

Turned out he was a preacher from Minneapolis canoeing with a church group.

With him was his son.

He was also named Mike Sager.

And so it was, on a rainy, Easter Sunday afternoon, after seventeen days and sixty-eight hundred and forty-some-odd miles, by air and by Avis, most of it spent clutching MapQuest printouts, that I found myself on Sager Hollow Road in the Great North Mountain Range of West Virginia, face to face with a large man in a camouflage hunting cap and a woman in an ankle-length denim skirt, a black lace doily pinned to the top of her head. They loomed above me on their elevated porch.

Being a Mike Sager of diminutive stature (since meeting all these other Mikes, I'd begun thinking of myself as shrimp Mike Sager), I obviously posed no threat. Hearing me out, taking in the absurd but heartfelt explanation of my mission—the twenty-fourth telling; fairly polished by now—the man on the porch proceeded to break out into a large smile, formidable in scope and completely infectious, appended at either end by deep dimples, the frequent appearance of which, I was soon to learn, had helped seal the election of one Michael Davis Sager—Mike to his friends, a lumberman, factory worker and elder of the Salem Mennonite Church—as Mathias High School's Class of '78's biggest flirt.

I took a seat in the front living room, which was warm and filled with ladybugs, one of which alighted on the top of my bald head, causing a ripple of ice-breaking laughter. Among the gathered were the Sagers' three daughters, age seventeen and up (two of them in hip-hugger jeans, the eldest in riding breeches), a son-in-law, and a family friend. They were getting ready to walk down to the end of Sager Hollow Road, to the home place—where Mike's dad grew up, bordered on three sides by the national forest—for their annual family Easter-egg hunt.

I was about to pull out my tape recorder when Mike—for months I'd been thinking of him as Mennonite Mike, but he was nothing like I imagined —entered from the other room carrying a metal box. It was battered and oxidized, as old as the hills. Out of it he retrieved a piece of sheepskin, a land grant from the Commonwealth of Virginia to John Sager, Sr., for 640 acres, dated 1794.

Then, Mike's wife, Patrice, handed me with a genealogy book, which included an article she'd written about the four Sager brothers who had immigrated here from Germany via Pennsylvania. When she left the room to make a copy for me using her flatbed scanner and computer printer, her eldest daughter, Elizabeth, a paralegal, stepped forward with Mennonite Mike's high school yearbook. Besides being biggest flirt, it turned out, Mike was all-state in basketball, with long, unruly hair and thick, mutton chop sideburns befitting the era.

After the initial flurry, everyone settled into chairs; all eyes turned to the stranger. I told them about Las Vegas Mike, police captain Mike, pistol-packin' Mike and his wife/cousin Deann Sager-Sager, about politician Mike (I skipped the part about him being a "fag lover"), and, of course, about Georg Mike, the most colorful Mike Sager of all. I told them about the Jewish and non-Jewish Mike Sagers, and about Yaakov Labe "Louis" Sager, my great-grandfather who'd lived just across the mountains from here. "He peddled fur pelts, I peddle stories," I told them, hamming it up a bit, feeling very much at home. "I guess I haven't come that far."

Patrice looked at me thoughtfully: "When I was doing my research for the genealogy article, I spoke to this expert in Texas, his name was Bill Sayer. And he told me that all the Sagers in this country, no matter what the spelling, are related to one another if you go far enough back."

The room grew quite for a few thoughtful seconds, the kind of thing that happens in these types of living-room visits, the only sound the flutter of ladybug wings. Then Mennonite elder Mike spoke: "I guess it's true what they say: we're all related under the skin."

Mike Sager: A random collection of nine letters from the Latin alphabet, arranged into two groups, one space in between. Three syllables, easy to say. A name that leaves room in a conversation for the next sentence. Not a fancy show-off name, not a cool, exotic name, not a tragic name like Dick Kuntz. A name with no baggage, no connotation. A name I've built from the ground up.

Mike Sager: A name attached to a whole slew of us, it turns out.

Several grew up fatherless, most are tall, several have black hair and blue eyes. Some are Jews and some are Germans; one was a German who looked like a Jew. Several are men of religion; many are men of ideas; all of them were generous, at least with me. Accuweather Mike and Las Vegas Mike, both out of Brooklyn, apparently unrelated, had the same distinctive way of using their mouths, bringing to mind a Christmas nutcracker soldier. Politician Mike's resemblance to old Georg Mike is just pain eerie. Almost all of them had some woodworking in their family tree. A random sampling of American men with nothing in common but a name.

Yet, with each meeting, came an almost instant feeling of kinship. And each meeting ended, I don't mind revealing, with a manly bear hug—except with high school Mike, who gave me a pound.

What's in a name?

To me, everything.

Call us *all* Mike Sager.

Esquire, July 2005

Acknowledgments

Thank you for the gift of wonderful assignments: David Granger, Peter Griffin, Lisa Hintelmann, Art Cooper, Lisa Henricksson, Jann Wenner, Bob Love, Bob Wallace, Alice Gabriel, Terry McDonell, David Hirshey, Bill Tonelli, Clay Felker, Michael Schrage, Jim Morgan.

Thank you for representing: Mollie Glick, Jeff Frankel, Phil Raskind, Brian Lipson.

Thank you for believing: Will Balliett, Morgan Entrekin, Barry Siegel, Don Graham, Bill Regardie, Jack Limpert.

Thank you for mentoring: Walt Harrington, Steve Jones, Hunter S. Thompson.

Thank you for supporting: Beverly & Marvin Sager, Wendy Sager, Lawrence Alfred, William H. Sager, Sam Freedman, Pete Earley, Tyler Cabot, Jamison Stoltz, Steve Cohen, Henry Schuster, Terrell Lamb, Chris Janney, Richard Ben Cramer, Geoff Diner, Marshall Keys, Al Baverman, David Kelley, Hesh Beker, Steven Sulcov, Michael Elizondo, Carter Harris, Peter Mehlman, Sheila & Ed Weidenfeld, Michael Tisserand, Patrick Beach, Colleen O'Connor, Richard Karpel, the Association of Alternative Newsweeklies, Patricia Pierson, Helene Rubinstein, Nancy Jo Iacoi, Fran Kessler, David Katz, Brendan Vaughan, Ross McCammon, Robert Scheffler, Kevin McDonnell, Tom Colligan, Victor Ozols, Dan Torday, Doug Cantor, Buddy Kite, David Walters, Luis Veronese, Shaun Dillon, Peter Jacoby, Edwin Lap, Steven

Nusinow, Gary Cohen, Greg Wiener, Yvonne Negron, Galya Button, Ania Dylewska, Megan Cohen, Wade Smith, Christopher Dale.

Thank you to all my students; to all the members of the Ministry for Wayward Writers; and to all my colleagues on the faculty of the Literary Journalism program at the University of California, Irvine.

Thank you to my wife, Rebekah, for her love and for the gift of fatherhood.

And most importantly, thank you to my subjects—without you, there would be no stories: Roseanne Barr, Sandra & Bob Younger and all the residents of Wildcat Canyon, Brooke Burke, Jesse Epstein, Marc Cuban, Tom Araya, Dave Lombardo, Kerry King, Jeff Hanneman, Lynn Clark, Steve Bean, Col. Bob Sinclair, O'Shea "Ice Cube" Jackson, Desmond Gorges, Heather & Shun Ducksworth, Tim Hovland, Mike Dodd, Sinjin Smith, Karch Kiraly, Steve Obradovich, Al, April, Rosemary, Butch, Walter, Deb, the members of the Elite International Swingers' Club, Diana & Mike Ditka, Glenn Sanberg, and all Mike Sagers not myself.

Permissions

The following stories were first published in the same or slightly different form in *Esquire:* "Fact: Five Out Of Five Kids Who Kill Love Slayer" 2/92; "Deviates in Love" 10/92; "Old" 9/98; "The Secret Life of a Beautiful Woman" 4/99; "Is Ditka Nuts?" 10/99; "Yeaahhh Baaaaaby!" 4/00; "The Multitudes of Roseanne" 8/01; "The Marine" 12/01; "The Man of Tomorrow Goes to the Prom" 10/03; "Is Something Burning?" 3/04; "Mike Sager by Mike Sager" 7/05; "Fifty Grand in San Diego," 7/06.

The following stories were first published in the same or slightly different form in *Rolling Stone:* "The World According to Amerikka's Most Wanted Rapper" 10/04/90; "Revenge of the Donut Boys" 10/01/92.

"Almost Famous" was first published in *GQ* on 2/96.

"My Man Desmond" was first published in *Manhattan, Inc.* on 9/87.

"Volleyball Gods" was first published in *Playboy* on 7/85.

About the Author

Mike Sager quit law school after three weeks to work the graveyard shift as a copy boy at the *Washington Post*. Eleven months later, he was promoted to staff writer by Metro Editor Bob Woodward. He left the *Post* after six years to pursue a career in magazines. Currently he is a writer-at-large for *Esquire*. His first collection, *Scary Monsters and Super Freaks: Stories of Sex, Drugs, Rock 'n' Roll and Murder*, was a *Los Angeles Times* bestseller. His first novel, *Deviant Behavior*, will be published by Grove/Atlantic.

A former contributing editor of *Rolling Stone* and writer-at-large for *GQ*, Sager has also written for *Vibe, Spy, Interview, Playboy, Washingtonian*, and *Regardies*. For his stories, he has lived with a crack gang in Los Angeles; ex-pat Vietnam veterans in Thailand; a 625-pound man in El Monte, California; teenage pit-bull fighters in the Philadelphia barrio; Palestinians in the Gaza Strip; heroin addicts on the Lower East Side; Aryan Nations troopers in Idaho; U.S. Marines at Camp Pendleton; Tupperware saleswomen in suburban Maryland; and high school boys in Orange County.

Sager has read and lectured at the Columbia University Graduate School of Journalism, the Medill School of Journalism, the Yale Law School, and many other forums; his work is included in three textbooks presently in use in college classrooms. Each spring, he leads a popular workshop at the University of California-Irvine, where he is a Pereira Visiting Writer. Many of his stories have been optioned for film. A graduate of Emory University, he lives with his wife and son in La Jolla, California.